THE RIDDLE
OF THE
CASWELL MUTINY

SÉAMUS BREATHNACH

The Riddle of the Caswell Mutiny

Universal Publishers/uPUBLISH.com
USA • 2003

ISBN: 1-58112-577-1

www.uPUBLISH.com/books/breathnach.htm

DEDICATION

In Memory of Clare (Barker), a sailor of Cork

Other Works by the Author:

A History Of The Irish Police
(From Earliest Times.,..)
Publishers: Anvil, 1974

Emile Durkheim On Crime And Punishment
(An Exegesis)
Dissertation.com, 2002

Contents

Acknowledgements............vi

Introduction..................viii

Chapter 1: An Old Crew.................................. 1

Chapter 2: A New Crew................................... 16

Chapter 3: Mutiny.. 36

Chapter 4: Counter-Mutiny............................. 58

Chapter 5: The Trials of Bombos...................... 76

Chapter 6: Letters And Petitions....................... 97

Chapter 7: The Case Of Thomas Crowe.............. 112

Chapter 8: A Double Execution......................... 132

Chapter 9: Hue And Cry The *Caswell*................. 146

Chapter 10: The Trial Of Joseph Pistoria
(*Alias* Francesco Moschara)...........................168

Chapter 11: The Execution of Francesco Moschara
(*Alias* Joseph Pistoria)....................................178

Chapter 12: Aftermath And Epilogue.................193

Appendix A..........................211

Caswell Calendar................. ..221

References.......................... 223

Index...227

ACKNOWLEDGEMENTS

As might be imagined I have many debts to pay for kindnesses rendered while compiling this book.

Amongst these creditors is my friend Padraigh O Snodaigh to whom I am indebted for more years than I care to remember. The debts extend as much for casual as for studied contributions over the years. At present I am indebted to him for reading the script before completion and for making some suggestions.

I wish to thank Niall O Cearbhaill for reading a further draft, not to mention those O Snodaigh-inspired discourses at *Club an Chonartha*.

I wish to thank Tom Rice for his comments and his companionship, the exchanges in the Eire Og Football Clubhouse, the post-prandial analyses in Teach Dolman and elsewhere in Carlow.

I wish to thank Frank Taaffe for opening his considerable library to me, his family for support, and to Brid for making my sojourns and stopovers in Athy so pleasant and memorable.

I also wish to thank Larry Darcy, Martina Darcy, 'Pod' Shaw, Mary Walsh, Betty Byrne, Monica-Byrne O'Malley, Stephen Fleming, Jacinta Schweppe, and 'Patsy' Hearns for their encouragement, enthusiasm and humour.

I owe much to the National Archives, to the front desk operatives, and to Gregory O'Connor in particular for his earlier advices and assistance.

I wish to pay special thanks to Cobh Library and to the Belfast, Dunlaoire, and Cobh Maritime Museums.

My gratitude to Penny Rudkin (of the Special Collections Library, Southampton City Council, Civic Centre, Southampton, SO14 7LW) for some useful hints and, in particular, for informing me of the exhibition, 'Under sail - Swansea cutters, tall ships and seascapes 1830-1880,' which was held at the Glynn Vivian Art Gallery, Alexandra Road, Swansea.

I was very fortunate to have made contact with Jane Phillips (at the Glynn Vivian Art Gallery, Alexandra Road, Swansea) whose assistance was invaluable.

I am also very grateful to Valerie Hart, Librarian, the Central Library, Civic Centre, Southampton, SO14 7LW, the National Maritime Museum, Park Row, Greenwich, London, SE10 9NF, and the Public Record Office, Ruskin Avenue, Kew, Richmond, Surrey, TW9 4DU.

I also wish to thank the staff at the Carlow County Public Library, Tullow Street, Carlow, the reference section as well as public desk assistants.

I am indebted to several Web Sites, some of which are given in the Select Bibliography.

For his efforts and immediate responses to my queries concerning past issues of *Sea Breezes* I owe a special debt to Paul Adamthwaite, Ph.D., Executive Director of Archives and Collections (ACS), a Charitable Canadian Society, 2, Gladstone Avenue, PO Box 125, Picton, Ontario, K0K 2T0, Canada, with a very useful website a <http//www.AandC.org>

I wish to thank the students of Criminology at CDVEC (City of Dublin Vocational Education Committee) for their curiosity and enthusiasm throughout the eighties and nineties, and for the Saturday morning seminars on *Historical and Contemporary Issues.*

I wish also to thank the less fortunate students of DIT (the Dublin Institute of Technology) for their courage over the years, and for their moral stamina in staying with the criminological discipline, even in the face of such inordinate and institutionalized sleaze as became synonymous with DIT from 1992 onwards.

Seamus Breathnach
Dublin Institute of Technology, 2003

INTRODUCTION

Fear of the contingency of life is part of the human condition. While controlling some things that govern our lives we acknowledge the existence of other forces about which we can do little or nothing. In every walk of life people have to make choices, even when they are not in full possession of the facts. In this sense each of us enters endless relations without our will, knowing that we never have full possession of 'all the facts.'

This fact of life is no less true for sailors, who live a life at sea, and in the 1870s they had their own peculiar concerns with which to cope. For our purposes -- which is to locate the parameters in which the story of the *Caswell* mutiny can best be related -- these concerns can be reduced to four. There was the possible fear of redundancy or displacement and/or a diminution of a sailor's self-esteem (brought about by the development of steam). There was the definite fear of death (arising out of the ordinary and every day hazards of service on the high seas). There was also the constant apprehension of government on board a ship, which means, possible cruelty or personal violence from above (captain and mates) or rebellion from below (able bodied seamen), the one no doubt arising from the fear of the other. And finally, there was the sometime fear of racism, violence, or mutiny amongst one's fellow crewmembers.

These four concerns apply exclusively in peacetime and were above and beyond the rigors of the sailor's ordinary life at sea. One doubts whether we can understand a sailor's lot in the 1870s; but if we look at these individual loci of possible apprehension, we may the more easily come to terms with comprehending something of what it must have been like.

Sail, Steam and the Suez Canal

With the European colonization of overseas territories came a dramatic increase in international trade from the mid-18th century onwards. Trading ships sailed along recognised trade routes, including the monsoon and wind corridors of the world. Perhaps the two greatest inventions, which impacted on imperial commerce, were steam and the telegraph. First developed in Britain at the end of the 17th century by Henry Newcomen, steam was further improved by James Watt in 1769, and was used in

Introduction

ships in the early 1800s. Even if it initially needed coal stations, steam-powered vessels improved reliability and speed. They were also ingeniously free from the constraints imposed by winds and tides. The fear of displacement by steam was probably the most general and the least immediate of a sailor's concerns. It is evident to us in the twenty first century that sail was eventually destined to be replaced by steam and, eventually, by nuclear power. In retrospect these progressive signs were unmistakable.

To take but two obvious if preliminary examples all we need do is to consider the enormous growth in the military and commercial use of ships or recall the opening of the Suez Canal.

Steam's greatest assault on sail arose -- not surprisingly -- from its military potential. Throughout history the military demand for innovation persisted apace with the drive for national and international power. The sole purpose of 'a man of war' was to carry guns. In size, as well as in science, the deep focus of the State was on a ship's military capacity. Henry VII's most famous ship the 'Great Happy' or 'Henri grace a Dieu', weighed 1,000 tons, carried 349 soldiers, and housed 301 mariners and 50 gunners. That was in 1514. By adding 85 sea-going vessels to his fleet, Henry managed to hold the balance of power in Europe.

The value of sail-power or sea-power was never to be forgotten by the British. By logical extension it initially translated into the equation that more sails invariably meant more guns and better and bigger ships. Innovations were devoutly to be wished, and in the 1770s, copper plating was introduced to make the fleet firmer and faster. In the 1830s experiments in steam at Chatham began the eclipse of sail from a military standpoint, and by 1860 the *Warrior*, an iron clad teak warship, virtually made everything else obsolete. Its single-engine steam capacity only operated when challenged -- otherwise it sailed as a simple deterrent, concealing its prototypical capacity, at first as a steam-ship, but eventually as a nuclear submarine or as an Air Carrier. Hardly had the dust settled on the arguments about where to put paddles and propellers, when nuclear power found its way into the one-time coalbunkers.

But while nuclear power was some distance away in 1876. If we look at the contemporary ships, we find that most were concerned with size and capacity. The latest ships -- the HMS *Baccanta* and *Boadicea*, for example, had been newly launched at Portsmouth, while the HMS *Euralus* was still under construction at Chatham. These weren't ironclads of the line, but rather swift unarmored corvettes used (like the *Nelson* off the Clyde)

Introduction

for cruising as well as 'looking after merchant vessels.' The more mature
ships ranged from 3000 tons (the HMS *Volage*) to 5782 tons (the HMS
Inconstant). Between this 3000-5782 ton-range lay others like HMS
Euralus, which, while under construction in 1876, had a projected weight
of 4070 tons; its engines propelling at 5250 indicated horsepower. The
Euralus was expected to carry sixteen guns -- fourteen 4-and- a-half tons,
and two 64-pounders, as well as a range of torpedoes. Its length between
perpendiculars was 280 feet, its extreme breadth 45 ft 6 ins. and its depth
in hold 15 ft 3 ins. It was being built to carry 400 tons of coals and its
complement of officers and men was no less than 350. Already over three-
and-a-half years had been spent on her construction, her keel having been
laid on March 15, 1873. And by October '76 she was as yet litle more than
half finished.

However impressive these military-type ships were, perhaps the best
statistic to demonstrate how far the capacity for British shipbuilding had
come was to be found on the Clyde; for nowhere had the shipbuilding
industry flourished more than on the Clyde, which, in November 1876,
employed no less than 40,000 workers. Not only that, but it was reckoned
at that time that the Clyde's shipyards alone could re-build the whole of
the British fleet in no more than two years.

There is no denying that coincident with steam came the widening of the
world's waterways. Accordingly, in November 1869, the opening of Suez
(forever associated with the Slave's Chorus in Verdi's Aida) celebrated
the 'shortcut' to the East. This meant that steamers, now loading up with
coal at Gibraltar, Port Said, and Aden, enjoyed an enduring advantage
over the sailing ship. However glorious the history of sail is, in the
1870s it appeared to many that, for the first time, sail's lucrative commerce was not just threatened, but was in time displaceable. Fortunately
this did not happen suddenly, nor was it considered a realistic threat to the
clippers of the '70s.

The worth of a small vessel like that of the *Caswell*, with a respective net
and gross weight of 499 and 517 tons, can only be gauged against the
undeniable thrust for bigger, better and more efficient ships. But just as it
would be foolish to deny the State's military expectations, so, too, would
it be equally foolish to exaggerate the effects of those expectations. In the
civil and commercial world of the 1870s, far from being threatened by
steam, sailing barques like the *Caswell* were at the peak of commercial
demand and were prized accordingly.

Introduction

Before Suez, for example, sail tonnage reached a high of 4.6 million tons, whereas steam -- by gradual improvements -- shipped only 0. 8 million tons. Even five years after the Suez Canal opened -- that is three years before the *Caswell* mutiny occurred -- sail carried 4.1 million tons to steam's 1.68 million. Aided by colonial wool, jute from Calcutta, and grain from San Francisco, sail held its own and even made a comeback.

As Basil Lubbock has convincingly argued (in *The Last of the Wind-jammers* (vol. 111, Glasgow, 1975), it was only in the eighties and nineties that sail's great markets finally surrendered to improved steam. In the nineties the demand for large steel windjammers was undeniable, but this was twenty years after the *Caswell* mutiny, and even then, the four-mast barques could still give the steamers a run for their money on the open seas.

In the 1870s, therefore, the eventual if dismal destiny of sail may have been visible but was not as yet felt except in the most rarified circles. For most people, steam merely pronounced the value of sail as a commercial venture, and, under its competitive stimulus , says Lubbock, 'Sail came to its perfection'. The clippers of the seventies were reckoned to be the most beautiful ever launched, the most perfect being that composite of wood and iron called the *Torrens*, an Adelaide passenger ship launched the same year as the *Caswell*. The *Caswell*, of course, was no less elegant if built for cargo, and, if not superior to the American Cape Horners launched in the eighties, she was perfectly admirable in her time.

That being the case, one might have expected the captain of the *Caswell* (and the owners and the insurers) to pay due attention to the selection of crewmembers as well as to their treatment and well-being. The commercial status of the *Caswell* deserved no less. And since both of these matters were firmly in the hands of the captain, much depended on his personality and judgment.

Hazards on the High Seas

So, if the sailor had no fear of displacement, what other fears did he have?

The second -- and by far the more significant -- external concern of seamen in the 1870s arose from the natural hazards attaching to life on the high seas. These included disease, disasters, and assorted accidents. If we look at each of these briefly, it will be apparent that most fatalities increasingly came from accidents. Mutinies, by contrast, if not infrequent, were numerically minimal when compared with the other risk factors facing a sailor who chose his ship at random.

In the case of disease, the story of the discovery of the prophylactic properties of limejuice is a convenient example. It happened that during the blockade of Toulon in the summer of 1793, many of the ships' companies became afflicted with scurvy. It became such a threat that Lord Hood, then commander in chief in the Mediterranean, forbade ships carrying scurvy from entering port, and in effect prohibited them from obtaining even necessary supplies! His Lordship was provident enough, however, to allow one ship into port for the express purpose of obtaining lemons for the use of the fleet.

This incident was most fortuitous, for, in due course, due largely to the consumption of lemons, it became evident that the incidence of sickness in the Royal Navy fell from one-in-four to one-in-ten annually. This welcome discovery progressively relieved the clogged hospital bays on the ships themselves as well those in dry dock.

In time, the general supply of lemon-juice provided other valuable advantages to the navy, not least in the ability of ships' companies to continue at sea for longer periods than hitherto had been the case. The lemon subdued scurvy. And with the widespread and gradual improvement in general hygiene, coupled with the introduction of an ample supply of beef and vegetables (again by Lord Hood) -- particularly during their service in blockades -- other longterm advantages were to follow.

This did not mean that medical mishaps were brought under foreseeable control. Hardly! As late as 1895, for example, the *Trafalgar* traveled from Cardiff to New York and then to Batavia, where to avoid Java fever, the men were virtually imprisoned. Some sailors escaped and one was recaptured. Unfortunately, when he was taken on board, he infected the crew, and. many of those on board the *Trafalgar* died of Java fever. Later still, in 1907 when the *Cape Horn* arrived at Falmouth, she docked with beriberi, killing one and hospitalising others. In short, the fear of contagion on the high seas was ever present. One need only recall the history of fever, plague, dysentery, small pox, typhus, cholera, malaria, and other diseases too numerous to mention, to realise the contribution made by modern medicine to the longevity of the average sailor.

But for our purposes it must be realised that disease was only one form of possible hazard -- and a minor one at that! Other hazards, by contrast, inclu-

Introduction

ded accident, collision, wreckage, ice, fire and fog, as well as countless others too numerous to mention.

As the following brief extract demonstrates, the mortality rate for sailors in the 1870s had multiple as well as decvastating causes.

"1873, Jan. 22. -- British steamer Northfleet sunk in collision off Dungeness, 300 lives lost

1873, Nov. 23. -- White Star liner Atlantic wrecked off Nova Scotia, 547 lives lost.

1873, Nov. 23. -- French line Ville du Havre, from New York to Havre, in collision with ship Locharn and sunk in sixteen minutes, 110 lives lost.

1874, Dec. 24. -- Emigrant vessel Cospatrick took fire and sank off Auckland, 476 lives lost.

1875, May 7. -- Hamburg Mail steamer Schiller wrecked in fog on Scilly Islands, 200 lives lost.

1875, Nov. 4. -- American steamer Pacific in collision thirty miles southwest of Cape Flattery, 236 lives lost.

1878, March 24. -- British training ship Eurydice, a frigate, foundered near the Isle of Wight, 300 lives lost."

The above extract, taken from the *Sinking of the Titanic and Great Sea Disasters* (edited by Logan Marshall - see also Website at <ftp//ftp.biblio. org>) acquaints us with the general sea-faring risk in the 1870s from random causes other than disease. Deaths from mutiny, which brings us to our third concern, were by contrast quite insignificant numerically.

Government Onboard

Perhaps what fascinates people about mutiny is not so much the numbers killed as the social and political relationships that bring it about. Mutiny is rebellion at close quarters. It is first and foremost about a captain and his crew, and how that relationship is formed and fractured. It is about understanding why a crew, against all the odds, including its own self-interest, should turn on its captain with venom and hatred. Unlike disease, the source of mutiny does not reside in a force outside human control, nor is it ever the result of accident. Quite obviously, it is the product of human will, and ought, therefore, to be amenable to reason.

In this sense the actions of the captain and crew of the *Caswell* should also be amenable to reason. And even if it is at the turn of the twenty first century that we reflect upon a matter that occurred in 1875/6 -- when full details and records are hard to come by -- we can, nevertheless, sketch some aspect of that mutiny, delineate its contours, and, where possible, fill up the canvas with some colouring. Towards this end it is necessary to say something of the government of the sailing ship, particularly through our historical image of both the sea captain and his crew.

Thus far we can see how the need for benevolent autocracy on board ship was universally appreciated and constantly justified. Disease and plague always called forth severe government -- one which all too often imposed conditions that would quarantine the crew for days and weeks. It is axiomatic to say that in times of plague the individual survives by virtue of group action. In the interests of survival all hands have to act as one. This also meant, of course, that --whether by way of excuse or genuine concern -- a ship could within seconds be turned into a floating prison, too often with a tyrant at the helm.

Sea-Captaincy
For centuries the ferocious character of the English sea captain was bound up with the fortunes of the fleet and the rise of the nation state. At first, in the age of discovery, the captain was seen as a patriotic explorer, (Columbus, Magellan. Drake and Raleigh), then as the defender of Faith and Fatherland (Granville, Frobisher, Gilbert, Howard of Effingham, and Nelson), then as a free-for-all buccaneer (captains Henry Morgan, and Henry Avery), as an adventurous pirate (captains Teach, Gow, and Kidd), and latterly as either an Officer in the Royal Navy, a Gentleman or as a simple laissez-faire entrepreneur in the Merchant Navy. Little need be said about the patriotic explorers; for whether we talk about Europe or the Argentine, the West Indies, Hong Kong, the Philippines, Mexico, North or South America -- there is hardly a country outside China in which we will not find a goodly supply of full-bodied admirals and conquistadores cluttering up every public square from Trafalgar to Trinidad. And O'Connell's Street in Dublin (before the demolition of Nelson's Pillar by the IRA) was no exception. To a great extent the sea captains carried autocratic cruelty across every gangplank, as if it were a perquisite of government upon the high seas. Whatever their personal profiles, they were held up in the public mind as patriots with personas as prominent as their statues.

Introduction

Until the publication of Alexander Exquemelin's *De Americaensche Zee-Rover* little or nothing was realized of the inner autocracy of a ship's government. The book appeared in Amsterdam in 1678 and in London in 1684. Only then did the reading public get a glimpse into the buccaneering persona. The sacking of Panama in 1671 by captain Henry Morgan helped to correct the patriotic pomp in which Drake and the Elizabethan explorers basked. Throughout the first quarter of the eighteenth century -- perhaps the high point of piracy on the high seas-- murder, rape, robbery, and pillage became synonymous with sailing. In his famous account of piracy, Charles Johnson (another *nom de plume* of Daniel Defoe?) selected his captains because of their crimes. Accordingly, in his '*General History of the Robberies and Murders of the most notorious Pyrates*' (London, 1724), there is hardly a sea-pirate, with the exception of Anne Bonny (the Cork lass tried in Jamaica in November, 1720), who did not die a most violent death; or whose head, like Blackbeard's, did not eventually decorate the end of a Bowsprit.

Yet it is through the medium of 'high literature' that these very violent sea captains are romanticised. In the person of the sea captain, violence manifests itself in defence mode, defending the faith, or, later on, the realm or, later on, in defence of personal honour. It only becomes social when Defoe's famous novel entitled, *The Life and Strange and Surprising Adventures of Robinson Crusoe* was published in 1719.

Hitherto it was argued that *Crusoe* was based upon the experiences of Alexander Selkirk, who ran away to sea in 1704. Selkirk requested to be left on an uninhabited island in the Juan Fernandez Islands some hundreds of miles off the coast of Chile. He reputedly spent over four years there before being rescued by a crew of mutineers. This most Christian of anarchists then contrives to cultivate a servant (a native, 'Man Friday'), while being, at the same time, beset by cannibals -- the moral of *Crusoe* being to demonstrate that society and hierarchy are two social imperatives which imply a third, namely, the need for a captain -- preferably one with an English accent who sits at the governmental helm of things. This moral is further evident in *Crusoe's* two sequels, *The Further Adventures of Robinson Crusoe* (1719) and *The Serious Reflections of Robinson Crusoe*, (1720). The violence and autocracy of the virtuous sea captain is unashamedly continued in *The Life, Adventures, and Pyracies* of the famous captain Singleton, (London 1720) and *The King of the Pirates, Being an Account of the Famous Enterprises of captain Avery* (1724). Both Singleton and Avery are depicted as exploitative egoists, violent if needs be, and rational rather than reasonable.

Introduction

A century later the English-speaking sea captain became suitably refined. Even when Herbert Melville's *Moby Dick* connected the New England Quakers with cannibalism, the quiet dignity of captain George Pollard was assured. In general, however, the focus began to shift from the rugged captain to the sea-faring experience itself. In the 1820s accounts like *The Red Rover* and *The Pilot, A Tale of the Sea,* by James Fenimore Cooper (Two Vols. New York, published by Charles Wiley, 1823) brought home the excitement of exploits in the Americas. Again patriotism featured significantly, and the psychotic sea-captain was being refined considerably.

The Common Sailor

From concern with the denizens of the quarterdeck to concern for those of the forecastle, is a long way to travel; for quarterdeck and forecastle may be only yards away on a ship, they are also as distant and as dismal as class relations are on land, the difference being, that on board ship one end of the town cannot at any time turn its back on the other. And to introduce these onboard tensions to the world, it soon became apparent that the common sailor -- not at all unlike the common twentieth century 'cowboy' under Hollywood management -- had to be sterilised before his pedestrian concerns could be brought to bear on public consciousness.

At first he was Christianised (even Quakerised) by Thomas Lurting (*The Fighting Sailor Turn'd Peaceable Christian:* HTML at voicenet.com; London, 1711). And only two centuries later could he be introduced to the fair sex, when he was romanticised in a sentimental way by Margaret Marshall Saunders (*Her Sailor: A Love Story*: Boston, L.C. Page, 1900). Later still, as sail had lost its savagery, the sailor became sanctified by age both by S. T. Coleridge's 'Ancient Mariner' and F. C. Woodworth's '*Stories by Jack Mason, the Old Sailor',* (NY. 1851). Woodworth, under the pseudonym, 'Theodore Thinker,' wrote a series of 'old-man-of-the-sea' stories laced with blueberry-pie morality, recalling the adventures of whaling and travel. These stories were aimed at a younger generation with a growing interest in sea-faring adventures.

With the exception of the *Mutiny on the Bounty*, very few serious works touched upon the internal dynamism of government on the high seas, and when they did, they pointed up the exact same moral dilemma. There have been several movies made of *Mutiny on the Bounty*, not least because it harvested a crop of concerns that is common to all of us, even in our every-day lives. It is this gripping moral dilemma in which we recognise ourselves

xvi

immediately. And through it we identify with the subject matter of the mutiny, which resonates throughout all cultures. In Act III, Scene 1, Hamlet shouts it from world end to English-speaking world end:

"To be or not to be, that is the question:
Whether it is nobler in the mind to suffer
the slings and arrows outrageous fortune
or to take arms against a sea of troubles and
by opposing end them?"

This is the question that Fletcher Christian poses when he can take no more of Captain Bligh's cruelty. Everywhere in the river of life we are all called upon to try and stop the flood, 'to take arms against a sea of troubles' and somehow end them. How we respond to violence is at the centre of our identity' it is what rivets us to Hamlet as well as to the *Mutiny on the Bounty*.

It is also the question which, in even graver terms , confronts Martin Luther, the religious reformer. And he answers: 'Hier stehe Ich; Ich kann nichts anders.' 'Here I stand; I can do no other.' And on a less elevated plane it also constitutes the *Riddle of the Caswell Mutiny*.

It is by virtue of these concerns that Richard Henry Dana, Jr's account of his experiences in the early nineteenth century have become so important. In his *Two Years Before the Mast* (The Harvard Classics, 1909-14), this young Harvard student reminded his readers of the less savoury side of a seaman's life. When he shipped out of Boston in August 1834 on the brig *Pilgrim*, he witnessed many things, but none had left such an indelible impression on him as the unnecessary flogging of two colleagues -- Sam, and John the Swede. Not unlike what happened on the *Bounty*, Dana demonstrates how a ship could be transported within minutes into the most violent abode. What is of particular importance to us, and to our understanding of the *Caswell* mutiny, is the group dynamic, or the effective chain of reactions to the captain's abuse of power. Because of this single issue we have dwelt at length -- and, hopefully, profitably -- on Dana's extraordinary narrative.

The nameless captain had apparently been picking on people for a few days. He had already threatened the cook with a flogging for dropping some wood on the deck. Now he was reproaching Sam, who was 'a good sailor,' even if he was a little 'slow.' John the Swede and others were standing by the main hatchway when they heard the captain's voice

Introduction

' raised in violent dispute' down in the hold: -

> "You see your condition! You see your condition! Will you ever give
> me any more of your jaw?" No answer; and then came wrestling and
> heaving, as though the man was trying to turn him.
> "You may as well keep still, for I have got you," said the captain.
> Then came the question, "Will you ever give me any more of your jaw?"
> "I never gave you any, sir," said Sam; for it was his voice that we heard,
> though low and half choked.
> "That's not what I ask you. Will you ever be impudent to me again?"
> "I never have been, sir," said Sam.
> "Answer my question, or I'll make a spread eagle of you! I'll flog you, by
> G-d."
> "I'm no negro slave," said Sam.
> "Then I'll make you one," said the captain; and he came to the hatchway,
> and sprang on deck, threw off his coat, and rolling up his sleeves, called out
> to the mates -- "Seize that man up, Mr. A__, Seize him up! Make a spread
> eagle of him. I'll teach you all who is master aboard."

With this the crew and officers followed the captain up the hatchway,
and after repeated orders the mate laid hold of Sam, who made no
resistance. They then carried him to the gangway. It was at this stage
that another crewmember responded.

> "What are you going to flog that man for, Sir?" said John the
> Swede, to the captain."

Upon hearing this, the captain turned on him and ordered that he be
put in irons. John the Swede went peaceably aft to the quarterdeck,
while the captain attended to Sam. The captain was going to whip
Sam personally while the crew 'grouped together in the waist', and
Dana began to feel sick and angry at the sight of a man being 'fastened
up and flogged like a beast.' Having lived with Sam for months, Dana
said that he regarded Sam as 'his brother.' Describing his mixed reactions, he reflected:

> "The first and almost uncontrollable impulse was resistance. But what
> was to be done? The time for it had gone by. The two best men were
> fast, and there were only two beside myself, and a small boy of ten or
> twelve years of age. And then there were (beside the captain) three
> officers, steward, agent and clerk. But beside the numbers, what is
> there for sailors to do? If they resist, it is mutiny; and if they succeed,
> and take the vessel, it is piracy. If they ever yield again, their punish-
> ment must come; and if they do not yield, they are pirates for life. If
> a sailor resists his commander, he resists the law, and piracy or subm-
> ission are his only alternatives. Bad as it was, it must be borne. It
> is what a sailor ships for."

This last sentence is striking in its ambiguity. When one thinks about it , it is very difficult to understand what Dana means. He is hardly saying that sailors should stoically accept even inhuman conditions or breaches of their human and constitutional rights with impunity! Or is this what he actually expects from sailors? How much is endurable short of self-defence?

Further on in the episode Dana writes:

> "Swinging the rope over his head, and bending his body so as to give it full force, the captain brought it down upon the poor fellow's back. Once, twice six times. "Will you ever give me any more of your jaw?" The man writhed with pain, but said not a word. Three times more. This was too much, and he muttered something, which I could not hear; this brought as many more as the man could stand; when the captain ordered him to be cut down, and to go forward".

> With this the captain now turned his attention to John the Swede. According to Dana, he stood on the quarterdeck, bareheaded, his eyes flashing with rage, and his face as red as blood. He was swinging a rope and calling out to his officers, "Drag him aft! Lay hold of him. I'll sweeten him, etc., etc". Having conceded to a peaceful flogging at first, the Swede then began to resist, but was subdued by the officers. And when he was made fast, he turned to the captain, who stood turning up his sleeves and getting ready for the blow, and asked:

> "Have I ever refused my duty, sir? Have you ever known me to hang back, or to be insolent, or not to know my work?"

> "No", said the captain, "it is not *that* I flog you for; I flog you for your interference, for asking questions".

> "Can't a man ask a question here without being flogged?"

> "No", shouted the captain; "nobody shall open his mouth aboard this vessel, but myself", and began laying the blows upon his back, swinging half round between each blow, to give it full effect. As he went on, his passion increased, and he danced about the deck, calling out as he swung the rope: -- "If you want to know what I flog you for, I'll tell you. It's because I like to do it! – Because I like to do it. It suits me. That's what I do it for". The man writhed under the pain, until he could endure it no longer, when he called out, with an exclamation more common among foreigners than with us-"Oh, Jesus Christ! Oh, Jesus Christ!"

> "Don't call on Jesus Christ," shouted the captain; "he can't help you. Call on Captain T__. He's the man! He can help you! Jesus Christ can't help you now!"

Introduction

At this juncture Dana tells us that he could look no longer. His blood ran cold and he turned away in disgust and horror. He revisited the scene with thoughts of revenge, but, again, 'the falling blows and the cries of the man' called him back to reality. At length the Swede was cut down. Every one else stood still at his post, while the captain, 'swelling with rage and with the importance of his achievement' strutted the quarter-deck, calling out to the crew:

> "You see your condition! You see where I've got you all, and you know what to expect! You've been mistaken in me -- you didn't know what I was! Now you know what I am!"

> "I'll make you toe the mark, every soul of you, or I'll flog you all, fore and and aft, from the boy, up"

> "You've got a driver over you Yes, a slave driver -- a negro-driver! I'll see who'll tell me he isn't a Negro slave!"

Shortly after this John the Swede's back was swollen and covered with stripes in every direction. He asked the steward to ask the captain to let him have some salve, or balsam, to put upon it. "No," said the captain, who heard him from below; "tell him to put his shirt on; that's the best thing for him; and pull me ashore in the boat. Nobody is going to lay-up on board this vessel."

Dana also recalls his fear that John the Swede, whom he regarded as a violent man and who was armed with a knife, might mutiny. In fact he didn't. Dana also noted that the captain was probably armed. He also pointed out that the option of resisting for either Sam or John (and Dana?) meant that they 'would have had nothing before them but flight and starvation in the woods of California, or capture by the soldiers and Indian bloodhounds, whom the offer of twenty dollars would have set upon them.'

The sleepless nights of the men groaning in pain settled a gloom over everyone, and made Dana reflect:

> "I thought of our situation, living under a tyranny; of the character of the country we were in; of the length of the voyage, and of the uncertainty attending our return to America; and then, if we should return, of the pros-pect of obtaining justice and satisfaction for these poor men; and vowed that if God should ever give me the means, I would do something to redress the grievances and relieve the sufferings of that poor class of beings, of whom I then was one."

Introduction

There are many lessons to be learned from Dana's account - which is why we have dwelt upon it so long.

First of all, we can see that what began with the captain's distemper and his threat to the cook was soon followed up by his bullying of Sam. This in turn led to Sam's public flogging. This public humiliation affected the crew, particularly John the Swede, who could not suppress his sense of injustice, so he fled to the side of the oppressed. Before long the whole crew was upset, but none of the others, including Dana, said anything. The captain continued his abuse, revealing even further depths of cruelty and an utter contempt for those in his charge. In such circumstances considerations of mutiny are no more than thoughts of self-preservation. Dana and the crew of the *Pilgrim* were now caste in the mould of Hamlet and Fletcher Christian, to rebel or to be bear witness to enormous injustice?

The second lesson we learn is somewhat more difficult to come to terms with, and when we compare Fletcher Christian with Richard Dana Jr., both of whom are faced with Hamlet's dilemma, then we can appreciate how difficult the problem is.

Not all men live with the discipline (or the future prospects) of Richard Dana. Some men are present-dwellers; they are less apt to defer gratification, whether that gratification comes from the assurance of future vengeance or from a sense of delayed justice. Moreover, such men have a morality of action, rather than one of reaction or introspection; they demand redress now, concurrent with the offence, rather than hereafter in retrospection, whether that retrospection is recounted in a court of law or in a novel. Richard Dana vowed to redress 'the sufferings of that poor class of beings', of which he was temporarily one. He did not vow to redress the injustice he saw done to Sam or John the Swede. Moreover, the redress he envisaged would follow only ' if God' should ever give him the means to do so. Some men of action (Christian Fletcher and Hamlet, for example) might argue that he had the means to redress the injustice before his eyes, and that he did not need God to provide the wherewithal for that redress.

The problem with Dana's account is the problem with Dana's morality. His relation with the captain (and the cruelties he was inflicting) was no more constrained that Christian's was to Captain Bligh or, for that matter, Hamlet's relation to his Father-in-law, the King of Denmark. Unlike Hamlet and Fletcher Christian, however, both of whom felt constrained to act, Dana, on due consideration, decided not to. He admitted that he felt compelled to act but decided not to do so -- hence that problematic phrase "Bad as it was, it must be borne. It is what a sailor ships for."

Men of action invariably wish to redress wrong spontaneously, wherever they find it. It may be quixotic, but not everyone is endowed with the fortitude and restraint, which Richard Dana exhibited. In point of fact Dana went on to practice law and politics. And during the operation of the Fugitive Slave Law, he acted as counsel on behalf of the fugitives Shadrach, Sims, and Burns. Abraham Lincoln appointed him United States District Attorney for Massachusetts. But this is still beside the point. The question is and was: Should Richard Dana have spoken up like John the Swede, and taken the lash? Or, alternatively, should the crew have revolted and at least restrained the captain? Maybe there are some occasions when, under severe provocation, mutiny *is* the moral thing to do.

It is desirable that we analyse Dana's narrative a little further.

There is obviously a great difference between what one feels when injustice is done to oneself, and what one feels when it happens to others in our presence. When we are personally confronted with unkindness or cruelty, we have a choice. We can resist it or bear it. It is peculiarly within our individual power to make such a decision. If we choose to bear it, it is because forbearance is very much a part of our character, of our individual psyche, of our peace-loving stoical personality. Proverbs and truisms applaud and encourage such forbearance as a virtue. Hence we hear that 'Great minds suffer in silence." We are content with our own unique sense of restraint and fortitude. We choose to bear 'the whips and scorns of outrageous fortune' rather than 'take arms against a sea of troubles and by opposing end them.' If we are Christian, we say we 'turn the other cheek.' We 'grin and bear it.' This we do personally, and for ourselves. We could, of course, take action -- or at least we say and believe that 'we could take action', thereby emphasizing the fact that we have made a virtuous and stoical decision to bear up to the adversity in question. If we did actually take action, it would assuredly be by way of some kind of alternative outcome -- alternative, that is, to our agreeable self-esteem and, possibly, to our life style as well. In this way we can see that we are authors of our own tolerance or martyrdom.

But when strangers are confronted with unkindness or cruelty in our presence, something else happens: we are pitted in a different mould. We are summoned to witness evil, to look on, to be excluded from the action. It is others who are suffering while we remain silent. We can neither adopt the pain stoically nor ameliorate it in the person of others. We are forced to witness cruelty, and the harsh truth is that we cannot bear to watch others suffer unnecessary pain, even the pain that we would stoically endure ourselves. Hamlet is activated out of a love for justice and for the memory of his murdered father, Luther does it for truth, integrity and the state of Catholicism under a corrupt Papacy. But Christian Fletcher and John the Swede are no less high-minded; they sacrifice themselves for others.

What inflames us most, perhaps, is the wanton cruelty to helpless others. Our most intimate sense of justice is ravaged. All our most sanctified senses of civilized living come forward and demand redress. It is the march of the righteous and, because it cannot be borne by us personally , it compels us to action. By the same token, those who in our presence, inflict gratuitous pain and suffering, especially on innocent or inadequate people -- people who have not got our privileges, our restraint, our education, our fortitude, our affection - they soon become the object of our most forceful and violent feelings. What first gave us character is now in utter revolt and cannot be subdued or, alternatively, can only be subdued with enormous difficulty. Even when we see animals badly treated, we rebel with a violence that is disproportionate to our ordinary character. Our revolt is intended to edify the wrongdoer, but only after peace is secured.

That is why 'teaching someone a lesson' has far too often become associated more with violence and vengeance than with education. That is also why in some circumstances spontaneous violence is the only lesson in morality possible. I do not mean premeditated violence or war carried out in retrospect or, indeed, war that is not defensive in nature, but action that is designed to 'teach the enemy a lesson.'

At a personal level, the problem with humans is not so much that they are diabolical, but rather, like John the Swede, they are angelic:magnificently angelic. Sam submitted to a flogging by a cruel captain, John the Swede voiced his objections and took the whip, and Dana lived to tell the tale. Had someone taken action, we would have had a capital trial for mutiny. Wherein lies morality then? In the captain? In Sam's submission to unjust and brutal discipline? In John the Swede's quixotic if magnanimous gesture? Or in Dana's narrative? And if they had resisted, what court could capture the moment in which they all ineluctably and ineffably took part? For many people spontaneity has its own morality, it holds its own court, and who is to say it is not the highest court in every land!

As the nineteenth century wore on, the increasing press coverage of mutinies and court cases, gave rise to a more realistic picture of life at sea. The image of the English-speaking captain remained somehow unscathed if not sanctified. Writers like Joseph Conrad and John Masefield and a myriad of lesser writers, taught us both about idealized captains like *Lord Jim* as well as reluctant seamen like *Dauber*. They also focused our attention on the general conditions of life then obtaining at sea.

But high literature is not always a good guide to great morality. *Lord Jim*, to my mind, is a case in point. It is a story of the redemption of a British naval officer who is damned initially for his cowardice, then lionized as a selfless hero. The novel may have been fiction, but the initial act of cowardice and dishonor was, it is believed, based on fact. The story (1900), originally intended as a short story, was enlarged into a novel and opens (as does the film) with an account in 1880 of the British first mate, A.P.Williams, who, with other officers, abandoned the steamship *Jeddah*, after it sprung a leak. In abandoning the ship they also abandoned the Muslim pilgrims who were now facing certain death. By sheer good fortune another captain in another steam ship happened by and brought the *Jeddah* to safety. In the film of *Lord Jim* the Jeddah becomes the Patna, and the story relates how the guilt-ridden British naval officer seeks redemption for his initial mistake. He finds it in helping islanders win their freedom.

That *Lord Jim* sacrifices himself in the process is more logical than real; and even if it was real, the hero is caste between two simple poles, one of cowardice and one of bravery, these being the dominant ethical values of both the writer and the protagonist. Breaking your word to a boatload of people, who will assuredly die because you have deliberately misled them, is hardly redeemable, especially if the tale follows hot on their miraculous survival. It is rather like pleading guilty to an act of pedophilia and later claiming, 'anyone can make a mistake' by way of defence. Moreover, to redeem one's soul by self-immolation does not to my mind excuse the initial wrongdoing. What Conrad has done to redeem his English-speaking sea captain is -- it appears -- done out of a debauched celebration of the art of story-telling -- hence the triumph of egoism over altruism.

The English-speaking captain survived in the public mind - even to the present day - in the approximate persona of James Onedin, protagonist in a popular television serial, *The Onedin Line*. He is meant to be understood as the best of a bad lot, the 'lovable rogue.' Even in make-belief the anti-hero is untouched by the slave trade, questionable contracts, and 'dodgy' merchandise. By implication every scam and questionable enterprise is to be excused by captain Onedin's early penury, especially his do-or-die necessity for success, which we, the viewing public, are meant to understand implicitly. Hence whatever pathologies are revealed, they are transcended by our common ambition and acquisitiveness, our shared indulgence in some common drive to escape some ghetto of European or American ordinariness. To assist us in thinking well of Nineteenth Century sea captains, captain Onedin is portrayed as less aggressive than his contemporaries. Diametrically opposed to this make-belief background we have the word of Basil Lubbock that real bullies abounded throughout the period:

> "It must be admitted that there was a type of man found on the quarterdeck in sail who has become almost extinct in steam. This was the sea bully. One of the most notorious of these buckos was Captain Bailey of the big full rigger *Dovenby Hall*. He was a terrible brute with an uncontrollable temper, a ready fist and vilely blasphemous tongue. He was murdered by his coloured steward on the passage home from San Francisco. At the trial both Bailey's wife and daughter testified that they could not live with him, and the steward got off with a life sentence." (*The Last of the Windjammers*, Vol. 1, Glasgow, 1975, p.49)

By the turn of the twentieth century, what had been romantic and patriotic had now become comic. As far as the British Isles were concerned the last of the rapacious pirates survived solely in Penzance where, with Gilbertian humour, they flirted ferociously, did their indentures meticulously, and captured the odd Major General, whose daughters they married.

Even the secrecy surrounding advancement in the 'Queen's Navee' was fully exposed by the Chorus of HMS Pinafore:

CHORUS:

Now landsmen all, whoever you may be,
If you want to rise to the top of the tree,
If your soul isn't fettered to an office stool,
Be careful to be guided by this golden rule:
Stick close to your desks and never go to sea,
And you all may be rulers of the Queen's Navee!

However beguiling television videos and good yarns are, they are the product of the twenty first century. For our part the belligerence of the English sea captain prevailed well into the 1870s and after. He was neither romantic, nor patriotic nor comic, but the remnant of the high pirate era, when violence at sea was a way of life. How the twin forces -- of the need for commerce, and of the responsibility for order on board ship -- are forged in the personality of captain George Best remains in the realm of conjecture, until, that is, it is revealed to us through evidence. We can only judge of these things from the evidence available and presented. The standards we apply -- either to the need for order on board or the need for commerce abroad -- derive from the ordinary expectations that we would exercise ourselves in a location and a time that bespeaks these dual ideals.

Thus far, then, we know that the competition of steam did not diminish the value of either the *Caswell* or her crew. We know that seamen faced very dangerous hazards at sea, even if mutiny did not itself bulk large as a major hazard. In this respect the role of the sea captain is crucial. Upon his persona depended the moral ethos of the ship, particularly when that ship carried a mixed crew. But how dangerous and unusual was the 'mixed crew' in the 1870s?

Racism and the Mixed Crew:
It has been said that the *Caswell* mutiny was primarily due to the mixed crew on board, as if the mixture of Greek and British sailors was the sole cause of the mutiny. Mixed crews in the age of sail were practically as traditional as the art of sailing itself. From earliest times multi-racial and multi-national crews abounded. Even at Trafalgar the crews were mixed, the 'black watch', it is said, growing numerous enough to relieve the 'white watch' on alternate shifts. Moreover, Lubbock tells us:

> "Practically every nationality in the world has a representative on the lower deck in Nelson's fleet -- and with the usual result, the German, the Dane, the Dutchman, the Dago, the Souwegian and the Finn gradually assumed the ways and the outlook of the Britisher, often married an English girl and gave his sons to the Empire." (Lubbock, Basil, *The Last of the Windjammers*, Vol. 1, Glasgow, 1975, p.62)

Even the Nantucket Quaker-Whalers aboard the famous *Essex* in 1820 were mixed of race -- and captain George Pollard lived on to see them eat each other, not out of hatred, but out of hunger. Twenty years later R.H. Dana Jr. observed that in his time three quarters of the crews were mixed. In this connection we might also remember that the word 'sailor,' as opposed to 'mariner' or ' oarsman', only becomes popular in the era of mercantilism, when unbridled movements of trans-national and migrant workers, whether captive, conscripted or recruited, were mobilised by the Nation State. The oarsmen -- rowing to the beat of a drum or the sound of the lash -- had served the needs of the Greek city-state, as well as the Roman and Medieval fleets of southern Europe. As military vessels, their fearful traffic held sway well into the eighteenth century but, because of their enhanced size, speed, and firepower, the sailing ship took over. At least that was the case with the ocean-going Atlantic vessels. In the coastal waters of the Mediterranean, things were otherwise designed; the highly maneuverable galleys were still in use and the galley sentence was meant to secure a continuing supply of labour.

These two nautical traditions (with their origins perhaps going as far back as the Holy Roman Imperial split between Byzantium and Rome) were so different in fact that over the course of the sixteenth and seventeenth centuries they gave birth at either end of Europe to two quite opposite penal regimes. On the one hand the Mediterranean States introduced the galley sentence while the northern countries founded the Workhouse. If we are going to examine the mutiny on the *Caswell*, or any other mutinous ship claiming a mixed pedigree as its source, it behoves us to look briefly at how the penal and punitive aspects clung to the sailing ship well into the nineteenth century.

Galleys

Throughout the 16th century European poverty was increasing apace with an expanding population. The new crime and the new plague were called 'vagabondage.' The feudal order was in a state of collapse, and private retainers and soldiers were being disbanded and turned out of the old manorial estates. Enclosure movements shed the land of its 'structurally unemployed' laborers and yeomen. The influx of bullion from the New World gave rise to an increase in prices. Basic necessities rose faster than wages, and the agencies of poor relief were choked off in the general struggle between Papal power and the rise of the Nation State. Power was passing from Pope to Prince, from the Saviour of Souls to the leaders of nations. It was England versus Spain in the sixteenth century, then England versus Holland in the seventeenth. Pirates became patriots, and begging and pillage abounded in the cities and ports of Europe -- the only organizers of discarded labour centered on the urban factories and the workhouse.In the south, galleys required hundreds of oarsmen rowing in unison. The triremes of ancient Greece had used them to great effect. The work was strenuous, dangerous, and severely disciplined. In times when demand for oarsmen was not met with an adequate supply, the wages of the fleet rose abruptly, and where excess demand remained, the fleets supplemented the labour force with galley slaves. These slaves came from the ranks of Turks and North Africans who may have been bought or taken captive in war. When the growing fleets of the 15th and 16th centuries could not satisfy the demand for oarsmen, the authorities looked to the criminals to

augment the ranks of the fleet. Condemned convicts whom the State
wished to kill were now pressed into the service of the military. From
Spain, Italy and France the Galley Sentence spread north, to the Netherlands in the 1520s and to Belgium and Austria in the 1550s.

The galley sentence was so terrible that, according to one authority,

> "The wretches condemned to it would sometimes sever their own
> arm or hand in order to escape it. The practice was even so com-
> mon that a decree of 1677 made it punishable by death."

At a time when corporal punishments were so countless and cruel,
capital punishments were seen as their mere extension. The galley
sentence in the North was to prove short-lived, not least because of
climatic conditions. Climate notwithstanding, under Elizabeth plans
were made to create an English galley fleet. In 1597 a statute authorized
the banishment of vagabonds or, alternatively, their conscription into the
galleys by the courts of quarter sessions. The execution of felons was
stayed. These included robbers, but not murderers, rapists, burglars or
witches. The act aimed at salvaging the strong and the able bodied. In
time it widened, further executions were stayed, reprieves were granted,
and galley sentences were encouraged.

A Commission in 1615 authorized the transportation of felons 'fit to be
employed in foreign discoveries or other services beyond the seas.' The
preamble of the 1615 Commission followed the language of the 1602
Commission in that the monarch ordered that some of the 'lesser offenders' condemned to die be redeemed by corrective punishment and by
service profitable 'to the Commonwealth in parts abroad.'

Notwithstanding a congery of purposes -- namely, to avoid the severity of
the medieval blood sanctions, to correct the offender, and to exploit his
labor -- they all had the punitive instinct in common, and it was this that
motivated the workhouse, the prison, and, to a lesser extent, the nineteenth
century sailing ship. Imperial expansion also moulded the policies of banishment and transportation. Generally speaking, however, the galley sentence
was short lived in the North, and increasingly gave way to the bridewell or
workhouse, which mirrored in the north what the galley sentence did in the
south. In the 1550s a bridewell, the former Royal Palace in London, was
converted into a workhouse or 'house of correction.' A bridewell in
Norwich soon followed (1565), then a workhouse movement, begun in
London and Norwich, soon spread to Amsterdam, Antwerp, Paris and the
cities of the German Hansa.

Introduction

The bridewells filled up with young vagabonds, 'sturdy beggars' and 'disorderly' persons, all of whom were compelled to work to sustain themselves. Just like the ship or later on, the prison, the workhouse was designed to introduce the inmate to the regimen of honest labor. It would train him in a working skill, and it would reform his character through discipline and moral instruction. The close trade connections between the Netherlands and England inspired the Dutch to exploit their labour in a similar manner. Religious instruction, penal reform, and the exploitation of labour, became the *rasion d'etre* of the Tuchthuis (Amsterdam, 1590s), the Zuchthaus (Bremen, 1615) as well as the Belgian Workhouses. In time a model workhouse was set up throughout Europe's major cities (e.g. Lubeck, Hamburg, Danzig, Breslau, Vienna, Leipzig, and Frankfurt), including Belgium (e.g. Antwerp, Brussels and Ghent). Such was the supportive connection between the use of the criminal law and the forced exploitation of labour, that its worst aspects were never reformed until the middle of the eighteenth century. This reform was reflected in Cesare Beccaria's slim *Treatise on Crimes and Punishments*, which became the focal point of reform throughout Europe. The Italian criminologist was by no means the originator of growing European resistance to the blood sanctions. On the contrary, talk of reform had begun long before Beccaria -- but his was the decisive blow against the old monotonous and religious theatrical cruelties of the *ancien regime*. The ship, whether propelled by oarsmen or by sail, played an important part in the displacement of these medieval blood sanctions. In so doing it helped as an intermediary in giving birth to the modern prison system. 'Hulks' and 'convict ships' were used as floating prisons on the Thames, the Liffey, and occasionally on the Lee. The ship was also used as a means of transporting convicts to the new plantations in the Americas, Australia, and New Zealand.

Transportation, or the wholescale removal of thousands of convicted criminals from one country to another became a European policy. It managed to divide the world in two, such that people quite sensibly spoke of two worlds, the 'old' and the 'new' world. To talk disparagingly about 'mixed crews' or to conceive of them as odd or undesirable is hard to take seriously. Whatever objections the British had to a 'mixed crew' such objections would have to be more specific and would have to arise out of some more specified political or personal circumstances.

Generally speaking, however, the penal disciplines, the tensions of former times, survived in the work ethic of the nineteenth century sailing ship. In some ways the sailing ship was worse than the workhouse for here the gender gap was complete and absolute; and whatever considerations might be afforded to regimens that included women, none attached to a sailing ship. Seamen picked oakum and had as grueling a regimen as obtained in any northern workhouse. Sailors were expected to work and never to slouch or relax.

It will soon become apparent that the crew of the *Caswell* came from two different sailing traditions, the one from the Mediterranean and the other from the Atlantic. It was as if the *Caswell* had inherited an overarching history of which her captain and her crew were perfectly unaware.

======

Chapter 1

An Old Crew

Old Swansea Town
Now our storms are over,
And we are safe on shore;
We will drink success
To all the girls,
And the one that I adore.
We will drink strong wine and brandy too,
And we will make those taverns roar;
And when our money is spent and gone,
We'll go around Cape Horn for more, fine girls

Chorus
Old Swansea Town once more,
And still we live in hope to see
Old Swansea Town once more.

(Contemporary Welsh Ballad)

Christos Emmanuel Bombos was the son of a Greek sea-captain. Some
people say he fled his home in Attica for the love of a woman. If so, he
was neither the first nor the last sailor to lose his bearings in love's maels-
trom.

Perhaps it explained how he came aimlessly to Buenos Aires and how
and why, in August 1875, he signed on with a British ship. Whatever
passions drove him forward, whatever fortunes attracted him hither, like
most men his age, he yearned for adventure. And where better to find it
than on a British barque? Bombos was young, open and eager for the
opportunity to meet other nationalities. He would see the sea through
British eyes. It would be an experience to remember, one about which
he could hereafter tell his father, his family and his friends.

Little did he know that by the time he had finished his short tour of duty
he would be arrested on board ship and tried in Ireland on a charge of
murder. Had it been otherwise he might have heard 'Old Swansea Town'
sung, if not by the mixed crew of the *Caswell*, then by some other crew;

1

for it was customary amongst the "old copper-ore men" to sing their way off Swansea's North Dock. After rounding Cape Horn the return trip was sweet, and on touching *terra firma* , it is said that they couldn't resist a stave or two of the old shanty.(See *Swansea Cape Horners Remember*, Swansea City Council, Leisure Services Department, Maritime & Industrial Museum)

But what he never knew about, Bombos never missed. In due course he was to learn about other things, including the circumstances under which he first clapped eyes on James Carrick, a young attractive ambitious Scot. Within the space of months Carrick would become both his friend and his mortal enemy. Almost a year later, as he awaited his execution in a Cork Gaol Bombos would recall their first encounter:

> "I… shipped from Buenos Ayres with the barque *Caswell*. When I went on board I saw Dunne and Carrick in irons. The Captain had put them in, and after 13 days gave them their liberty."

The story of the *Caswell* mutiny is very much about these two young men, Christos Bombos and James Carrick, and how they related to each other and to the crew and captain of the *Caswell*. But it would be wrong to give the impression that the drama on board was confined to two or three people. Quite the contrary; it was more particularly about a small community of 16 men and their self-contained government on board what is, after all, a small, floating country, an island measuring no more than 155.5 feet long, 28 feet broad and 16 feet deep.

(It will be observed that we refer to the *Caswell* as female, not solely to compensate for the exclusively male makeup of her crew, but also because it feels more convenient — almost traditional -- to do so. It is also preferable to the use of a lifeless ' it.')

In the nineteenth century the South Wales port of Swansea developed an important trade in copper and other non-ferrous metals. Cutters, tall ships and seascapes -- they all combined to create a sailing-ship preserve where 'doubling the Horn' was still a fashionable and daring thing to do. One man, captain James Bevan is reputed to have rounded the horn no less than 56 times 'without losing a ship' (*Sea Breezes*, number 236, August 1965). Amongst the Swansea pioneers (in the smelting and refining of copper ore on a substantial scale) were John Henry Vivian and Sons. Their enterprise began with the introduction of the famous Hafod Copper Works to the district in 1810. It was copper that increasingly made the difference, such that Swansea got the name of being a 'metallurgical metropolis'. Eventually Swansea became one of the leading ports in the United Kingdom. By the 1830s the ore-smelting reached industrial proportions.

At first, huge quantities of copper ore were imported from Cornwall, Cumberland, and Anglesey. This gave birth to the renowned Swansea 'copper ore' barques. And when the Cornish ports were worked out, these barques -- hungry for copper -- scoured the' ore ports' of Spain, Cuba, South Africa and South America.

Home expansion saw the opening of Swansea's North Dock in 1852 and the South Dock in 1859. This expansion enabled the larger sized vessels to have access to the port. And from then until the 1870s the copper ore trade flowered phenomenally. Swansea in the 70s outstripped any comparable port in the Bristol Channel, including Bristol itself. Even Cuban ore was bye-passed in favour of the richer deposits on the west coast of South America. Swansea now shipped ore from Chilean ports (Valparaiso, Caldera, Lota, Antofagasta, Tocopilla, Taltal, Carrizal, La Serena, Copiapo, Coquimbo, and others), which connections gave rise to the name 'Copper Ore Cape Horners.' The passage to and from Swansea meant that Cape Horn with its ferocious gales and head winds had to be 'doubled.' The barques themselves became objects of inspiration, and in due course Swansea developed a pilot boat-rig, which was unique to the port of Swansea and, incidentally, recognizable by mariners all over the world.

Into this maritime nest the *Caswell* was born in 1875. She was built at Dumbarton by McKellar, McMillan & Co, registered in Swansea, and christened the *Caswell* in Welsh waters. Her pedigree was pure – *secundus ad nullum* - the product of the most loving and skilful hands that bore the stamp of seamanship in *Gross Britannia*.

Paradoxically, the *Caswell* was ancient in her infancy and infant in her ancestry. On the one hand, her character was one that stretched as far back as commercial man could see, even to Phoenician times. On the other, she was unique: at birth she was blessed with what had been denied to her ancestors; she had iron! All in all, she was an original -- with all her genes in their proper place. Not only had she oodles of history -- with Celtic, Roman and Norse blood in her veins -- but she also had wire in her rigging, three masts on her deck, and iron in her hull. She was new and she could glide and tack against the wind with the best. We must also conclude

that she was a very attractive ship, not least because we can see it for ourselves. Back in 1876, as she lay in Queenstown harbour, at least one artist
fell under the spell of her unfurled allure, and, thankfully, has provided
this book (and the *Illustrated News)* with a most sought-after sketch.

In due course the *Caswell* was given her official number - 70492. At
long last , her deck was polished, her name was painted, and her time
had come. She soon slipped her moorings and, like a fledgling swan,
opened her wings to the breadth of heaven and flit to Glasgow – all
499 tons of her!

Despite her charms and the ceremony that surrounded her delivery, she
was destined for foul winds rather than fair. Hers would not be a long or
a happy life. On the contrary, she would not live beyond her twenty-fifth
year, and tragedy and violence would mar her from the first. Even if she
was designed to carry her cargo across the most disturbed seas, and to
plough the worst squalls, the *Caswell* was but one of a legion of small
Welsh vessels for which such chores were commonplace. She was built
for endurance, and she had the heart of a cheetah. It was the men in her
life who caused her to lose her self-esteem, so to speak; to live a life that
turned out to be short, brutish and bloody. No sooner had she been baptis-
ed in Wales than she was delivered over to unhappy men.

On July 1st 1875 the *Caswell* sailed out of the port of Glasgow and turned
her back on Blighty. Her destination? Buenos Aires. Her Captain? Mr.
George Best, a Londoner who had married the daughter of Chief Constable Allison, Swansea's finest! While there are few available accounts or
descriptions of Best, he was in fact quite well known. He was even
thought well of in some circles. According to *The Cambrian* (May 19,
1876), a Welsh newspaper, he "was a man rather above the average
height, of ruddy complexion, dark hair and handsome appearance, and
seemed a genial good fellow. When irritated by incompetent or unwilling
hands, he may have been somewhat Choleric and sudden." The irony
surrounding his character is, perhaps, best exemplified by N.L. Thomas'
anecdotal reference in an article in 'Sea Breezes,' which puts him firmly
in the Valhalla of sea-captains (number 236, August 1965. See also "The
Story of Swansea's Districts and Villages" by N.L. Thomas).

> "...In their day, some of the best-known captains were Maddox of
> the *Ocean River*; Bully Best of the *Caswell*; Fisher of the *Pacific*;
> Hugo Jago of the *Florence Danvers*; and David Mendus, Castle,
> Shearer, Bevan, Rosser, Briscoe, Grove, Finch, David Lewis and
> Jenkins."

An Old Crew

***

Before proceeding further perhaps we might mention two items. One
describes the division of labour obtaining on board ships like the *Caswell*.
The other simply asks what affect the sea has had on young minds.

Within a short period of time two crews—or the better part of two crews—
were to man the *Caswell* in swift succession, and although their numbers
differed, their functions remained much the same. The first crew left Glasgow and numbered nineteen; the crew that would leave Buenos Aires on
the return trip numbered sixteen. Who were these men? What kind of people were they? What inspired young sailors to go to sea back in the 1870s?
And of equal importance: what were their respective duties vis-à-vis each
other? How, in other words, were ships like the *Caswell* governed?

We have already commented on some aspects of the history of the sailing
ship. But in the nineteenth century there is a conscious recognition of an
almost anthropological longing for the sea. Even the irreverent Buck Mul-
ligan in Joyce's *Ulysses*, pays homage to the sea's overall significance.
He no sooner castigates the "snotgreen sea," and the "scrotumtightening
sea", than he instantly recalls its original authority. "Thalatta! Thalatta!"
he cries: "She is our great sweet mother." For our purposes the ancient
caresses of this Goddess are best exemplified by reference to two compet-
ing voices.

The first of these is the popular and contemporaneous account by John
Masefield (1878). In his poem *Sea-Fever* Masefield captures the sea's
seductive power. At first an image is sprung, then an urge is released,
then it becomes a yearning, a desire, a conviction and eventually a fever.
By the third stanza, the poem offers a philosophy, a virtual lifestyle, to
every poet, dropout, and antiglobal-capitalist on earth. Indeed , the offer
is made to young men of every age, to yield right-of-way to the siren
in their souls, and, against all the odds , to get out, turn on, and hurry

"... Down to the seas again to the vagrant gypsy life.
To the gull's way and the whale's way
Where the wind's like a whetted knife
And all I ask is a merry yarn from a laughing fellow-rover,
And quiet sleep and a sweet dream when the long trick's over."

An Old Crew

A more cautionary contrast is provided by Richard Dana Jr. who, as we have already seen, surrendered himself as a young man to the call of the sea. His experiences and views, if not as poetic as John Masefield's, are nevertheless as valuable in the present context. With Protestant precision he cautions against what Masefield most promotes.

> "There is a witchery in the sea, its songs and stories, and in the mere sight of a ship, and the sailor's dress, especially to a young mind, which has done more to man navvies, and fill merchantmen, than all the press-gangs of Europe. I have known a young man with such a passion for the sea, that the very creaking of a block stirred up his imagination so that he could hardly keep his feet on dry ground; and many are the boys, in every seaport, who are drawn away, as by an almost irresistible attraction, from their work and schools, and hang about the decks and yards of vessels, with a fondness which, it is plain, will have its way. No sooner, however, has the young sailor begun his new life in earnest, than all this fine drapery falls off, and he learns that it is but work and hardship, after all. This is the true light in which a sailor's life is to be viewed; and if in our books, and anniversary speeches, we would leave out much that is said about "blue water," "blue jackets," "open hearts," "seeing God's hand on the deep," and so forth, and take this up like any other practical subject, I am quite sure we should do full as much for those we wish to benefit."

Between these two views of life at sea lies an ocean of difference. In some ways they are hardly reconcilable. But rarely do people in circumstances short of war live entirely in either polar extreme. Thankfully, they inhabit both such worlds at the same time and pick and choose as befits their personality what suits them. For our part we can safely assume that whatever attraction pulls those who take to the sea, they enter relationships somewhat without their will, but expect nevertheless to fulfil their dreams by so doing. If you bring it down to a choice between these two opposites, I have no doubt but that the poet shall take the day; for, thankfully, young men shall be forever young, and, like Dana himself, they will surrender to the siren in their souls -- and have a bash! -- no matter what the cost, no matter what the risk, no matter what the price.

On a more practical level, however, a ship's crew has to operate as a community; it has to function with respect to the captain and itself. If every member of the crew could experience the same dream, then they certainly could not experience the same labour, the same status or the

6

same privileges. However idealized or ignored the seaman's lot was in the nineteenth century, he could not conceivably operate without some hierarchy, some chain of command within which his duties and responsibilities were defined vis-a-vis the ship , the captain, and the crew.

As one might expect, the captain, like Alexander Selkirk, was lord of all he surveyed. He could come, go, and stand watch as he pleased. He had an American President's powers to declare war, a High Court Judge's capacity to dissemble and to find guilt, and a Surgeon's power over life and death. When he ordered someone to be put in irons, his orders were more effective than a *lettre de cachet* signed by Louis the Fourteenth, committing some hapless musketeer or other to the Bastille. More than any other public or private body, he could in honesty say,' *L'etat, c'est moi!'* -- and mean every word of it. His orders were, therefore, unnegotiable, and were obeyed implicitly. The captain could not only make and break his officers, but he could do what Kings and revolutionaries couldn't: he could transfer his officers from the quarterdeck to do duty amongst the proletariat of the forecastle, and vice versa! Like every member of that small minority of people who, at one time or another, enjoyed totalitarian power over others, he was ever alone, and possibly very lonely as well. He was a being -- a bit like God -- who, perforce of habit and occupation, had to commune with himself. When the anchor was raised and the gangplank cleared, the *Caswell*, like every other ship that ever was, floated away like a self contained colony under an omniscient, omnipresent, omnipotent and personal governor called, 'Captain, Sir!'

The chief mate on such a colony was second in command. He had several other names including 'boatswain' and 'first mate'. His function was to take responsibility for everything of a practical nature on board ship. He is what the civil service is to the government; he converts policy into action, including the ordinary everyday details of running the ship. In the nineteenth century he kept the logbook. He had special responsibility for the cargo, and was to a large extent answerable to the owners and insurers. Moreover, since the captain was often too dignified to crack jokes or socialise with the lower orders, whatever levity or laughter his chief mate exhibited was invariably regarded as manna from Heaven, but countenanced by the captain.

By contrast the second mate was a general dog's body who tried to bridge the quarter-deck and the forecastle. He had charge of the boatswain's locker. He was also the general provider of working materials for the seamen. He could be found working at anything , and anywhere from the Topsail to the captain's quarters. His greatest difficulty was maintaining the obedience of the crew with whom he worked and, let it be said, at a wage which at any time was far greater than theirs. Not surprisingly the common sailors always suspected the second mate. For one thing, he was always on deck setting the pace and pushing the crew. He was compromised in his duties ; for at the same time as he worked the crew, he ate and slept in officer's quarters. In some ways the second mate had no home; for it sometimes happened that because of his duties he never ate with the captain or the first mate, but rather ate at a second table or, alternatively, he ate after the captain and chief mate had dined.

The captain, together with his first and second mates, constitute the essential government of a ship. They were to the *Caswell* what the Prime Minister, the Deputy Prime Minister and the Minister for Finance are to government on land. land. It doesn't really matter how many members of parliament there are, real power lies with some two, three or four people gathered around the PM. So, too, with a sailing ship, the only obvious difference being that a ship is so small that none can run away or hide from the captain's gaze, be it benign or -- God forbid! -- baleful.

Politically speaking, the steward was in a peculiar position -- one that was forged by his personal relationship with the captain. As servant of the captain, he had sole charge of the pantry, and this did not endear him either to the crew or to the first mate. The first mate disliked him because he had charge of something over which even the first mate had no control, and the crew distrusted him because he was too close to the captain to be either toyed with or taken seriously. It was easier to distrust him.

In comparison the cook was the crew's personal saint. He had the power to launder or dry someone's wet clothing. As well as being in a position to proffer a place to smoke for those on the night watch, he would also apportion the food. Petty culinary privileges kept him immune from gossip and secure from verbal attack. Both he and the carpenter slept at night, a rhythm that approximated landsman's hours. Except when' all hands' were called on deck, they both avoided the watch, and on that account, added some stability to an unsteady ship.

The watch itself divided the rest of the crew into larboard, led by the chief mate, and starboard, led by the second mate. When one watch was off, the other was on, thus dividing up the day into 6 shifts of four hours each, and dividing the ship into those 'on deck' and those 'below'. Of course, bad weather or other unforeseen circumstances might change this routine, but ships obeyed the watches routinely.

An Old Crew

The monotony of the repetitious-watch was broken by means of the 'dog watch', that is, they broke, say, the four-to-eight watch, into two two-hour watches, thereby creating seven rather than six watches altogether. This device had many useful aspects: it preceded the setting of the night watch, it was also an opportunity to bring all hands on deck at the same time, and it reshuffled the rotation of the watch such that each day the watches worked different hours. At eight o'clock, eight bells are struck, the log is marked, the watch is set, and the wheel relieved. The relieved watch goes below and the galley is shut up.

At daybreak there is an orgy of washing and scrubbing. The "scuttle butt" is replenished with fresh water, and the decks are swabbed. At eight, the day's work begins anew, and the work goes on till sundown, with the exception, that is, of an hour for dinner.

The importance of the above relationships were reducible to the following wage differentials once described by N. L. Thomas:

> "Ore Ship captains were generally paid £9.10s a month;
> Mates £4.10s, and able seamen between £2.5s and £2.10s."

The *Caswell* was new and, unlike older ships, needed less attention in order to remain clean. She was built at a cost of £10,000 and when she left Glasgow she had been no more than 30 days at sea. She was pure and pristine and none the worse for her first crew who were mainly Scotsmen. Loaded with iron water pipes, she left the port of Glasgow and turned her face to South America -- her first long haul. It took seventy-three days before she sailed into Buenos Aires, where, to the delight of the crew, she discharged her cargo. The voyage, according to one report, " was pleasant and prosperous." However well intentioned this remark may have been, it actually transpired that the *Caswell*'s first excursion across the Equator was not without tension. It is the exact nature of this tension, her birth pangs as it were, that has never become fully known or fully explored. On the whole, it must be inferred that the voyage was less than ideal, and that it prefigured the on-coming mutiny.

The remainder of this book tries to piece together something of the events, which led to the mutiny -- and to shed some light on its antecedents as well as its awful consequences. The prologue to the mutiny began somewhere between Glasgow and Buenos Aires.

An Old Crew

The nineteen-man crew, described as 'adequate' when they left Glasgow, was shocked and demoralised on arrival in Buenos Aires. Except for the officers, the carpenter, and the two apprentices, the rest of the crew left. This, in effect, meant that thirteen crewmembers left the ship and, as the government spokesman had later pointed out to the Queenstown Magistrates, none of them had been 'discharged'. As we shall see later, only three members of that crew eventually made it back to Blighty.

In the meantime the crew, soon to be scattered to the seaports of the world, ensured the secrecy of the *Caswell*'s first major voyage. From Belfast to Bahia, sailors, then as now, shared information about where to go, what voyages to embrace, what ships were available, what captains to avoid, who was at war, what experiences to forget -- all of them seeking a well-run ship, a half-decent skipper, a fulfilling life-style, and a better place to be. Few of them would avail of the opportunity to tell publicly the real stories behind naval government on the high seas, at least not while they were in harness, so to speak.

Throughout the later trials and the publicity surrounding the mutiny, not one of its first crewmembers came forward or volunteered any information as to what happened on the outward voyage. And were it not for the courage of Edward Warner, a seaman who had sailed with Captain Best eleven years earlier, the world would never have known anything of the atmosphere Best was capable of creating on board a ship under his command. This unique account can be seen hereafter under references to the *William Leckie*.

***

The *Caswell* was to remain in Buenos Aires for a full six weeks. Before she could sail again, captain Best had to solve two problems. First of all, the *Caswell* needed cargo. Secondly, and more importantly, the captain needed a crew. Perhaps because he was preoccupied with getting a cargo he did not properly apply himself to hiring a crew. Whatever the market conditions were for able-bodied seamen in Buenos Aires, especially for a boat with a bad reputation, the captain was glad to recruit without discrimination. Maybe he felt he could not make up the shortfall of sailors from the available English labour pool, or maybe they would not sail with him. Perhaps he did not want men who spoke the Queen's English. Whatever it was that made life difficult on the first voyage, the question now for captain Best was: could it be avoided on the second leg of the journey?

Again, our curiosity cannot penetrate the captain's subjective reasoning, and the facts are not plentiful enough for us to be categorical about his motives.

All we know is that six men remained on after the Glasgow trip -- the captain himself, two mates, the carpenter and two young apprentices. The captain wanted a complement of sixteen for his return trip, so ten others had to be recruited, that is, nine sailors and a steward.

When a young lad called Neville, the captain's first steward on the outward voyage, left the *Caswell*, Emmanuel Griffiths, a coloured, inoffensive Welsh teenager replaced him. While we cannot be certain of it, the steward was probably the first to be recruited. Thereafter according to the most contemporaneous account, eight of the remaining nine crewmembers were recruited as follows:

> "In the room of those paid off, the Captain shipped two Maltese seamen, brothers named Gaspard and Joseph Pastoria; three Britishers named James Carrick of Rothsay, and John Dunne of Bristol, able seamen, and a cook. There was also a Greek named Christos Baumbos.

> As they were two short, Baumbos asked to go ashore to fetch two men. He was granted permission and returned with George Peno and Nicholas Morellos, two men of ill repute. (Greeks)." (The *Cambrian* newspaper of Swansea, 12th May 1876)

This decision by the captain to delegate authority to a stranger and to allow him to recruit on his own behalf is not as strange as might first appear. Whatever Bombos did, he is more likely to have done it on the captain's instructions. Otherwise such a method of recruitment was reckless and cavalier. The captain knew that Bombos could only recruit from an even more limited and sectional pool of the labour market than he himself could. But that, perhaps, was his intention. What possessed Bombos to recruit 'Big' George Peno and Nicholas Morellos was the captain. It is only later on in the case that we learn that captain Best wanted a 'mixed' crew. Bombos simply did what he was told, never questioning the whys or wherefores. It turned out to be the worst decision that either captain Best or Bombos ever made.

Within a month or so of the interviews being completed -- if, indeed, there were any interviews -- eight sailors and the captain's steward had been recruited. This left the desired complement of 16 men short one man, an Irish man named Rourke, who was probably recruited before or at the same time as the British. We must assume that Captain Best was satisfied with his very mixed crew. He now had sixteen men, and most of them had experience. They comprised six men from the original voyage, mostly Scottish, a Welsh steward, an Irish man, two newly recruited Maltese brothers, the Pistorias, a Scottish sailor named James Carrick (taken on in September), an English sailor named John Dunne , a German cook called Rook Agineau, and three Greeks (taken on in September). The three Greeks were respectively named Christos Emmanuel Bombos, George Peno, and Nicholas Morellos.

From the outset it should be pointed out that the three Greeks were not strictly Greeks. 'Big George' and Nicholas Morellos were probably more Turk than Greek. The only definite Greek was Christos Bombos, the son of a Greek sea captain. And it was highly unlikely that Bombos knew the other 'Greeks' beyond a coffee-bar acquaintance before he recruited them. This does not mean that George Peno and Nicholas Morellos did not know each other, although the likelihood is that they didn't.

One should also point out that there was considerable confusion, not just with the nationalities of the crew but with their names as well. The two brothers Giuseppe and Gaspari Pistoria, for example (a.k.a. Francesco and Gaspari Moschara), were accepted throughout as Maltese. In the 1870s there was good reason for foreign sailors to pretend to be Maltese, and many of them who got their hands on a ' Maltese Discharge,' which they either bought or borrowed, enlisted as Maltese on the docks of Cardiff or in other ports across the Empire.

The Maltese, to protect their good name from being tarnished by mutinies committed in their name, wrote several letters of protest to the press and the Board of Trade. Certainly Giuseppe Pistoria revelled in anonymity with respect both to his name and his place of birth. Throughout this narrative we, too, shall refer to them as Maltese where the text or context seems appropriate, but, as we shall see, they were in fact natives of Sicily. Apart from the widespread use of contrived names and nationalities, the foreigners' names were used indiscriminately. Bombos is called both "Bambos" and "Baumbos," Morellos is called "Morales" and "Morach-lis." Gaspari is spelled "Gaspard", and Joseph or Giuseppe is called 'Giuseppi' as Christian name and "Pistoria," "Pistorie," "Mescara," and "Moschara" as surname.

An Old Crew

For our purposes we shall refer to them throughout by the names listed below, except where we are otherwise obliged to use another name or when quoted in a third-party text or context.

All in all, then, the makeover crew of the *Caswell* consisted of the following sixteen persons:

1. George Edward Best, the captain (44), English.
2. William Wilson, the first mate, Glasgow.
3. Allan McLean, the second mate, Glasgow.
4. Peter MacGregor, the carpenter, Dumbartonshire.
5. Charles McDonald (16), an apprentice from Skye, and
6. Walter Chisholm Ferguson (16 yrs), an apprentice from Glasgow.
7. Emmanuel Griffiths, the black steward, (19) Welshman (Replacing a chap called Neville).
8. September 28th: James Carrick (25-30), able seaman, of Rothsay, Liverpool. (Scottish), recruited in Buenos Aires.
9. John Dunne (25-30), able seaman, Bristol, recruited in Buenos Aires.
10. Michael Rourke, able seaman, Irish.
11. Rook Agineau, cook, German.
12. Nicholas Morellos, able seaman, Turk/Greek.
13. George Peno, able seaman, known as' Big'George, Turk/Greek.
14. Giuseppe Pistoria (37), able seaman, (a.k.a. Joseph Moschara), Sicilian.
15. Gaspari Pistoria, able seaman, Sicilian, brother to Giuseppe.
16. Christos Emmanuel Bombos (24), able seaman, Athens, Greek.

Perhaps it should also be noted that many commentators, including those on the Press, and the trial judge, tended to accept the return crew as numbering fourteen rather than sixteen. As *The Cambrian* put it:

" The number on board the ship on her return voyage was 14 all told; and the proportion of British to foreigner was eight to five, with the coloured steward neutral."

This figure of 14 only applies if we exclude two of the crewmembers. Because Michael Rourke (Irish) and Rook Agineau (German) abandoned ship very early on in the return voyage, they are inclined to be left out of the reckoning, most commentators reckoning only from the time of the mutiny rather than from the time the *Caswell* left Buenos Aires. The real number of crewmembers, then, was 16, and the original ratio, if such has relevance, was 10 British to 6 foreigners, and that treats the Irishman and the coloured steward as British and puts the German amongst the 'Greeks.'

How this crew was to knit together, to harmonise its multiple cultures, temperaments and nautical skills within a confined space and for a long duration under a unified government was hard to imagine. Already the English crew was loose in speech. They taunted the foreigners. They addressed Bombos commonly as 'Sambo' -- a definite "put down", a name that perhaps was all the more symbolic because some forty years earlier the *Beagle*, carrying the most precious of cargo in the form of one Charles Darwin, had passed the same way as the *Caswell*. It was ironic that Darwin who pointed so convincingly to our common ancestry (not just 'Sambo's') was used to initiate a racist reference, even if it was harmlessly intended as sailors' banter in the 1870s.

One thing that could hardly be ignored was the firm belief that something had happened on the outward voyage from Glasgow. All commentators after the trial of Bombos acknowledged this. Some laid the blame to the captain's charge: but none could say what specifically had transpired. For the moment it is sufficient for us to raise some questions. Why was the crew discharged? Why did they not want to rejoin the *Caswell*? Why would so many of them prefer to hang about the docks of Buenos Aires rather than sail back to Blighty? It was bad luck for a ship on her maiden voyage to repel its crew. Perhaps some of the crew, now ' black-balled' by their skipper, quit Buenos Aires and headed for Brazil or Uruguay. Perhaps a spell in the pleasure houses of Rio de Plata with the possibility of another ship sailing from Monte Video commended itself to the crew, or perhaps they sought to put a greater distance between them and what-ever it was about the *Caswell* that they wished to forget.

However much of a mess had been made on the outward voyage, and however much the captain may have been at fault, the good thing was that he now had six weeks in which to reflect and begin anew. It was within the captain's grasp to put the past behind him, to learn from his mistakes, and to make the voyage home so much sweeter than the one that brought him outward to Argentina. This was the bright side; for here, indeed, was what the Gods reserve for the chosen few; here was a second chance, the kind of second chance that *Lord Jim* craved and fully responded to; an opportunity for captain George Best to make life better for his new crew, his ship, and himself. It was Buenos Aires; it was 1875; Christmas was coming and , apart from Turkish-European relations, all was well with the world.

======

Chapter 2

A New Crew

SIR JOSEPH: You've a remarkably fine crew, Captain
    Corcoran.
CAPT.: It is a fine crew, Sir Joseph...
SIR JOSEPH: I hope you treat your crew kindly, Captain
    Corcoran.
CAPT.: Indeed I hope so, Sir Joseph...
SIR JOSEPH: Never forget that they are the bulwarks of
    England's greatness, Captain Corcoran.
CAPT.: So I have always considered them, Sir Joseph...
SIR JOSEPH: No bullying, I trust—no strong language of any
    kind, Eh?
CAPT.: Oh, never, Sir Joseph.
SIR JOSEPH: What, never?
CAPT.: Hardly ever, Sir Joseph.

        HMS Pinafore/Gilbert and Sullivan

From its inception the new crew presented problems. No sooner had the three Britons, Carrick, Dunne, and Rourke, entered their indentures than they were at loggerheads with the captain. On hearing that they would be sailing with Greeks they forthwith refused to sail. What was never clearly explained, at the trial or elsewhere, was why. Why did they feel that they could not ship with Greeks? And in 1875 whom did they mean when they referred to Greeks? Moreover, why, if they felt that way, did they sign on with captain Best in the first place? The easy answer to this question of course is that they had signed their indentures before discovering that they were -- or would be -- part of a mixed crew. And then, presumably, it was too late to change their minds. Or perhaps captain Best held them to their contracts or -- worse still -- tricked them into signing up with him.

In fairness to the captain, it must have appeared obvious to him that these recruits were insolent if not downright mutinous from the beginning. For what captain could endure being dictated to by three new recruits, particularly on issues which were reserved to his authority and to his authority alone? It isn't every sailor who, on first acquaintance with a new crew and captain, would voice his objections on hearing ship's policy. Nor is it every captain who would deem it necessary to acquaint crewmembers with his policies respecting past or future personnel. It is more likely that when captain Best heard his new recruits voicing their objections, he felt that it was an insufferable impertinence. No doubt captain Best made his feelings evident. But these, it would appear, were not enough to arrest the obstinacy of the British seamen.

So why did the British persist?

Obviously their feelings ran deep, deeper than could be expected at the time. Even with the benefit of hindsight one cannot fully appreciate how persistent and courageous the sailors were about their convictions, particularly when their objections proved to be prophetic. Whether such objections were racist or well intended is hard to say. At the time there had been some distrust of Greeks especially Turkish Greeks -- probably because the newspapers at the time carried accounts concerning Greek and Turkish tensions as well as one particular mutiny which inflamed all concerned. Since seamen always had recourse to their own experiences regarding such matters, it is no surprise to learn that they probably learned about the *Lennie*-mutiny in advance, and this -- rather than any political matter -- sparked their rebellion. Seamen, it should not be forgotten, were notoriously superstitious. But that does not mean that they were ill informed. On the contrary, they always had their own communication system, especially when it came to mutinies. Before examining the general and particular tensions prevailing at the time, let us look closer at what we know of the objections raised by the British seamen, and how they were received aboard the *Caswell*

Given that the crew had such strong objections, one must concede that it was better to have them heard in the calm of Buenos Aires rather than half way round the Horn. One can only imagine the captain's response to his new recruits. When he refused to be swayed by their objections, the seamen protested that they wanted to go ashore to see the Consul. The captain refused. He was troubled and preoccupied at the time, not just with holding his crew together, but also with the task of securing a cargo.

The seamen remained adamant and pressed their argument further. They repeated their demand -- maybe several times -- to see the Consul. The captain responded by putting all three in irons.

We know how persistent the sailors were -- before they were put in irons, the clash of wills had already given way to violence on the captain's part. And even this violence did not deter them. MacGregor, one of the old crew (and very much on the captain's side at the time), when later questioned about this, gave the following replies:

> Question: I believe there was some difference between the captain and the English crew at Buenos Aires?
> Answer: There were some words between them, and Carrick, Dunne, and Rourke were put in irons. On that occasion Dunne received a wound in the head. It was before he was put in irons. He was wounded.
>
> Question: By whom was that wound caused?
> Answer: By the captain with his baton. Rourke was kept in irons for seven days, Carrick was four days in irons, and Dunne was six days or about that.
>
> Question: I believe the captain was afraid to release the men 'all-at-once'?
> Answer: Not that I know. The reason they were put in irons was that they wanted to go ashore to see the consul. But the captain refused to allow them to do so. Shortly after the foreigners came on board they did not to my knowledge make complaints of the treatment they received and the food they got; the food was served out that we signed the articles for, and even more than the allowance."

To the objecting British seamen, they were 'Greeks', but to MacGregor they were 'foreigners' The foreigners, it should be said, with the exception of Giuseppe Pistoria, had little or no English and, in any event, were never a party to the antagonism between the captain and the British crew. Even if the 'Greeks' had made enquires as to why the British had been incarcerated at the time, they may not have been told why. If this was so, they were hardly in a position either to change or to question the captain's actions. Moreover, if they had known why their fellow sailors were being beaten and put in irons, presumably they would have applauded the action of the captain rather than sympathise with the British seamen. The 'Greeks' may even have made efforts to allay British fears.

It is ironic, to say the least, that this objection to sailing with Greeks although testified to in court, did not arise out of any referable antagonism; for such an antagonism is nowhere mentioned by either party to the other, either in evidence, in the newspapers, or in Bombos' account. The objection to sailing with Greeks was hermetically sealed between the British and the captain, and between the British and the court. Not once did the Greeks take issue with this objection; it is as if they were never conscious of it, so therefore they never mentioned it. Moreover, all the evidence leads us to conclude that the Greeks identified quite readily with the British sailors rather than with either the captain or his officers -- which was hardly likely had they known at the time why the captain put the three objectors in irons!

***

There were two probable sources grounding the objections of the British seamen, one was long term and somewhat removed, and the second, the more realistic probability, was the occurrence of a recent mutiny believed to involve Greeks. We look at both of these probabilities in turn.

Long-term antagonisms:

The British objections to sailing with Greeks are probably traceable – in part at least -- to the rise of the British Empire and to the decline of the Ottoman Empire. In the latter half of the nineteenth century the Ottoman Empire fought two wars with Russia. The Crimean War (1854-56), which allied France, Britain, and the Ottoman Empire against Russia, and which concluded officially with the Treaty of Paris. Following this, Russia renounced both her right to intervene in the Balkans as well as her obligations to protect Orthodox Christians within Ottoman.

Throughout the 1860s and early 1870s there was a movement, which, concomitant with widespread Western investment, sought to europeanise the Empire. The idea was that Ottoman should adopt Western political institutions including an elected parliament and a written constitution. This secularisation of Muslim beliefs was met with predictable resistance, and in 1876 the sultan was deposed by a *fetva* obtained by Midhat Pasha, a reformist minister sympathetic to the aims of the Young Ottomans.

In 1877, due to the threat, which the Ottoman Empire posed to Serbia, the Ottoman/Russian war resumed. Eventually, under the Treaty of San Stefano, Ottoman holdings in Europe were reduced to Eastern Thrace while independent Bulgaria enjoyed Russian protection.

Russia's dominant position in the Balkans became the focus of other European interests, towards the alleviation of which the Congress of Berlin was called in 1878. At this conclave, by European consent a shrunken Bulgaria came nominally under Ottoman hegemony. Serbia and Romania became independent. Bosnia and Herzegovina (Ottoman provinces) came under Austrian administration, Cyprus became a British protectorate and Russia received Bessarabia and the Caucasus. Later on, in 1882, Britain began its occupation of Egypt. These were all traumatic losses to the Ottoman Empire, and that is not to mention the French seizures of Algeria and Tunisia.

These tensions led on to greater events in the realignment of Europe, but in the meantime they involved Bulgaria and Greece -- particularly Thrace and Crete, and the strain in Greco/British relations took a turn for the worse: British troops were killed and justice was nowhere visible.

On July 8, 1876, the *Illustrated London News* published several sketches showing Europeans being insulted in the streets of Constantinople. Yet another provocative drawing sketched some Europeans in chains being examined by the Insurgent Pasha of Widdin. In one report the *News* commented:

> "The die is cast. Hostilities between Turkey and Serbia in alliance with Montenegro have commenced. They were begun by the latter, and, according to Turkish telegrams, echoed and re-echoed from other places to the advantage of the Turks... A new chapter of history has been opened touching the relation of the Turks to their Christian fellow-countrymen - or, perhaps, it may turn out to be, of the Sultan to the other Powers of Europe - the contents of which it would be presumptuous as well as futile to foretell."

By September 16 a monster open-air meeting was held at Blackheath and people came to hear Mr Herbert Gladstone speak about 'Turkish Atrocities'. And it wasn't until November 18, that an armistice was proclaimed in Paratjime.

Obviously these latter events, only in so far as they arose out of earlier events, could possibly have influenced the *Caswell* objectors. But when coupled with some striking earlier events, they may well have had some currency. In 1870 there had been a particular incident that may have survived in some memories. This happened at Oropus, where several British soldiers had been captured and massacred. British hackles were raised, and a cry went up to have those responsible brought to justice. Lord Clarendon insisted at the time that he personally be allowed to take part in the examination of the brigands

Contemporary frustrations may be gleaned from the following *Times*-correspondent's report from Athens on May 19:

> "The English Government is using every means for bringing to light the whole truth relative to the circumstances that permitted the capture of our countrymen near Athens and led to their murder near Oropos; but the Greek government continues to pursue its policy of deceit and hostility to publicity.

> Brigandage will be sure of finding recruits as long as amnestied brigands are seen walking publicly in the streets of Athens in a more independent position, and drawing higher pay than veterans in the King's service. Their presence tends to nourish discontent in the army. Experienced officers and good soldiers who have been doing their duty against the brigands in the mountains for years feel deep indignation when they come to Athens and see amnestied brigands strutting through the streets.

> In the rich and splendid dress which is the pride of every Hellenic heart, the veteran envies the gay habiliments of the criminal; and resents the injustice of statesmen who flatter brigands and neglect honourable service. It requires no special knowledge of the state of Greece to understand that this open impunity granted to brigandage must demoralize society, and to believe that no effectual measures can be adopted to suppress brigandage as long as this state of things continues. Everybody sees that it was the duty of Mr Zaimis, a Minister of the Interior, to order every amnestied criminal drawing pay from the Government to quit the capital on the 12th April, when he heard of the capture of our countrymen in its vicinity, and to order them to reside at Auaphe or Skyros, or somewhere, to prevent their communication with brigands at large.

Great activity is displayed in pursuing brigands at present, and
the existence of brigandage to a considerable extent in the Peloponesia is now admitted by the patriots who lately declared that
only the calumniators of the Greek nation could say that such
a thing was possible, for that all the brigands came into the
country from Turkey. A brigand chief of Elis, named Agaera,
has been killed near Patras, but another named Kourkoubas, of
Argos, still infests the mountains of Argolis and Arcadia with his
band. In Locris, and Aetolia, and Acarnunia several brigands
have been killed, and others taken, but both Takos and the
remains of his band of murderers and Spans with his band have
escaped the pursuit of troops in Attica and Boneotia."

After 14 hours' duration, seven prisoners were sentenced to death – a
remedy that found its echoes seven years later in the blockade of the
ancient city of Salonica. But British appeasement did not follow.

By 1876 tensions in Turko/British relations were again coming to the fore
and the objection to 'Greeks', meaning members of the Ottoman Empire,
past and present, became credible.

This was one possible source of the objection, though one might reasonably argue that the 1870 incident was too early to matter, and the misfort-
unes of the Ottoman Empire were also too late or too remote to influence
behaviour between the denizens of the *Caswell*. Which brings us to the
second and more likely source of antagonism, namely, the recent mutiny
on board the *Lennie*

The Lennie Mutiny:

In 1875, on or before the time the British crewmembers came on board
the *Caswell*, the sailing world came to know of a boat called the *Lennie*.
The *Lennie*, a fully rigged 950- ton ship registered at Yarmouth, Nova
Scotia, left Antwerp for New Orleans. The crew had an assorted mix.
There was captain Hatfield, of Liverpool (a Canadian), an Irish mate, J
Wortley, and the Second Mate, a Scotsman named Richard Macdonald.
Then there were four Greeks, three Turks, an Austrian, a Dane, an Engli-
shman, a Belgian steward, and a Dutch cabin boy. In its composition,
not to mention other aspects of comparison, the *Lennie* was to resemble
the Caswell with an uncanny and prophetic fatalism.

And like the *Caswell*, the *Lennie* had trouble from the start. The captain
and the mixed crew were simply not getting on. At the subsequent trial,

allegations of brutality were made against the captain, but they were never sustained. "Certain it is," stated one account, " that the treatment was not excessively brutal, and with such a crowd forward (*meaning the Greek mix of seamen*), discipline would have to be stiff."

The friction between captain and crew soon came to a head in the Bay of Biscay. On the 31st October the steward awoke to the sound of a row on deck. He heard the captain call out in a choking voice,'as if his throat was cut'. He then heard five shots being discharged amid much prancing to and fro on deck, as if some of the crew was frantically chasing after some others of the crew. Then eleven mutineers came down to the cabin and intimated that they 'had finished.' By this they meant that the mutiny was over and that the captain and his two mates had been murdered.

Apparently, all hands had been tacking ship, the Mate was tending the headsails on the forecastle, and the captain was "aft with the Turks and Greeks." In slacking away the braces, one of the Greeks made a mistake and drew down the wrath of the captain, who swore at him. The Greek couldn't take it; he sprang at the Captain and stabbed him. With that, the second mate went to the rescue, but he, too, was murdered. It was said later that the mutineers knew nothing about navigation, and on that account -- it was suggested -- they spared the steward.

The ship had been on its way to America; but the mutineers, intending to go to Greece and scuttle it, asked the Steward to navigate to Gibraltar. By all accounts the Belgian steward, named Van Hoydonck, with the assistance of the cabin boy, Henri Trousselot, craftily stalled the ship and anchored in *Ile de Re*, off the French coast. After lying at anchor for some days, during which time Van Hoydonck managed (by means of sending English and French SOS messages in bottles) to notify the authorities, six of the mutineers went on shore. It wasn't long before a gunboat came in answer to distress signals hoisted by Hoydonck, who, meanwhile, armed himself with a revolver, and defied the remaining five mutineers. The five murderers were arrested, and the use of the telegraph led to the capture of the other six the same night.

All in all the trial resulted in three Greeks and a Turk being sentenced to death. Van Hoydonck was rewarded with £50, and at Antwerp received the Knight of the Order of Leopold. The cabin boy, Henri Trousselot, received the Civic Cross of the Second Class.

It was the news of the *Lennie* rather than anything else, which most likely spooked the British seamen. The *Lennie* mutiny happened almost concurent with the enlistment of the *Caswell's* new crew. Of course the trial and execution of the mutineers had not as yet transpired; but the news concerning the murder of the captain and his mates would most likely have reached all their ears. The subsequent events of the *Lennie*, as we shall see, were to dog the proceedings governing the *Caswell* -- almost as if both mutinies had arisen from one and the same set of circumstances.

It is perhaps this closeness and similarity of mutinies which tends to make us forget that the *Lennie* happened first in time, and that the *Caswell* just didn't succeed it chronologically, but arose in great part because of it, and because of the objections make by the British seamen as a result of it. In this sense, the objection to sailing with a mixed crew ostensibly arises from a most unusual conviction (or prejudice), and was shared and supported, perhaps, by other sailors at the time. Whether it was a conviction or a prejudice, it unhappily matured, as we shall see, into a gruesome prophecy. The question is: was it self-fulfilling? Or did it arise out of a remarkable or sensible insight into the scheme of things? That the seamen so readily admitted their fear of sailing with Greeks in an Irish court some months later only demonstrated how conducive the climate was at the time to voicing such opinions. Unfortunately Captain Best never really learned any lesson from the *Lennie* mutiny. Quite the contrary; he preferred to ignore the news entirely.

In effect, of course, only three sailors objected. Giuseppe Pistoria, perhaps the most educated of the foreigners, had some fluency in English, while Bombos and Big George Peno had only a smattering of broken English. Moreover the Greeks were lately recruited - so that, if they did not already know about the objectors, then there was no good reason to inform them, lest they, too, refuse to sail. On the other hand, if the British were being disciplined for some other reason , then the foreigners were hardly in a position to discover it. And the captain was even more unlikely to communicate such disciplinary matters to any but the recipients of such discipline.

If the punishments or terms of incarceration in irons were intended to fit the crime, then we can only conclude that Rourke (with seven days detention) must have been the first, the loudest or, possibly, the most unremitting offender. Dunne (with six days detention) was close behind Rourke, and Carrick (with four days detention) was a mild if resolute third. What was said about insight or prejudice must now be scaled to meet the differential punishments. And since Michael Rourke jumped ship at Valparaiso, obviously out of conviction with his first impressions, it can only be assumed that he felt strongest about sailing with Greeks, or about the crew generally, or about the captain. On this reasoning, Michael Rourke must have been extraordinarily shrewd or unboundedly bigoted; for what transpired afterwards had nothing to do with him, save and in so far only as his initial actions pointed uncannily to the subsequent events which were to rock the *Caswell* to the core.

Nor was Michael Rourke the only savant. Things must have become unbearable at Antofogasta as well; because here we find that the German cook, Rook Agineau, also jumped ship—and neither he nor Rourke were ever heard tell of again. Their names hardly ever appear in the subsequent files or correspondence. And when the *Caswell*'s strength is mentioned, as we have already pointed out, a complement of only fourteen men is invariably referred to, the two who jumped ship being left out of the reckoning. Moreover, since they jumped ship and disappeared, subsequent events made it impossible to deny or corroborate the initial story as to why the three British were put in irons. The veracity of the story is left totally in the hands of James Carrick and John Dunne.

***

It was an unedifying state of affairs to say the least. The British had hardly been recruited when they found themselves in irons, while Bombos was recruiting for the captain. In addition, according to Bombos, the captain had already 'broken their heads'. Before Rook Agineau jumped ship, he was so appalled and scared by the captain's swearing and general abuse that he could not get on with his work.

On one occasion (according to Bombos) Rook was ordered by the captain to go to the wheel and keep to the wind. He did so anxiously. Pressed by the captain, he shouted back: " I cannot go nearer to the wind, as the sails won't draw." The captain cursed him and his sister in unintelligibly foul language. Agineau was too afraid to be offended. He was so naive that he asked the crew how the captain came to know that he had a sister. But the captain wasn't finished. He rushed at Agineau, caught him by the head and assaulted him on the deck, where he remained insensible for three hours. As yet the Greeks had no particular reason to hate the captain. They witnessed several assaults, but these assaults were inflicted solely on the British seamen - and now, for the first time, on the German cook!

Indeed, it was the British who had most reason to fear -- and, perhaps, hate -- captain 'Bully' Best. On one occasion (according to Bombos). when it was James Carrick's turn to take the wheel, Carrick said: " I will give £6 to whichever of you will kill the captain." This alarming statement was reputedly said to all those present at the time. Nicholas Morellos of Samos replied, "Why don't you kill him yourself?"

For the moment nothing more came of this loose talk. But from the start it was clear that the mix of nationalities was a gamble that could easily backfire. Mixed nationalities aboard British ships were not a novel idea. On the contrary, they were almost traditional, particularly in the merchant or mercantile navy. It should not be forgotten that Britain was an Empire and, eventually, a Commonwealth, given for centuries to a division of labour that required the expertise of other nationalities. And whether we move backwards or forwards in time we will find examples where mixed nationalities proved disastrous; but these account for a tiny minority of cases, which hardly reflect upon the vast majority of voyages that are perfectly enhanced by the excitement of a nationality mix.

In respect of mutinies that leaned against mixed crews other than the *Caswell* itself, two examples should suffice. The first , the mutiny on *The Lennie*, as has already been noted, occurred at the same time as the *Caswell* mutiny, and the other, the mutiny on the *Leicester Castle*, took place in 1902.

Because of its mixed crew, and its closeness in time to the happenings on board the *Caswell*, the *Lennie* logically suggested itself as a likely vessel for comparison. It was so apt, not just because its malefactors had been tried at the Old Bailey (May 2), some two weeks before the *Caswell* had been towed into Queenstown (May 13), and almost three months before the first *Caswell* trial (July 27) but also because its relevance in time was indisputably paramount. At one stage the conclusion of the *Lennie* trial was reported on the same page as that of the *Caswell*. The impression being made on the reading public in Ireland (and perhaps on the future *Caswell* jury) may be gleaned from a perusal of the following two references carried by the Times on Tuesday May 23. Under the heading 'The *Caswell* Mutiny,' it was reported that:

> "Mr Joseph Cartwright of London who acted as interpreter on the trial of the Lennie mutineers, was sworn as interpreter in this case, and it was arranged that the evidence should be first written out by the clerk of the court, and then read to the prisoner..."

Elsewhere under the heading "The Lennie Murders," it was also announced, inter alia, that:

" The execution of the sentence of death passed upon the prisoners
Matteo Cargalia (alias France Peter), Giovanni Carcaria (alias Joe,
the Cook), Puscalos Caludia (alias Big Harry), and George Calda
(alias Lips), will be carried out next Thursday morning; and although the evidence left no doubt of their complicity in the terrible
crime(s) committed aboard the Lennie, still it would be a satisfac-
tion to the public to know that the prisoners since they have been
under sentence of death have made statements that came almost to
a full confession of their guilt. They have been constantly visited
by the Rev. Mr. Melenthus, the Rector of the Greek Church in
London wall, and they appear to have conducted themselves, with
the exception, perhaps, of the prisoner France Peter -- who has all
along exhibited a dogged and sullen demeanour...

   Although all appear to be born in Turkey they profess the Christian religion in accordance with the rites of the Greek Church...
they demand the Greek Archimandrite - for they have no English
... It was their intention to have killed the steward and also the
boy at the time the other murders were committed, they owe their
lives to the fact that none of the men on board were able to navigate the vessel and they were therefore reluctantly compelled to
place confidence in the steward. An appeal has been made to the
Secretary of State on behalf of Joe, the Cook, on the grounds that
he acted under the intimidation of the other prisoners and that he
was not proved to have taken any share in the active murders."

The fear of mixed crews was slow to leave the all too personal nature of
government at sea. The *Leicester Castle*, the property of Joyce & Co.,
was built in Southampton in 1882, and in 1902 (July 26) it left San
Francisco bound for Queenstown with a mixed crew. On this occasion the
crew was made up of American, Irish and Dutch nationals. There were
others who had been shanghaied to make up the full complement -- but that
had no bearing on the mutiny. If we are to believe captain Peattie, all
went well until about 10.30 pm on the night of the 2nd of September,
when three Americans named Hobbs, Sears and James Turner, tried to ·
take over the ship. They first tried to arrest the captain who refused to
surrender. He received five revolver wounds in the struggle. Less fortunate was the second mate, Mr Nixon, who tried to help the captain. He
got shot through the heart and died. It was thought that the mutineers
planned to murder all the officers on board, confiscate the ship, and make
off with it.

As things turned out, the mutineers were glad to escape on a 'frail raft' made up of a few planks and three cork cylinders, which, it was believed, went to pieces, the three Americans perishing on the high seas. Why the Americans wanted to mutiny in the first place was never convincingly explained. Some grievance, real or imagined, was suggested, but never specified. After the mutiny and after a rest captain R. D. Peattie, a native of Paisley, and an obvious graduate from the old school of hard knocks, arrived in Queenstown to resume his duties. He also reported and wrote up the event. By all accounts he made a remarkable recovery, never appearing like a man with four bullets still in his body.

Fear of mixed crews, then, particularly those with a Greek or so-called Greek element was a rather enduring aspect of nineteenth century mercantile navigation. And why we have gone to such lengths to explicate that fear is to try and understand the initial fears of the sailors who raised objections to sailing with Greeks. Thereafter, it might help us decide whether the mutiny was a self-fulfilling prophecy, a racist prejudice, an organisational disaster or a brilliant prognostication. All we can say is that such fears were grounded in contemporary realities.

Valparaiso

Captain Best's second problem was to find a cargo. Cargo was the life of trade, and without it the *raison d'etre* of commercial sailing was unthinkable. But where to find suitable cargo was neither obvious nor guaranteed. With cargo in mind captain Best sailed out of Buenos Aires and headed south, past the Falklands towards the Cape. They rounded the Horn, and sailed as far north as they had come south from Buenos Aires. Captain Best knew full well that when he passed Puerto Montt, the *Caswell* had left one of the stormiest seacoasts in the world behind her.

It was later alleged that he had worked his crew hard - that in fact he had beaten them, abused them, and kept them hungry as they sailed around the legendary Horn. The Cape lay midway between Buenos Aires and Valparaiso. The history of the difficulties of the Horn needs no elaboration. Cook had been there, and he had travelled from east to west and back again - no less than what the *Caswell* was to do. The 'Beagle' had also been there. It wasn't an idle observation that some circumnavigators like Drake preferred the Straits of Magellan to the risks of the Horn. And although copper and iron barques like the *Caswell* were admirably suited to the task, at the same time, there was no denying the fury of the Horn's Westerlies and the raw squalls that hammered the deck and masts with indescribable ferocity, or the greybeards that rose some 40 to 60 feet tall

to engulf the barque like a little child swaddled in the great limbs of an
angry bear. Whatever else they were, captain Best's mixed crew were no
mean seamen; to deny them food on such a perilous voyage -- if true --
was both foolish and unforgivable.

A sailor's grub back in the 1870s was hardly taken with great relish.
Since there were no 'fridges', the food was coarse, dry and salty. Fresh
meat was impossible to preserve for long after leaving port. There was a
heavy reliance on salt beef and pork. Ship's biscuits became proverbially
riddled with weevils, and rations were customarily scarce by the time the
Cape was rounded. Peas and pea soup was the order of the day. It often
happened that there was no cooked food for weeks. Because of the
weather the cook was unable for long periods to use his galley, where
in any event, there was only room for one man. To deny the crew such
unappetising fare was provocative as well as unconscionable. It should
not be forgotten also that the apprentices and stewards were only teen-
agers with little or no experience. Bombos was 24, Joseph Pistoria was
37, Big George, whatever his age, was large and corpulent and presumably needed food like the rest. As for the rest of the crew? Most were
between 20 and 30 years of age, and all felt the pangs of hunger.

The three days spent at Valparaiso could - and should - have been a
refreshing break for a deserving crew, had it not been for the repressive
attitude of the captain. Even if it was too inconvenient to backpeddle to
the greater metropolitan attractions of Santiago, a brief surrender to the
delights of the Vina del Mar would have done the crew no harm. Instead,
the tensions between captain and crew surfaced yet again. This time the
captain allowed the cook on shore - but in so doing, he refused to give
him a penny of his wages. Having sailed around the worst waters in
Christendom, the *Caswell*'s young German cook, Rook Agineau, found
himself for the first time for weeks on *terra firma* and not enough pesos
in his pocket to make temptation probable. And there was much to tempt
a young man with an appetite. His nose would have led him to the local
empanala (a mix of meat, onions, eggs, olives and raisins cooked in a
flour pastry); his taste buds must have been tempted by the savoury *bife
a lo pobre* (steak and chips), which would have proved every bit as
salubrious as the gaucho beef of Argentina. How the German cook must
have gulped at the sight of the huge lobsters from the Juan Fernandez
islands, at the abundant abalone, the sea urchins, the clams, prawns and
giant *choros* (mussels), as generously provided as Chilean wine. Had he
been paid his due, he would have tasted a variety of sweet *chicha*
(brandy) or, indeed, the Pisco liqueurs of Chile. Here was a cook who

was in Chile, yet he could not taste of its foods, its fish, its wines, not to
mention its casinos, or its late night cabaret.

No wonder, then, that in his despondency Rook Agineau sought out the
British Consul at Valparaiso. He wanted to complain about captain Best
and conditions on the *Caswell* generally But the Consul allegedly made
nothing of it. He simply refused to listen. He probably felt that he ought
not attend upon a (foreign) seaman's complaints against his captain, especially in the captain's absence. One thing is apparent, he never visited
the ship, or gave Agineau to understand that he would check out his
complaints, much less that he would act upon them.

This singular failure to respond must have created a bad impression on
Rook Agineau. It most probably also created a mood of frustration and
despair amongst the crew.

The English seamen, perhaps more so than the foreigners, understood
only too well the powerlessness of a British sailor. Britain's empire was
in no small measure bound up with the glorious cruelty of its sea captains,
and the manner in which they 'disciplined' their crew. To complain to the
captain was to risk being put in irons or being flogged mercilessly. And
even if there was no suggestion of any floggings on the *Caswell*, every
British sailor knew that to complain about one's captain was to run the
risk of being branded a 'trouble-maker' and suffer the captain's distemper
throughout whatever voyage he decided upon. To men who could not comprehend English, however, the captain's abusive language and bad mann-
ers suggested great cruelties to come, and the loose talk amongst the crew
exaggerated those fears. Now that it was known that the Consul would not
listen to Rook Agineau, the crew's fears , now ignored, were allowed to
spread and magnify. It was going to be a long trip and, from the start,
things augured quite unfavourably.

After three days it became clear that there was no cargo to be had in
Valparaiso. It was time for the *Caswell* to raise anchor and move on.
They sailed past Coquimbo, and climbing north into Capricorn, dropped
anchor at Antofogasta. Here the *Caswell* loaded with Saltpetre. It was
here, also, that the loose talk on board ship took on a rather dangerous
dimension. The second mate, McLean spoke wildly and wrecklessly to the
'Maltese', Giuseppe Pistoria. As has already been pointed out, Giuseppe
could speak English with some fluency. McLean let it be known that the
captain intended assassinating them (the foreigners), and throwing them
overboard as soon as they left Antofogasta.

30

Maybe it began in fun, as often happens when young men play on each other's weaknesses. Or perhaps McLean enjoyed making play on the sensibilities of the foreigners or exaggerating the significance of his rank. The foreigners, because of their obvious disadvantage in English, were gullible, insecure, and the inescapable object of in-house jokes. It could also have been the result of a simple if rampant racism on the part of McLean and the English generally - a racism that had already caused the able bodied seamen to be clapped in irons. If the seamen had spoken such words, they might well have been construed as an intention to destabilise the crew, so that something untoward and vengeful might happen to the captain.

If McLean's intention was to spook the Greeks, then it certainly worked. Pistoria came to the forecastle and spoke with great vigour and urgency to the Greeks. Notwithstanding the fact that, according to Bombos, he spoke in Italian, they nevertheless understood. (From this it also becomes apparent that it was only the English who thought that the Pistoria brothers were in fact "Maltese"). In any event McLean could hardly have calculated the effect of his loose talk. The foreigners were all horrified - and if it was ever intended as a joke, it soon lost its humour.

As it happened there were a few English ships in port and one night the captain invited three other skippers to dinner on board the *Caswell*. A visiting sailor, whose name nobody remembered, thought it expedient to rouse the sleeping crew of the *Caswell* from their bunks. "Get up," he said urgently in Italian, " till I tell you something." Giuseppe Pistoria and James Carrick were among those present.

"I heard your captain say to the other captains that he would kill you and throw you overboard as soon as the ship leaves Antofogasta."

This alarmed Pistoria. He translated everything for the Greeks, and then concluded:"This strange mate says the same things as McLean says". He now had alarming corroboration of his initial fears. And he was in such a state of trepidation that at midnight, when the captains were going away, he (Pistoria) stole up to the gangplank to see if he could eavesdrop on the company of captains.

This preposterous homicidal design on the part of the captain was soon confirmed yet again by what Pistoria heard or thought he heard that night. He claimed that he heard captain Best repeating some accusations against his crew. Pistoria could not imagine that perhaps -- as is quite likely -- the captains were discussing the *Caswell*'s maiden voyage and

31

that Best was defending himself against the rumours of his former crew, why they had been discharged, why they were unhappy, and how the *Caswell* was going to manage the return trip with a mixed crew. There was no doubt but that they were talking about crews, ships and incidents. What else do captains of ships talk about? Indeed, it is quite likely that captain Best was talking about crews and accusations; but it is quite preposterous to imagine that he was deliberating with other captains how he was going to dispose of his own crew. Towards what end would he wish to do such a thing? And how would he sail without them?

A little learning is a dangerous thing, and Pistoria's English, however 'fluent' was hardly fluent enough to pick up on the racy or passionate exchanges between the English captains. Nuances, inflections, assorted rhythms, sarcasm, wit, understatement, humour etc.- all these turns-of-phrase are often assumed by those who speak 'egoistic English', that is, words which appeal to immediate consciousness. In such a context, while words are being spoken, they have to be repeated, dwelt upon, and added to, to convey literal, narrow meaning and usually in the present tense only. But spoken English, like all matured languages, carries a rich tapestry of meanings and tenses quite removed from those who are not nurtured in it. In any event Pistoria had heard enough. He came back and told the Greeks what he heard. And what he heard was enough to convince him that their captain was a scoundrel who wanted them all dead as soon as they made way upon the high seas.

Notwithstanding their fears the foreigners did not feel ghettoised in any respect. On the contrary, they confided in their fellow English seamen, with whom as sailors they identified. As far as they were concerned, the animus – in so far as they knew anything of it -- lay between the captain and his crew. The mates and steward would probably side with the captain against the seamen. But if they were to save their own lives, foreign and English, they would have to take action. Mutiny was the furthest thing from their minds. What they proposed to their fellow seamen was that they would stop work the following day and go and tell the Consul of their dilemma. According to Bombos the English, who knew full well what it was like to oppose the captain, refused to work this proposal and declined to suggest any better solution. What Bombos does not say, however, is that the English also knew that they had several gullible and malleable crewmembers on board. It must have dawned on the English that if they wanted to create trouble for the captain, then all they needed to do was to stir up the Greeks a little further. What may have begun as a joke was now elaborated upon and confirmed by other sources also. It must also have been apparent to the English, now that the worst

fears of the Greeks were confirmed, that they were even more gullible
and impressionable than before, and this made them more passionate
and more easily spooked.

Christos Emmanuel Bombos was a moderate and thinking man, but he
sensed the danger and had heard enough. He later claimed that he intended to jump ship. He even asked permission of the captain to go on
shore on the pretence of buying cigars. His real purpose was to see the
Consul. The captain refused his application. Maybe the captain saw
through his intentions. Everyone , it appears, wanted to see the Consul.
At the height of these tensions the captain thought best to refuse all
shore leave and the crew was kept under watch all through the night.

After Antofogasta, it was time to return home. The *Caswell* was bound
for Queenstown for orders. The captain did not intend to enter or stay at
any port along the way. This, of course, also meant that there would be no
opportunity for the English to avenge the ill treatment meted out to them
by their captain. Paradoxically, they were now forced to work at close
and dangerous quarters with those whom they hoped never to work with,
and who had been inadvertently responsible for having had them clapped
in irons. They also had to work under the constant gaze of Captain Best.

***

On Friday the 1st of January 1876 the Saltpetre-laden *Caswell* set its sails
for Queenstown *en route* to Bristol. Without their cook it was, perhaps, to
be expected that the vital item of food was sure eventually to provoke some
reactions. The Greeks complained about it, and throughout Saturday the
crew was kept at work, with little or no food in their stomachs. According
to one report "One of the crew was laid up with sickness-- whether real or
feigned is unknown -- which made them two short." This report in the
Cambrian did not name the two, but one was Bombos.

On Sunday evening Bombos lay sick in his bunk. The first mate, Wilson,
told Big George Peno to come and relieve Bombos. Big George refused
to take up the relief. Two reasons were given for this, but to understand
them in their entirety we have to appreciate how the two watches were
manned at the time. They were manned as follows:

Watch One   Alternative Watch

Allan McLean, Second Mate   v William Wilson, First Mate

Big George	v	Carrick
Bombos	v	Dunne
Gaspari	v	Giuseppe

When Big George refused to take up the relief, he did so - according to Bombos - because:

    a) He did not speak good English, and,
    b) He claimed it was unfair.

What he meant, of course, was open to conjecture, but it would appear from the lineout of the watches that one was predominantly Greek and the other was predominantly English. In the case of Giuseppe Pistoria, since he had 'fluent' English, it did not matter so much. He could serve on either watch -- and, perhaps, it was desirable that the brothers Pistoria should have been on separate watches as well. Big George probably meant that he would be isolated on the English watch and that it was irrational to shift the person who had least English to a watch in which he would be least effective.

His second reason merely meant that if he transferred, he would in effect be doing a double watch. However invalid these objections may have been, it was apparent that Big George did not want to transfer.

    "Let others go", he said to Wilson.

    " You must go," insisted the first mate; " because if you won't, I shall go and tell the captain."

    "I won't go ", repeated Big George.

And with that, the first mate went off to complain to the captain. The captain, brandishing a revolver, came to the forecastle with the first mate by his side. He ordered Big George to his watch at gunpoint. Big George again refused, saying, " Let other men do it...." The captain insisted on his going, and then Big George said to him:

> "Why have you come to the forecastle with a revolver? - To kill me? It is usual for Captains - when they want the sailors - to send for them on the cabin. And if they do not obey order to write their conduct in the logbook or put them in irons until we arrive in England."

"I will put you in irons," the captain threatened.

"Put me in irons!" said Big George, defiantly holding out both his wrists.

The captain may have been taken aback by this show of logic and daring. Alternatively, he may have reasoned that men in irons can't work -- or perhaps he thought it imprudent to proceed with his threat. Whatever the reason, he more or less backed off and satisfied himself with a promise from Big George that if Bombos remained sick, he would turn out at ten o'clock. With that the captain left Big George, but not before asserting his authority. "I don't come forward among Greeks without being well armed," he said. " I have got a revolver, and mean to use it if necessary."

At ten o'clock Bombos was still confined to his bunk. Big George, on the other hand, made no appearance. According to one account his insubordination was overlooked and the watch went on with one man short. This incident was significant; it was a foretaste of unsettled and diametrically opposed wills, a foreboding of things to come...

Apart from this incident, nothing of significance occurred until Monday when the crew was at work. Carrick and Giuseppe Pistoria were having a conversation. According to Carrick, Pistoria had asked him casually whether he knew anything about navigation. (Carrick recalled this question later and, inferred from it that Giuseppe was at this early stage checking out who was 'disposable' and who wasn't). On the other hand Pistoria recalled quite a different conversation - a conversation that he related to Bombos. According to Bombos, Carrick used the opportunity to poison Giuseppe against the Captain. He allegedly said:

> "The captain wants to kill you as he killed a French man in the same way on the main yard. And at another time a boy at Antofogasta. He will do the same thing to you."

As has been already noted, this was not the first time that Bombos refers to the fears created by the English in the foreigners. In this context, and apart from the aforementioned incident, it might be reiterated that up to this point the captain had not raised his hand to any of the foreigners.

Chapter 3

Mutiny

"That country will have to learn ... that a republic cannot succeed till it contains a certain body of men imbued with the principles of justice and honour."

(Charles Robert Darwin (1809–1882):
The Voyage of the Beagle, chap. vii.)

At eight o'clock on Tuesday January 4 the morning relief came on deck. Big George relieved Carrick, Bombos relieved Dunne, and Gaspari relieved his brother Giuseppe at the wheel. The captain came out of his cabin and walked the quarterdeck. James Carrick was forward, and the first mate, William Wilson, was at the forerigging. The captain came off the poop in his shirtsleeves and straightway went to talk to Big George. Big George at this time had taken up work on the main rigging and had a knife in his hand. The captain said something to him that no one could quite hear. One would have expected him to say something about the roster and his failure to report for duty as promised. But there is no evidence of this

According to the sixteen-year-old apprentice, Ferguson, the captain ordered Big George to "ratline the main rigging." Whatever else was said, no one heard it. Whatever it was or however it was said, Big George lost his head. Not only did he stab the captain twice in the abdomen, but he also stabbed him in such a way as to "gut" or fillet him. Peter MacGregor saw it all:

"... I saw Big George jump down from the rail to where the captain was standing, and with his left hand on the captain's

36

breast, he gave two cuts in the captain's stomach, one down and one across, and his entrails came out."

Three times the captain cried out: "My God! My God!" Most of the crew witnessed it. The captain was standing on deck with his stomach ripped open and his bowels hanging out. He was standing on the deck and crying out piteously; he did not know himself. He neither stood nor fell. Before he fell Giuseppe Pistoria left the wheel, drew a revolver from his coat pocket, and shot him twice in the head. (MacGregor said three times). Carrick recalled a small blue mark on the butt of the captain's ear, caused presumably by the shooting.

The dying captain was then set upon and stabbed several times by the foreigners. As described by the witnesses later (and Bombos), it was reminiscent of the assassination of Julius Caesar, no British knife being raised either to slay or to defend. This was perhaps because the second mate, Allan McLean, while running to the assistance of the captain, was shot through the arm by Giuseppe Pistoria. After that he ran along the deck shouting to someone at the wheel -- "Put her back." But it was too late to reverse the ship or to do anything else with it. Bombos then stabbed him.

The First Mate

When the first mate, William Wilson, saw the captain being shot, he ran from front (for'ard) to the rear (aft) of the ship. Nicholas Morellos darted out of the galley, grabbed him and stabbed him. Big George did the same and Giuseppe (Joseph) again used his revolver to shoot him. During this episode Giuseppe led the affray; and the first mate, now shot, stabbed, and dying on the deck beside his captain, cried out, "Not me, Joseph", "Not me, Joseph".

"Yes," said Giuseppe, "you son of a sea cook ", and discharged his pistol into the first mate. Giuseppe, Gaspari, and Big George ran up to the poop. All three had revolvers.

The Steward

The steward, Emmanuel Griffiths (18), a coloured British boy, was in the relative safety of the cabin when Big George and Giuseppe came to the poop and called upon him to come on deck. As he was coming up the companion (stairs), Giuseppe shot him in the face. He fired two shots at him, then a third. It would have been more merciful had he killed him outright. But the steward was still alive. He didn't know where to turn. He ran round the companion. Big George followed him, caught him by the hair of the head, and dragged him into the cabin where he sought to force him to disclose where precisely the arms were kept. Bombos, fearing the worst (according to himself), said sheepishly to Big George, "don't kill any more." But George turned round to Bombos, obviously enraged at the distraction, and said - "If you say anything more I will kill you, too."

With that he dispatched the steward in the most gruesome manner. According to the evidence, Peno cut the heart out of his young body. When later questioned about this, Peter MacGregor testified: "I saw his heart on the deck, and afterwards one of the boys threw it overboard." James Carrick was also adamant that he " … saw on the deck portion of the heart of the steward." And young McDonald, the apprentice, spared by Giuseppe, also saw the steward being killed. "Big George seized him by the hair with one hand," he said, "and with the other he nearly cut him in two." He continued:

> "The steward when dying said to me, ' Tell my mother how I was killed'. Those were the last words he spoke. The steward's body was taken off the poop and placed beside those of the captain and mate. After the bodies were thrown overboard, I saw part of the steward's heart on the poop…"

Notwithstanding this plethora of direct evidence, one is still impressed by the evidence of Ferguson, the other teenaged apprentice, who, one feels, was nearer the mark when, more modestly, he stated that Big George "cut out his left breast." And if that wasn't enough, Gaspari also shot him in the ear.

Why the young coloured steward was hated so can only be imagined. Politically he stood too near the captain, and was on that account alienated from the crew. He was seen as the "captain's favourite." Why the mercantile services, not unlike the military or, for that matter, the Churches – why they have historically been allowed to exploit so many young men, is something of a mystery. The practices and protocols of these institutions, which rely so heavily on young tender novitiates, particularly before the use of bromide, have never been fully open to critical examination. And the history of Castrati, Roman or Turkish, does nothing to ameliorate one's misgivings.

Mutiny

The steward's mutilated body was carried down to the deck and fastened to an anchor.

The Second Mate

When Allan McLean, the second mate, was seen running past the door of the deckhouse, the foreigners hotly pursued him. He ran into the house and closed the door. Pistoria tried to get in through the window, and Big George tried to force the door. Giuseppe Pistoria called him out. McLean's first reaction was to hide himself inside the cabin. Eventually, however, he saw the futility of it. He came out and ran on to the poop and cried to Ferguson at the wheel to put the ship back.

He ran down the companion hatchway with Giuseppe firing at him and wounding him in the arm. He pressed forward and as he jumped off the poop Bombos stabbed him twice in the back of his shoulder. Gaspari then shot him. According to Carrick, "Peno had his arm around the second mate stabbing him and singing a song and Gaspari was shooting him in the leg." The second mate fell within a yard or two of where the captain lay.

Carrick also said that he saw Bombos give the captain 'one or two stabs' as he lay on the deck near the poop. How he saw 'one or two stabs', not knowing which, is rather difficult to envisage, as is his evidence of Peno's singing while he was stabbing the second mate - both testimonies reflect generally upon the quality of the evidence against Bombos, and the reluctance generally to testify too harshly. Bombos always maintained that he did much less than he was forced to, and that he at all times subverted what all the other foreigners and English were doing. Ferguson, the apprentice, however, was perfectly clear when he said he saw Bombos stab the second mate in the back. And this event was firmly corroborated by the others, particularly by MacGregor.

According to himself Bombos also took refuge in the deckhouse. He claimed that Peno and Pistoria had pursued him, that they eventually gave up on him, and that he could see all the goings-on from his hideout. He could see them all, he said, standing near where the captain, the two mates and the fallen steward were lying. After a moment's pause and after considering the awful vista ahead of him, he came out of the house and gave himself up. Given the weight of the British evidence against him, Bombos' view of himself must be taken, in parts at least, *cum grano salis*. Moreover, when one considers this evidence in toto , it becomes apparent why the mutineers would never surrender to cross-examination even if given the opportunity.

Mutiny

This means that Bombos' account is the only other account of the mutiny, and until now this has remained in Dublin's archives since 1876 (See Appendix A.)

Peter MacGregor, the carpenter, having witnessed the mutiny and having described the death of the captain, went on to say:

> "...The Greeks have knives and the Maltese revolvers. They were all gathered about the same spot about two minutes after the killing of the captain, and the crying of the mate. I saw the second mate then coming off the poop by the port side, and I saw Baumbos stab him twice in the back. Dunne took a handkerchief out of his pocket to tie it round the second mate's wrists, which were bleeding. I saw Baumbos come across to where the captain was lying and plunge the knife twice into his breast. The captain had life in him at the time, but his bowels were protruding. This was after he stabbed the second mate, and ran after him. ...
>
> While I was locked in my house, the prisoner and Big George came there crying 'Carpenter, Carpenter.' I said nothing. The prisoner tried to force in the window, and Big George tried to force the door with a knife. After they ceased speaking I left my house and came across the main hatch where the bodies of the captain, mate, second mate, and steward were lying. I had seen the steward before get shot in the ear when he came out of the cabin after the second mate. The steward was shot a minute or two before the second mate was stabbed. When I came out of my house it was to give myself up. At that time, the mutineers were tying the feet together."

The murders seemed to stop with MacGregor. He was put in mortal fear for his life, but he was extraordinarily lucky to have escaped the rage of the mutiny and live to 'tell the tale.' He also described the circumstances under which he was spared and the immediate events that followed:

> "The three Greeks and the two Maltese were there at the time. Joseph Pistoria spoke to neither. He told me to go down on my knees in the captain's blood and swear to my God to help them to the best of my ability. I did so, and then, I was told to wash down the decks. The bodies were tied to a kedge anchor, and Joseph told me to lift up the captain's head. The prisoner and all the others took part in throwing the bodies over. When I was at the captain's head I saw him putting his hand on his entrails to drag them -- as I thought -- to himself. The anchor broke away and I saw four of the bodies floating by the stern.

40

Before they were thrown Joseph lifted his heel and stamped it three times down on his (the steward's) head, saying: 'You black son of a b...' The steward was a colored man, about nineteen or twenty years of age. While washing down the poop I saw the steward's heart lying where he had been murdered.

After this the Greeks and Maltese painted off the name of the ship from bow and stern, and also from the boats. I was ordered to get them breakfast and I did so. I cooked and gave it to the foreigners, the prisoner being amongst them on the poop. Nicholas Morellos took command of the vessel and navigated her with the help of Carrick. The prisoner slept with us until the Maltese left us off the river Plate..."

While the mutiny flared, the Greeks intended to kill both the carpenter and the apprentices and, indeed, anyone who got in their way. Giuseppe Pistoria on the other hand, who had hitherto done so much damage, now insisted that the apprentices were to go unharmed. His will prevailed, and some believed that sparing the carpenter and the apprentices was purely because without them the Greeks could not navigate the ship. This unlikely reason was never reported at either trial. Not surprisingly , it soon became apparent , that demonstrations of loyalty to the prevailing crew were necessary. When these were secured, the carpenter came out and gave himself up. Also on Giuseppe's assurances the English appeared. And the assurances were honoured. Carrick, who had concealed himself in a coal-bunker in the deckhouse, reappeared. MacDonald also abandoned his lair, and Ferguson left the wheel.

When the carpenter was forced to his knees (as he later recalled, ' in the blood of my captain'), he swore to God, that he would assist the mutineers to the best of his ability. The others (according to less dramatic accounts) swore similar oaths of allegiancce to the new brotherhood. Then the Greeks 'kissed them to seal the agreement'. Peculiarly enough Carrick and Dunne were spared, not even threatened.

There were now four bodies to be disposed of. But first their legs had to be tied to the anchor. Big George took a rope and with the help of Giuseppe tied all their feet together.

Mutiny

"Get that kedge anchor along," ordered Giuseppe. The anchor was brought to where the bodies of the dead men lay. Big George cut off a piece of line and wrapped the rope first around the captain's body. He then made a 'close hitch'. Meanwhile the other bodies were brought to the same spot. Giuseppe cut the watch tackle and with it lashed the bodies to the anchor. The others assisted. The rope was then made fast, binding both bodies and anchor. Finally the crew heaved and pitched the lot -- anchor and bodies -- overboard. "We all assisted in throwing the bodies overboard", said Carrick - all, that is, except the McDonald boy, who was at the wheel, and MacGregor, the carpenter, who was at that time locked up in the Galley and who saw nothing of this.

Most of the witnesses present still believed that the captain and the second mate were still alive, even when their bodies were thrown overboard. Bombos recalled how, with one hand on his abdomen, the captain kept trying to keep his bowels from protruding, and the other hand was on the side of the vessel. Carrick also testified that the captain, "when being thrown overboard, grasped his protruding bowels…" Elsewhere he stated that "the mate and steward were dead before they were thrown overboard, but captain Best had life in him when he was thrown in the sea, and so had the second mate." It was sad that even as the bodies lay dead and dying, the mutineers had not as yet, outspent their fury on the young black steward. Giuseppe, still spurned at the daring of his own deeds, kicked him in the head before jettisoning his young gangly body over the side of the ship. "I could not say if the man was dead at the time," said Bombos later.

Nor did the bodies sink as planned. The anchor "got fouled" before it hit the water. The bodies came loose from the anchor and began to float apart. This occurred, said Carrick, precisely 'at Lat. 24 South and Long. 74 West.'

Nicholas Morellos brought out a basket of ham and eggs, and MacGregor and Carrick were ordered to prepare breakfast and serve it on the poop. Giuseppe then ordered the crew to wash the blood off the deck, and they did so. Bombos, Big George, and Gaspari got paint. They scraped the name of the vessel off the barque, bow and stern, and also from the boats. Over the plates bearing the name "*Caswell*", they painted the words "*Caswell* no more"

The foreigners then took possession of the captain's cabin and clothes. Big George ordered Morellos and Carrick to ascertain the ship's bearings. With that, they all went down to the cabin and Carrick pointed to their position on the map. Big George and Giuseppe, now in possession of a hatchet, locked themselves in the captain's cabin. They forced the drawers open, until Big George reappeared and said "money no get," and returned to the cabin. They locked the door again. Bombos thought he heard "the clinking of coin." Then George and Nicholas came out again and Carrick followed them up on deck, where Giuseppe was eating his breakfast. Giuseppe cried, "We will go to Valparaiso."

Thereafter the Greeks and the Maltese occupied the cabin and stateroom, and Bombos slept in the forecastle with the British until the 19th February.

In some ways it was apparent that the mutineers were dividing. As far as the Greeks were concerned, Nicholas was acting as master. But Carrick worked the ship on behalf of the Maltese and the British. Moreover, Bombos at this time was sleeping too comfortably with the British.

***

It took no more than a few minutes. The killing may have raged and the violence may have receded, but the mutiny was by no means over. On reflection some curious aspects about the whole episode began to emerge. Brutal though it was, it could not be put down to the general terror engendered by Big George Peno. When roused to anger, he was fatal. There was no doubt about his psychopathy, but, curiously enough, when left to do his work, he was quite bovine. He certainly would never have made a reliable replacement as a captain. But, by all accounts, he never tried to be captain. As Nicholas navigated with Carrick, Giuseppe – without opposition -- assumed command of the ship up to the time of his departure from the *Caswell*. After that the captaincy fell inexplicably to Nicholas Morellos. So, whatever ambitions George Peno had, they were certainly not inspired by his desire to tell others *qua* captain what to do or how to do it. That being the case, it is fair to ask: who engineered the mutiny? Was it a conspiracy? And was Judge Barry correct, when three years later, he said:

> "Either before or shortly after the vessel sailed, a conspiracy was formed by the foreigners to seize and carry off the ship, having killed all the English or so many of them as it might be necessary to put out of the way for the accomplishment of the piratical object".

Mutiny

This view was hardly correct. For one thing, there would be a letter waiting in Queenstown for Gaspari from his wife, whenever he should arrive there. So whatever conspiracy had been hatched, Pistoria's wife had not been informed of it, and it couldn't have been planned before they left Buenos Aires. This -- conceivably -- meant that the conspiracy had to have been hatched after leaving Buenos Aires. Secondly, why would the foreigners wait until the 4th of January to take control of the ship? And why would the Maltese, if they were party to such a plan, leave the ship as they later did? Furthermore, none of the mutineers really wanted to possess the *Caswell*. They were momentarily isolated on board its planks, but none of them ever really envisaged stealing the cargo or stealing the ship. If the judge had said that the timing of the mutiny and the coordinated manner of its execution strongly suggested prior planning, or, at any rate, a spontaneous revolt with minimum planning, then such a theory could be grounded more cogently on the facts.

That the Maltese had possession of firearms should not astound us either; because according to some accounts, they were allowed to possess such arms. One suspects, however, that some of the firearms had been stolen from the captain's quarters. The captain, of course, carried his own firearms and wouldn't go among the crew without them. The event of the mutiny demonstrated how, together, the foreigners seemed to share a common design, such that they executed the mutiny promptly and expeditiously. And even if Bombos does not refer to it in his account, it could hardly have been executed without some premeditation.

It was also apparent that the mutiny, whether the result of a conspiracy or not, was aimed essentially at the Captain and his officers. It destroyed only those who were not recruited in Buenos Aires, only those who had sailed out from Glasgow, only those whom, amongst the British, the captain had not punished. Conversely, those whom the Captain had punished, namely Carrick and Dunne, were spared, even when the reason for their punishment was their refusal to sail with Greeks. And while only one account inferred that all had to kneel in the captain's blood and swear allegiance, according to Bombos only the carpenter was made to do so. The point being made here is that the carpenter was the only survivor of the first crew and, because of the general antipathy, whether real or imagined, against the remaining members of the first crew, the least officer-like of them, the carpenter, had to humble himself before the foreigners. He surrendered himself and, like Carrick and Dunne, was then spared.

It was also true that after the mutiny Carrick became one of the principal men on the ship. For one thing he helped to navigate the *Caswell*. Secondly, after the mutiny the foreigners and British dined together.

Immediately following the mutiny the two Maltese, George and Nicholas, went down to the Cabin, and sacked the captain's stateroom. Peno complained because he found no money, and Giuseppe took a hatchet and began to hammer at something or other in the stateroom. After about half an hour they called Bombos down. According to Bombos he went down and asked them what they wanted. George said to him, " We will tell you: Do you value your life?" "Ho", says Bombos. " Of course I do. Who does not?"

Big George then said: "We will go to Valparaiso, scuttle the ship and kill the Englishmen and yourself. But if you wish to save your life, you can if you like"

Bombos replied: "I will neither kill anyone nor let you scuttle the ship; for these men have done nothing to me, and I have no spite against the owners."

Big George reputedly replied: "Since you do not wish to do as you are told, you will share the fate of the others".

After this alleged conversation Bombos said that he came on deck and told Carrick what George, Nicholas and the Maltese wanted to do, i.e. to kill them and him and sink the ship. "So", said Bombos, " we had better be on the look out."

This was Bombos' account to which we are somewhat partial, not least because it is he who will be on trial and, despite the trial, there is nowhere else that his account can get an airing. But Carrick's observations at this stage are also interesting. What perhaps was most curious and somewhat indicative of guilt was the change in arrangements directly after the mutiny. Carrick noticed, for example, that the Greeks had changed their clothes. Bombos had the first mates' shirt and trousers. And Big George had the captain's clothes. After January 4 Nicholas occupied the captain's room, George Peno the port berth, and Joseph the starboard berth; Gaspari, Bombos and the 'Englishmen' occupied the forecastle. Nicholas was proposed as master. According to Carrick, he (Carrick) " used to calibrate the time for the Maltese from the chronometer, while they in turn confirmed it by calibrating it from the sun". In some way this indicates a duality of authority, or a shared authority, which belies both the standoffishness of the British as well as the so-called universal hatred of the foreigners. To the contrary, after the mutiny the British were quite capable of intermixing with the Greeks, or so it seemed.

For some time after the mutiny the main question revolved around the endless speculation as to what the mutineers would or might do. And everyone, it seemed, had an opinion on the subject. In his narrative Bombos observed:

> "Gaspari Pistoria came up then and asked me what was I grieving about. And I replied 'why should not I, considering you are going to slay me.' 'Oh', says he, 'you need not be afraid'.
>
> I then asked him why did they wish to commit this frightful act.
>
> 'Which other way can we escape?' Said he.
>
> 'You do not know the coast', said I. 'As none of you have been here before, and if you scuttle the ship, you will be caught by the agents of the owners of the ship and cargo wherever you happen to go. Listen to what I suggest,' I said. 'We will take the ship back to Buenos Aires and you can go on shore with the ship back to England.'
>
> 'Well', said he, 'I will speak to my brother about it'".

Gaspari did so. But Giuseppe made no reply. Then Bombos went up to them and repeated what he said before.

> "We are in the majority," said Bombos persuasively; "and we could carry it out - since there are only two on the other side. If you mind what I say you need not care, as I understand their language and will listen to what they say and can report it to you, and then both yourselves and the ship will be saved.'"

The crew assembled and came to see Bombos. A proposal was put to Nicholas and George to the effect that if they should take the ship to Buenos Aires, the four of them (foreigners) could then go ashore in safety, leaving Bombos and the Englishmen to take the ship back to England. Of course this was Bombos' version, and in the absence of any other alternative or corroborating account, all one can say is that it is quite plausible. It was also curious that Pistoria saw the mutiny as an

Mutiny

attempt for him and his brother to "escape" from something or other, and their eventual departure from the *Caswell* confirms that opinion.

Peeved at his 'speechifying' Big George reached for his revolver and was about to fire at Bombos when the Maltese intervened. Here again Giuseppe Pistoria, who had no apparent compunction about shooting the captain and killing the mates and steward, saved Bombos' life, as he had saved the lives of the two apprentices. Apropos Bombos' proposal, the Maltese already had plans to quit the *Caswell* as soon as possible. In this sense it could not be argued that the Pistorias were pirates who wanted to seize the ship, sell it, and simply maximise their interests as pirates.

According to Bombos, George Peno regarded Bombos with great suspicion throughout. He told the crew to ignore his proposals, he cautioned the rest of the foreigners against his treachery, and told them that he (Bombos) would get them all arrested. They even argued about it for an hour and more.

This did not deter Bombos from eavesdropping on the cabin, where Nicholas and George conferred. At one stage he heard George suggest that they should kill the Maltese brothers, Christos, and, after them, the 'Englishmen.' They also talked about scuttling the ship and escaping to Valparaiso. In the event of being arrested they planned on saying that the ship caught fire and that all the crew perished. Bombos relayed this account back to the British and the Maltese on the forecastle

> "I will tell you something both for your good and for mine", he said mysteriously. 'If you do not wish to sink the ship I will tell you'.

> 'Tell us', they said, 'and we will not sink the ship'.

He then repeated to the Pistoria brothers what he had heard, and when they heard it, they hailed him 'as a brother'. They even trusted him to be armed. 'You take a revolver said Gaspari', giving Bombos a revolver.

Again he related the story to Carrick and Dunne. Carrick pleaded that while his proposals were all well and good he, personally, had 'no arms'.

"Take a halibut," said Bombos; 'and in addition, you have your own knife. I have a revolver since Gaspari gave me one. But you had better be on the lookout.'"

Mutiny

With that, they kept watch the whole night.

***

What does one do after a successful mutiny? Where does one go? How does one feel?

The group psychology of the mutiny had by no means spun itself out. Already the mutineers mustered without conviction, searching in themselves for direction. The *Caswell* shimmered in the winds like a sheeted ghost that could not rid itself of its history. It was laden with guilt. And guilt has no place on board a ship.

In this regard it should perhaps be remembered that death is always different at sea, and mutiny leaves an awful vacuum. On shore when a man dies -- he may even be a distant friend or relative -- the mourners assemble, people pray and weep and pay their respects, and the whole community comes in aid of the grieving family. If the pain is unbearable, then, for some, there is prayer, and for others, there is death's antidote, "*Uisce Beatha.*" There is also a ceremony of sorts, and the deceased (if not cremated) is eased into the earth, where a cross, a stone, or other such object marks the spot. Sometimes death is even expected, so that the onset of bereavement is anticipated and life's passing is marked by a ceremony, designed to catch by way of reflection the terror of time.

Because he is always both a citizen and a servant, time holds no terror for the sailor. His citizenhip is peculiarly coterminous with his service *en voyage*. Unlike the landlubber, he never gets old or tired or sick at sea, for when he signs on he has to be 'able-bodied', and not given to sickness. Naturally he does not expect to die on board. So death, if it comes, must come suddenly and shockingly, from some untoward, accidental or unnatural source.

Neither is there the hierarchy of family-members. Such roles are neither present nor expected at sea; for these relationships are transcended by a new order, a conscious communism, where status quo and common weal become one. A ship is not a collection of foreign recruits, but more like a panopticon of caretakers, wherein ship's structure and seaman's function miraculously merge. A unity of space and purpose predominates and a surrender to exigency rather than a triumph of power results. Despite the objection to sailing with Greeks, all seamen by definition share a common country just as they

share their board, their rent, their chores, their food, their lives. And if
there is a master's side at quarter deck and a common side at foc's'le,
between the two no river flows and no railway track is allowed to run --
for the seaman's deck was always common weal and, while on board,
his life was ever common wealth. At least this is the theory, the ideal.

The secret of the sailor lies in this: he knows that space and time are
always one. Between ship's bells, space has been socialized: to and fro,
tide and time, fore and aft, youth and age -- are binary ideas wherein
the heavenly bodies ebb and drift between the bells of birth and death.
That's why on board a ship a dead man never dies until the voyage ends.
En voyage the dead man leaves a space that is forever unfulfilled, and
although it goes unmarked, a sailor's absence is always noticeable. When
lost at sea, the sailor is irreplaceable; his voice is hushed, but he is never
silenced: whether from quarterdeck or forecastle, his absence is always
felt until the voyage ends.

A dead man on a ship is therefore always missed. When every watch is
mustered, his absence is most visible: all hands are reminded of the two
that are missing; it is self-evident. It isn't that the dead man is remembered so much as that he cannot be forgotten, because he cannot be replaced until the voyage ends.

That's why a ship at sea is probably the only place where a man's job is
guaranteed. His redundancy is always coincidental with some tragedy or
other, some violence, some untoward dislocation in the political economy
of the common weal. 'Man overboard', is no mere notification to the neighbours that something is amiss: it is a Hue and Cry, it is the cry of "Wolf" --
the Wolf cometh!. It is a summons to every sailor that the war against the
marauding sea has recommenced. This summons reaches back in Darwinian
time. It is in this sense that the loss of a sailor overboard is a social outrage:
his murder a universal fratricide -- but the onset of mutiny, is a kind of forest
inferno in which most if not all hands , by their own undoing, are necessarily
consumed. A mutiny knows no neutral zones: the gatherers and the scatterers
together inherit the same fire, whose fury , like a revolution, only manages
to subside when the social combustion has been spent and purged.

Put a dozen men or more aboard the same barque, ask them to round the
Horn. They become blood brothers fast, or else they perish in each other's
arms. And that's what they were doing on the Caswell. They failed the
first test – to become blood brothers – now they were perishing in each
other's arms. No; the *Caswell's* mutiny wasn't over: it had just begun.

Mutiny

Already, the ship was shorthanded -- which meant that a closer alliance between the Greek and British sailors was called forth. The absent voices echoed their interdependence at every turn and, at the same time, determined the mood swings of the remaining crew. There were some disturbing signs that the scenario that had been present prior to the mutiny was repeating itself again. Now we had the mutineers assuming the role of the dead officers, wearing their apparel, sleeping aft as they did, taking the watches as they did, and now they informed the British that Big George wanted to kill them in exactly the same fashion as the British intimated to the foreigners that captain Best wanted to kill them. Were these loose words primed to have the same or a similar result as they had before? Were Bombos and the Pistorias undermining Big George and Nicholas Morellos in the same way that the British had undermined their captain and his officers? Was 'history', as they say, about to repeat itself!

Now fastened to their accusers, the mutineers must have felt distinctly uncomfortable about their next move. Buenos Aires seemed like the best destination, if only because the Pistorias were magnetically drawn there. Gaspari's wife and family lived there, and this singular fact, coupled with Giuseppe's single-mindedness, seemed to weigh in favour of returning eastwards round the Horn again.

The announcement of their intention to leave ship gave rise to a new set of tensions and alignments. There was no hiding the disappointment of the 'Greeks' at this decision of the Maltese. What had hitherto been mere British versus Greeks-and-Maltese, was now more complicated. According to Bombos these tensions were due solely to his machinations; but in a climate of murder and intolerance, national insecurities were bound in any event to raise their head. In the cauldron, the Maltese (and Bombos) were siding significantly with the British, informing them at every turn of Big George's desire to have them killed. And this in turn kindled further suspicions in the Greeks. Maybe it was time that the Pistorias left!

Before reaching Cape Horn, a dispute developed between the Greeks and the Maltese. According to the *Cambrian*:

> "The Greeks wanted to kill the Englishmen, sink the ship and go ashore as shipwrecked sailors, but the two Maltese prevented them, as they wanted to get to Buenos Aires, where the wife of one of them lived. On arriving off the River Plate, the two Pistorias launched the lifeboat, and fairly loaded with their share

of the plunder, they took their departure. They warned the British
before leaving to look out for themselves, as the Greeks would
certainly kill them. The proposal of the Greeks now was that the
ship should be navigated to the coast of Africa, where plenty of
Greek ships were to be found. Baumbos thrashed the apprentices
daily."

(It should perhaps be remembered that the *Cambrian* must have
received its information from someone on board the *Caswell*, more
likely Carrick -- but it could have been MacGregor or Dunne, or all
three. It reflects the British view of what was going on. But to some
extent -- at least in so far as it purported to speak for Big George or
Nicholas Morellos -- it has to be taken with some circumspection.)

The Pistoria brothers and, separately, Bombos, seemed to sing the
same tune. The Greeks (meaning Big George and Nicholas Morellos)
they claimed, would have killed the British already were it not for their
separate intervention. Further, the Maltese assured the British that if
Peno tried to kill them, he would have to kill them (the Maltese) also.

Letters

On or about February 10th, off Cape Antonio, the Maltese decided to take
their leave of the *Caswell* and her crew. They again informed the British
of Peno's bloody intentions and, in exchange, requested a letter from
Carrick, exonerating them from all blame for the mutiny.

This letter and the reasons begetting it have more than one interpretation.
Bombos claimed the same virtuous motivation as the Maltese. He also
explained his part in the mutiny in the same terms as they did. But before
looking at Bombos' explanation, it is curious to contemplate why exactly
the Maltese wanted a letter at all. As far as the teenage apprentice (Ferguson) and the carpenter (MacGregor) were concerned the whole idea of writing a letter was an agreed stragagem whereby the Pistorias would obtain
help behind the backs of Big George and Nicholas Morellos. Whether this
was true in fact or not is beside the equally important consideration that
Ferguson and MacGregor thought it was true, thereby giving credence to
the notion that the Pistorias were well and truly trusted by the British and,
indeed, that they were *'escaping'* from the *Caswell* rather than leaving it.
Such inconstancy in the crewmembers' alignments invites one yet again
to question the whys and wherefores of the mutiny!

So, too, does the issue of the parting letters. How many letters were there? And what was their significance?

These questions cannot be answered with any certainty. The most likely explanation centres, first of all, on the need in the Pistoria brothers for some kind of recognition of their bona fides in the estimation of the survivors of the mutiny. Curiosity compels us to ask why, on the one hand, they required recognition of their good faith, and, on the other, why they thought that Carrick (and/or Dunne) should testify to it. On the face of it, they seemed, like Bombos, to requre British approval - demonstrating yet again their identity with the working crew, but also the recognition that what they did was not totally wrong.

Whatever its contents, and by whomsoever signed, the letter could not under those or any other circumstances carry anything smacking of an indemnity or an exoneration. Such powers did not lie with any person or group of persons on board the *Caswell*. And the Pistorias must have known this, or known it substantially. So, was the letter meant to reflect a mere personal certification of moral support? In this respect, why ask Carrick rather than Dunne or the Carpenter or the apprentices? Further, were the Maltese asking for Carrick's support - or were they asking him and the survivors to come clean -- to admit that the mutiny had been provoked or inspired by the British? Indeed, was it actually executed on their behalf, to save them (Carrick and Dunne) from the brutality of their captain and his officers?

In other words, did the Pistorias think that before leaving the scene of the slaughter they might have some written words -- by way of evidence – which confirmed their good intentions throughout the mutiny? If such were the unarticulated motives behind the letter, then who better to ask than Carrick? Was this, in other words, a debt that Carrick owed them? And now that they were parting, having liberated the British from their cruel captain, was it not time for the British to acknowledge it? The Pistorias must have thought that such a letter had some meaning, which means that, in their eyes, it was not tainted with coercion, and no matter how drafted or what its contents, it was given, as it was sought, between people who had at least some regard for each other.

On the other hand the letter may have been written in conjunction with another letter or undertaking that, once ashore, the Maltese would summon help in support of the captive British. In this vein we are told that the Pistorias promised to deliver it to the police in Argentina. It was never revealed if in fact they did deliver this letter. Ordinarily, for guilty men or men on the run. it would have been very foolish. for it would. for good or ill. have identified them as being participants in the mutiny. But. of course. they could have delivered a letter seeking help without disclosing their identity. and if they had another letter exonerating them. then for future reference their attempts at an indemnity would be maximised.

So, why didn't they summon help?

Maybe they did, and the prosecution did not reveal it. Maybe they never posted it. because there wasn't any letter seeking help: there was only a letter exonerating the Pistorias. which was held by them privately until such time as it might be needed. Thereafter it lost its importance and. eventually. its relevance. That was one letter.

If we look to Bombos' reasoning. we find reference of yet another type of letter. In his private account of what happened. he claims. *inter alia*. that he wanted to leave with the Maltese brothers. He said so at the time. His intention. he claimed. was to advise the English Consul of the mutiny. He then claimed that Big George prevented him from leaving the ship because. unlike the Maltese. he was not to be trusted.

Bombos also claimed that on foot of this failed attempt. his friend Carrick wrote a letter for him - a letter that was addressed to his cousin in Monte Video. This letter was to be delivered at a coffee house his cousin invariably frequented. In that letter Carrick beseeched the English Consul to send a man-of-war to arrest George and Nicholas and to liberate the ship. On his instructions. also. the Maltese were to be arrested on landing. And finally. to make the matter even more extraordinary. Bombos declared that such a letter was not only sent. but was presented to him when the ship eventually arrived in Queenstown. He also claimed that it was James Carrick who gave him the letter in Queenstown and who said: 'the Maltese are arrested'. Of course the Maltese had not been arrested. and these words would. therefore. have been a complete lie. So why did Bombos concoct such a thing? And why would Carrick lie and. at the same time. show Bombos a letter. which a 'liar' might equally conceal if he had a mind to? Was Carrick. even in Queenstown. playing games with Bombos?

Bombos insisted that he had seen the letter. that he had recognised it as his property. If produced. of course. the letter might have gone some way to prove his *bona fides* at the time of writing: but. given the evidence that the crew was prepared to marshal against him. it was hardly likely that it -- or anything else for that matter -- could save him from the gallows. (For Bombos' account see letter translated by Mr Yourdi in Appendix A)

Mutiny

What added to the confusion surrounding the Pistoria-letter was the fact that the letter was never produced. On the contrary, when Carrick mentions it during the trial, Pistoria's counsel vehemently denies its existence. Why he does so is somewhat of a mystery. One reason might be that if it was either produced or admitted, then questions as to why it was not delivered would arise, and that would demonstrate guilty knowledge and motive on the part of the Pistorias. In effect they left the British in the clutches of Big George Peno having given their word that they would see to their rescue when they reached Buenos Aires. To confuse matters further Giuseppe Pistoria admits of such a letter in his final utterances.

***

For the following rather different and additional account we are totally reliant upon Bombos, according to whom Big George got up one morning and gathered the Maltese and Nicholas Morellos around him. He intended to reveal his plan for the *Caswell*. "Have you agreed with Christos and the Englishmen?" says he to the Pistoria brothers. "Christos will play the deuce with you," he said.

"It is you that wants to play the deuce with us and not Christos", retorted Gaspari.

"We must do what I told you or else we shall have a general fight," said Big George.

"We four will go on shore at Buenos Aires and then Christos with the Englishmen can bring the ship back to England," said Gaspari.

Big George was not impressed. He had heard it before. " If we go to Buenos Aires," he said, "we will scuttle the vessel."

"We will see about that," the Maltese replied.

With that, things cooled. But when the *Caswell* came to St Antonio, tensions mounted. Anticipating what might happen, Bombos conspired with the Maltese. "George will propose to you to land at Monte Video," he said to Joseph Pistoria. " You can persuade him to go out with you. We can then set sail for England." Gaspari relayed the above information to the English. He also confirmed that "George would land at Monte Video and you can go back to England."

Big George was somewhat sarcastic about the arrangement. He still did not trust Bombos. "When you go to Monte Video," he said to the Pistoria brothers, "take care you do not take Christos Bombos with you - for as sure as you do, he will go and inform on you."

It was at this point that Bombos, who thought that all was agreed, said that he related all to Carrick. "You must write a letter to the Consul," he said to Carrick, "and I will take it to him, as I may be going on shore with the Maltese." Bombos' stated intention was to write a letter and get the authorities to send a man-of-war to arrest the crew. This, if it worked, would answer the oppression of Big George and Nicholas Morellos, but what about the Maltese brothers?

Here Bombos exhibited an uncharacteristic degree of Machiavellian treachery. According to himself he wanted to have the Maltese arrested also, the evidence of their crimes being contained in the letter which they (the 'Maltese') were to deliver on shore.

Carrick wrote the letter and gave it to Bombos. But things did not turn out as anticipated. Having obviously thought about it and, perhaps, listened attentively to George Peno more than he would like to admit, Giuseppe said to Bombos: "We will not take you ashore, but George will land at Monte Video with Nicholas."

Bombos could not hide his disappointment. "This is all the thanks I get?" he replied to Joseph. "But for me, George would have killed you."

" George says that you will inform on us, and that is the reason," replied Pistoria.

"If you do not wish to take me on shore, at least do me a favour?" said Bombos.

" What is that? ", says Gaspari

"I wish you would to take a letter for me to a certain coffee house, where my brother's cousin will get it"

"I will think about it," said Gaspari cautiously.

Mutiny

Bombos then contrived with Carrick as to what the letter should contain. Obviously they could not mention the role of the Pistoria brothers in the mutiny, lest Giuseppe should read it. So the letter was couched in language, which called for assistance from shore. The problem now was how to secure its delivery by the Pistorias.

On approaching Buenos Aires, Giuseppe and his brother prepared to leave the ship. Giuseppe ordered MacGregor to prepare a boat for him to go ashore. The carpenter took an axe and an adze and went to put a boat in order. This done, the Pistorias launched the boat and Bombos asked Gaspari, this time "in tears" to take his letter. He allegedly took it. And according to Bombos this letter was delivered. He was adamant that it was also sent to Queenstown for he had seen it there.

This letter was of the utmost importance to Bombos' account of the mutiny. It set him apart from both the Greeks and the Maltese and confirmed his loyalties, his benevolence, and his devotion to saving the lives of the British and that of the *Caswell*. It would also demonstrate that he was acting under the orders of the tyrant, George Peno. Giuseppe and his brother loaded the boat with two chests and several bags and boxes – some of it the captain's finery - and on or about the 19th of February, some 30 miles from shore, they disappeared in a life boat up the river Plate

The young Scot, Charles McDonald, claimed that two letters had been written –

> " One stating that the two Maltese were not guilty in the affair, and the other for an English man-of-war -- stating what had occurred, and mentioning that the Big Greek was going to murder us."

In some ways the notion of two letters made more sense. They also tended to corroborate Bombos' views.

Following the departure of the Maltese, several changes occurred.

For one thing the *Caswell* now came under the new command of Nicholas Morellos, who installed himself as captain. It also became apparent that the Greeks intended to sail the ship into Greek waters.

Bombos slept with the English until the Maltese left the ship, but afterwards he slept in the cabin with the other Greeks. He had been ordered by Big George to bring his chest into the other cabin and not to speak or mix with the English. If he did not comply, George threatened to kill him. With that he went to the forecastle, sat on the chest and said to Carrick: "This is no good -- bad for all men."

Carrick then helped Bombos to transfer his chest to the cabin. George was there. He was caught momentarily unawares. His eyes flashed defensively and he barked, "If you ever come down in this cabin whilst I am asleep, I will kill you."

***

Chapter 4

Counter Mutiny

Maura

There does be a power of young men floating round in the
sea,
And what way would they know if it was Michael they
had, or
Another man like him, for when a man is nine days in the
sea,
And the wind blowing, it's hard set his own mother would
be to say what man was it.

(Riders To The Sea by J. M. Synge)

Hitherto Bombos had slept with the British. With the departure of the
Pistorias he returned to bunk with the other Greeks. There were now two
distinct 'camps'on board the *Caswell*, and a counter-attack was always
probable. Whether it was fair or foul, or whether, indeed, it could have
been brought about without the help of a defector is a matter that is short
on reliable evidence.

That the counter-attack was savage, however much it was played down
by the British, is hardly surprising. But how it was organised and accomplished was almost subject to as much speculation as was the organisation
of the mutiny. The Crown lawyers and the Judges gave great credence to
a conspiracy theory, but the survivors, rather than express the violence in
such explicit terms, preferred to understate it. The surviving Greeks were
hardly likely to admit freely to murdering the captain and his men, no
more than the British were likely to emphasise the manner in which the
ship was re-captured. The Press, on the other hand, conscious of promot-

ing the heroic image of the British sailor, was nevertheless consistent in its early reports, and was, on the whole, much more apt -- in the interests of intelligibility-- to put a gloss on what the respective witnesses said.

When news of the counter-mutiny first broke, the Cambrian reported as follows:

> "About 3 weeks after the departure of the Maltese, on March 11th, the English crew staged their own mutiny. The day before, the Britishers, when they were able to act in concert, armed themselves...the Englishmen killed Peno and Morachlis while they were coming up the companionway later, and threw their bodies overboard. Baumbos received several cuts about the body and two on the head before he surrendered. He was put in irons, but was taken out later to have his wounds dressed, only to be put back in irons later when his wounds were better..."

The *Illustrated News*, which carried in the same issue articles and pictures of the Turkish war, gave the most graphic overview:

> "On the night of March 11, when Peno was keeping watch, MacGregor knocked him down and killed him with a hatchet.
>
> The noise aroused the other two Greeks, but Carrick and MacGregor ran to meet them in the cabin. MacGregor attacked Nicholas, who fired, but missed. Next moment the adze in the Scotsman's hand knocked away the rear door, but missing the Greek's head, it sunk into the side of the ship.
>
> MacGregor and Nicholas seized the weapon and fought for its possession. The struggle was a desperate one, for one or other of the men must die; but the strength of MacGregor told: he threw down the Greek and killed him with the hatchet on the cabin floor. Christos Bombos and Carrick had been meantime fighting desperately, Carrick with a hatchet against Bombos with a knife. Carrick wounded him in several places, and would have killed him had not MacGregor dispatched his man in time, when he turned on

Christos Bombos, struck down his arms, and they both
pinioned him. He was bleeding a great deal... they sewed
his back up with a packing-needle and thread, and the
wound held. They put him in irons and lashed him to the
main hatch."

McDonald testified as follows:

"... On the night of the 11th March I saw the prisoner
(Bombos) go forward three times. Suspecting him I followed the prisoner into the forecastle, where Dunne, the
carpenter and Bombos were. I saw him lying in a chest in
the forecastle. Bombos had been sleeping in the cabin at
this time. I afterwards went below, and about two o'clock
in the morning, while lying awake in the forecastle, the
carpenter came into the forecastle and said, 'Now, boys,
for your lives,' or some words to that effect. In a short
time I heard a great roar aft, and on getting on deck I saw
the big Greek lying on the poop with a knife in his hand.
I saw him crawl towards the companion, when Dunne
seized the adze and struck him in the head. I heard a great
noise in the cabin also, and saw Bombos led up captive.
He came on deck with Carrick and the carpenter after him.
He was put in irons by Carrick and Dunne, and was
removed to the deckhouse. He was wounded, and his
wounds were dressed and attended to..."

Since Bombos could not give evidence in his own defence, we
have to rely upon the translated account of events he made before
his death. In conjunction with that, we may also rely upon what
inferences we can draw from the cross-examination of the main
witnesses, in the hope that the questions asked of them were
prompted by instructions given by Bombos. Obviously his own
account is the more reliable concerning his views. And from it
we have to conclude – as one might expect - that the murders of
Big George and Nicholas Morellos were quite deliberate and
premeditated. That being the case, the assailants naturaly waited
until their victims were asleep, or at their most vulnerable , and in
Big George's case, when he was drunk. The English in their evidence will refute the notion that they caught the Greeks napping,
but will rather convey the impression that the counter-mutiny was
somehow more spontaneous, that it was not as savage as alleged,

and that the killings occurred on deck rather than in the Greeks' cabin.

According to himself Bombos was quite friendly with the English, not just because he was sleeping in the same room with them right up to the departure of the Pistorias on the 19th of February, but also because they had discussed all the action-oriented possibilities available to them under the tyranny of Big George. Bombos claimed that he himself proposed that Big George and Nicholas should be seized and brought back to England in irons. He further claimed that towards this end he faithfully reported all he heard concerning the Greeks, particularly about their plans to kill the crew, steal the *Caswell*, sell or scuttle it, and escape to the island of Samos. In return for this flow of information the English allegedly promised their informant anything he wanted when they all returned to England.

In furtherance of this camaraderie Bombos shortly afterwards intimated to both Carrick and Dunne that when George and Nicholas were asleep, they could go down below together, tie them up, and bring them to England in irons. Carrick and Dunne did not agree to this. They had their own ideas, formed no doubt by the increasing threats posed by the Greeks.

As expected, tensions between Greeks and British exascerbated. The British felt, perhaps with good reason, that Big George wanted to get rid of them. To pick a fight would have been the most direct way; but, when one thinks about it, if one has power, one's will is one's reason. If Big George really wanted to kill his prisoners why would he need to fabricate excuses, fights or taunts as a pretext for so doing? And why, if - as alleged -- he really wanted them dead, would he delay? Nicholas Morellos, of course, may not have been as confident of his sailing skills as had hitherto been thought – in which case any intentional executions may have been delayed until after they had sailed past the Falklands.

On or about the 9th March Big George came to the forecastle on spec. He came to MacGregor and drew his knife across his throat. He felt MacGregor had been negligent in keeping the watch. "This is not English ship", he said: "This is Greek ship, and I, Big George, am Commander. You must do everything I tell you." It was as a result of this threat that Bombos took issue with Big George. As MacGregor himself testified , "Baumbos heard this (knife threat). I saw him and Big George speaking loudly on the poop, as if they were quarrelling."

On another occasion when the boy Ferguson did something wrong with a rope, Big George threw his knife at him, and it whizzed past his head. It stuck in the deck. According to Mac Gregor, 'Big George intended to kill him.' In this manner tensions between the factions hardened, with the Greeks spying on the British to get an opportunity to kill, and the British suspecting every manoeuvre as a preparation for assassination.

Moreover, on the 11th of March, as Carrick later recalled, "the Greeks threw pea-soup into the faces of the English and subjected them to other annoyances, which led the latter to think that the foreigners were endeavouring to provoke a quarrel in order to assassinate them."

Things drew to a head when suddenly and without any warning, Carrick, Dunne and MacGregor conspired to take back control of the *Caswell*. Armed with an adze and an axe, they marched on the Greeks and caught them napping -- so to speak!

Big George

Although accounts differed, Bombos was emphatic that the counter mutiny was savage. He was adamant that while he and Morellos were sleeping, Carrick and MacGregor emerged from the deckhouse first and made for the poop, then they surprised Big George who was alone and probably drunk. The attack was carefully planned and precipitated by Dunne putting a cap on his head, after which " they went at George with hatchets and finished him." MacGregor, the carpenter, hit him on the head with a hatchet, and the others followed suit.

Bombos remembered being dragged on deck where Big George was lying down. He heard him groan, and saw Dunne take an axe from Carrick and "broke George's skull in three places."

Nicholas Morellos

Two views again prevail with respect to the murder of Nicholas Morellos.

Counter Mutiny

According to the British, Bombos and Nicholas were awake when they rushed below. They took the stateroom, Nicholas fired at them three times but to no avail. A struggle ensued, the Greeks were overcome . Nicholas and Bombos were wounded, and Carrick received some minor knife-wounds.

After the struggle, when command of the *Caswell* was secured in British hands, both Nicholas and Bombos had their wounds treated. In due course Nicholas succumbed to his wounds and Bombos survived to be returned for trial in Queenstown.

This essentially and unceremoniously is the British view. A minimum of violence was used.

Bombos' view is somewhat more sanguine. Accordingly, after the murder of Big George, MacGregor went below and found Nicholas Morellos asleep. He thereupon cut Nicholas' head off with an axe. "The pillow", said Bombos graphically, "still bears the mark of the axe."

Bombos claimed that he was himself awakened by a blow on the head. Further blows followed – which left him bleeding profusely. He also remembered hiumself staggering and falling in the middle of the cabin. He recalled asking Carrick: "Why are you trying to kill me? I have not harmed you. On the contrary I saved your life and the ship."

At this stage Charles Macdonald brought Big George's revolver from the cabin and Carrick discharged it into George's body. They then pitched him overboard.

Bombos was locked in the carpenter's house, where he remained half insensible for the next ten hours soaking in his own blood. The British then dressed his wounds and put him in irons and - headed for Queenstown.

The trouble with Bombos' view is that, if, as he claimed, he was asleep in his cabin when the counter-mutiny began, how could he know what happened to Big George, or, for that matter, whether George was drunk of sober when attacked? Inconsistencies like this take considerably from his account.

Counter Mutiny

Throughout their long voyage home, the *Caswell* only met two
other ships. Carrick asked both for help. The *Caswell* was very
short-handed, but neither ship could afford to part with even one
crewmember. One of them was a French barque, the *Le Gaal.*
It proved uneventful. The engagement with the second ship,
however, was described as follows:

> "While the *Caswell* was still at sea, but after the mutiny
> had been quelled, a strange thing happened. As she was
> "crossing the line" Carrick saw a sail a mile off, and made
> for her to regulate the chronometer. The vessel was the
> barque *Le Genile* of Dunkirk. An English boy on board
> complained of ill treatment and asked to be taken on board
> the *Caswell*. Carrick refused to allow him to do so without
> the Captain's permission, but the next day, the vessels
> being a quarter of a mile apart, the boy jumped overboard
> and swam to the *Caswell"* (The *Cambrian*)

Bombos also mentions the boy off *Le Genile* as a possible witness who might have testified to his ill-treatment, but no such
witness was called. While Bombos has many complaints, most
of them -- including the missing logbook -- centre either on
British treachery or ill-treatment.

Apropos the logbook, Bombos claimed that Carrick came into
the cabin one day and as soon as he clapped eyes on the logbook,
which lay on the table, he clamoured: "Throw it overboard; it will
tell against us." Bombos refused, but before he could say anything
more, Carrick seized the logbook and pitched it through the cabin
window into the sea.

As to Bombos' complaints about being ill-treated, they were multiple and sometimes unconvincing. His conviction, however, that
the British were indebted to him is quite pronounced. Recounting
his feelings, he states:

> " They came then and asked me if I was dead. I replied:
>
> 'Is this the return I get for saving you? I proposed that George
> and Nicholas should be seized, and brought to England in
> Irons. I repeated to you faithfully what I had heard, and you
> promised me, that if I saved your life you would give me

anything I wanted when we returned to England, and
hailed me as a brother -- and now you want to kill me'.

They then said: 'We will cure you, and not kill you.'"

Some of these exchanges, given the depth of violence already
perpetrated by all involved, strike one as much less significant.
Yet Bombos dwells on them so much that one suspects that he
relishes a 'good moan.'

"Then they brought a needle and stitched up my wounds and
anointed them with oil, and in a fortnight I began to mend.
At the end of that time they put me in irons and gave me
very little bread and water, and very often I went without
getting anything to eat the whole day, and they used to beat
me on the face with their clenched fists, which made the
blood run from my nose and mouth. I used to ask them
'Why do you strike me?' They would then reply: 'Because
you are a Greek.' And I said: "Is that the reason -- because I
am a Greek? There are good and bad amongst all nationalities."
I then asked for bread and they struck me, and repeated the
treatment when I demanded some water. Says I, 'If you do
not give me something, I will die'. Said they: 'That is precisely what we wish.' Said I: 'You had better take another and
finish me, rather than torture me in this manner.'"

What have these details to do with either the mutiny or the counter-
mutiny? They delineate a scenario wherein Bombos, after the mutiny,
is convinced that he was the only friend upon whom the British could
rely. In exploiting this friendship the British -- especially Carrick --
beat him, put him in irons, and generally treated him very shabbily
throughout the voyage back to Queenstown. While these allegations
are credible in the main, their particulars lack verisimilitude.

Take the incident on their way to Queenstown, when the captain
of one of the ships they accosted came aboard, and Carrick told
him everything about the mutiny. The captain then came to where
Bombos was tied up and said 'did you do anything?' Bombos
replied, 'No'. He also consoled himself that 'Carrick confirmed
my statement. Then the captain went away.' This innocence or
naïveté is revealing. It is hardly possible that if Bombos was
going to tell lies in his own defence he would rely upon such a
remarkably insignificant observation. He believed that Carrick's

confirmation, which was itself casual, to an indifferent third party, of the fact that in general he had not done anything wrong -- that this should rank significantly in his defence on charges of multiple murder and mutiny on the high seas. Bombos' concers lacked real balance.

It also contrasts with his later treatment, when -

> "Carrick came up to me with a piece of raw pork about 9 lbs weight and hit me across the face with it, and struck me in the nose twice with his clenched fist and said: 'if you ask for anything more, I will kill you'".

He stated further :

> "I want to return to England because I have not done anything. If I say anything it will be but the plain truth and nothing to your disadvantage. And they said:'You will not be rewarded by the owners, so when we are nearing home you had better take a small boat and land on the French coast'"

When he refused this offer, Carrick allegedly took a stick and began to strike him. Then he took a marling-spike and poked it in his eye. Young McDonald came up to him and said, 'If you do not land on the French coast, Carrick will kill you'.

According to Bombos, the whole crew wanted him to go on the run. But despite their continuous taunts and beatings he remained adamant and refused to go on the run. Even when he tried to sleep they poured cold water over him, such that he remained constantly damp and uncomfortable.

Finally, Bombos makes another one of those seemingly harmless observations, as he had done when the mutineers changed their clothes. This time, he observed that the counter-mutineers, Dunne, Carrick and MacGregor, began to wear the captain's clothes.

The above account and extracts by Bombos are taken from his account of the mutiny, which was translated at his Hellenic Majesty's Consulate, Queenstown. (See Appendix A)

What was not, perhaps, appreciated at the time, was the fact that Bombos had little in common with the 'other Greeks'. He had an extended family, and his father was a retired navy captain who lived with his wife in Athens and who was in receipt of a pension from His Hellenic Majesty's government. He was hardly the type to jump ship, and go on the run with his tail between his legs.

In some respects, these observations – however colourful – are perfectly irrelevant to his guilt or innocence. As far as the criminal trial was concerned his ill treatment, at the hands of his erstwhile conspirators, would not have been a defence to his part in the mutiny. And he may have known that. So why dwell on his ill treatment in such detail? Obviously he became disillusioned with the manner in which the British betrayed his friendship and his confidence -- despite his efforts to save them and the ship. In his opinion they owed him for risking his life on their behalf.

If we ignore the criminal law for a moment and follow Bombos' account of what happened, we find that, apart from their apparent imbalance,they nevertheless give rise to several questions.

Bombos was now the only foreign captive of the mutiny and the counter-mutiny, neither of which, on his view, were flattering to the British. In his person he became at once an embarrassment and a trophy. His captivity represented the triumph of the loyal British over the disloyal foreigners, and it confirmed the original suspicions of the British against sailing with Greeks. Here was the culprit. Let him translate his way out of four dreadful murders. Moreover, that he was alive at all was due to the mercy shown by the counter-mutineers. Even in the thick of murder, they showed mercy and restraint where they need not have done so.

There was no denying the fact that Bombos was an embarrassment. Carrick hardly relished the idea of affording him an opportunity of talking about the logbook, not to mention their 'friendship'. Before the mutiny the British egged the Greeks to revolt; during it they went into hiding; and after it they parleyed with the mutineers and obligingly assisted them in the government of the ship.

The relationship of the British with Bombos was at best risque. Before the counter-mutiny the British allegedly conspired with Bombos personally; during it they turned savage - like George Peno; and after it, they vacillated between killing Bombos, nursing him back to health , bringing him to trial, and allowing him to escape to

Counter Mutiny

France via the coast. Bombos simply knew too much about everything. Or was he just a mutineer who got caught!

Actions, of course, have always spoken louder than words, and it
was English actions that brought Bombos to Queenstown despite
his account of their treacherous and deviant behaviour. Under the
heroic command of Carrick, the *Caswell* steered its way towards
Queenstown. The mutiny had occurred on January 4th, the
counter-mutiny on March 11th, and they reached Queenstown on
May 13th. They had been at sea for four and a half months, they
had lost their captain and five men, and that did not include two
deserters. And still Carrick took them home, cargo and all. In the
morning light off the head of Kinsale a British gunboat, the
Goshock, went out to meet them. A boatswain, four mariners, a
carpenter and one watch of Bluejackets were put on board. The
crew was drained, the *Caswell* was taken in tow, spirits were
high, and all Queenstown came awake.

All of a sudden everyone was up and out of doors. There was
great excitement in the air. Even before the petty sessions opened
people gathered in serried groups in the streets. Expectations ran
high, and when Carrick, MacGregor, Dunne, and the other
survivors of the *Caswell* landed, they were – to quote the Cork
Constitution - "pursued by a crowd who were anxious to catch a
glimpse of the heroes of the mutiny." Like Trojans from the
fields of Troy, the sailors came home to a hero's welcome - a
welcome that was to follow them with wanton joy and excitem-
ment all the way to Bristol, where,

>   "People were allowed aboard at sixpence a time, the funds
>   going to the murdered men's relatives. Immense crowds
>   went aboard (more than a thousand the first afternoon), but
>   when it was found that people were cutting up the wood-
>   work for mementoes, the ship was closed."(Sea Breezes V.
>   15 November, 1931)

Moreover, the sixpenny onlooker could see for himself that " The
cabin of the vessel (showed) traces of a severe struggle....", not
to mention the fact that,

>   "There were 3 bullet holes in the State room, one where
>   Nicholas fired from the bunk when he and Bombos were

surprised by the Englishmen. The glass (was) broken, and there (was) a deep indentation on the partition frame of the berth caused by a blow of the hatchet." (The *Illustrated News*)

Notwithstanding the fact that they had several heroes in Queenstown in 1876, by popular acclaim one of them stood head and shoulders above the rest. It was becoming increasingly evident that everyone's favourite hero was the wily Scot. Here, in James Carrick, people were beginning to recognise a quiet Ulysses. In him they began to see the unassuming and considerable resources that had passed from the person of Homer to the person of James Carrick now resident in the cul-de-sac of Queenstown harbour. A real live unprepossessing crafty sailor. How often does one meet such a man – a Ulysses! Whence comes such another?

The *Illustrated News* observed:

> "Carrick, MacGregor and Dunne are young men 25 or 30 years of age. Carrick is a very intelligent man, with great firmness and determination."

The methodical manner in which he approached things impressed all and sundry, including the Press. Already he had done his part in the counter-mutiny, now he was to take command without dissent or objection. Instead of going to Rio de Janeiro he chose, against all the odds, to sail to Queenstown and protect both crew and cargo. Once he had worked out his 'resolution', commented the News, 'He scarcely ever left the wheel'.

> "The ship made fair time and the easterly winds drove her to the Irish coast, where on Friday week, the 12th inst. she was met by a pilot boat from Queenstown.
>
> Carrick hailed her (the pilot boat), and got one man on board, saying, in reply to questions, that his crew was sick. This showed the forethought and fidelity of the man...."

When they were sick and exhausted, Carrick had the presence of mind to consider the greater good of both the *Caswell* and her crew. The crew could not, apparently, 'work the ship up to Queenstown.' At first Carrick made it known that he wanted to

remain independent of the crew of the pilot boat. Later on the
Caswell 'fell in' with the pilot-boat again. This time Carrick per-
mitted three men on board, but not unconditionally. According to
The Illustrated News,

> "...In order to prevent them making a claim for salvage
> he drew up a paper which he made them sign, in which
> they bound themselves to accept a certain sum for their
> services."

But who was this thoughtful Odysseus who took charge of everything and who, with craft and equanimity, brought them in tact to
the shore of Queenstown harbour? "By parentage he is an Irishman," said the *Illustrated News*; "but by birth this brave young
man is Scotch." His leadership qualities were everywhere demonstrated without a heavy hand; for as the News was keen to
point out, the men responded almost naturally to his ascendancy.
This included MacGregor, who had :

> " ...Worked with equal fortitude and perseverance on the
> two-month voyage home; and under him Carrick's orders
> were always carried out."

By Monday the 15th of May the heroes had rested up and were
ready for the day's excitement. There was a distinct buzz in
Queenstown since the *Caswell* first anchored. But now it was
time to hear an account from the actors themselves.

The courtroom was packed to capacity. What the people had now
come to see was not so much their heroes as their villains: and
they weren't disappointed. Bombos was put forward and charged
with the "Murder (on the High Seas) of George Edward Best, William Wilton, Allen McLean, and Emmanuel Griffiths." There was
a hush when the Greek appeared in court. He was 24 years of age,
dark, sturdy, and 5 feet six inches tall. Whatever else went on in
court the dominant impression, captured by the *Cork Constitution*
(Tuesday, May 16th), was the unmistakable first impression that
Bombos created by his mere presence and appearance:

> "The prisoner who wore a red shirt looked very firm and
> defiant in the dock. In appearance he is thoroughly
> Grecian - his features, especially his nose, indicating his
> nationality. His eye, for he has only one that he can see

with, is very dark, the other having a cataract over it gives to his face a most sinister expression. Thus from his right hand side he is a rather good looking young man -- but his appearance from the opposite point of view is hideous, for the white surface over his left eye makes the other seem to glisten when he fixes it on one."

The *Constitution* was not the only newspaper to describe Bombos' appearance. The *Illustrated News* described him also:

"The prisoner, Christos Bombos, is a young, good looking man of 27, with closely cut whiskers, ending in an imperial; he has handsome Grecian features. He was dressed in a red shirt, a cap, light trousers and heavy seaboots. He speaks Italian fluently, and did not appear to care about his position. One of his companions killed in the final conflict, boasted of having killed two captains before."

The owners, W.H. Tucker & Co., Swansea, and their representatives were there; Mr Yourdi, the Greek Consul was there; there was a Representative from the Press, some Gentlemen from Swansea were present, and the locals thronged both inside and outside the courtroom. The Queenstown Petty Sessions were presided over by Captain W. D. Seymour (in the chair), A. Bremner, Major Longfield, W.R. Starkie, R.M. N. Beamish, and F. McCarthy. Bombos was represented by the Cork city Solicitor, J. T. O'Connell. Mr Yourdi, the Greek Consul had secured O'Connell's service. Unfortunately, however, O'Connell failed to make an appearance. Mr. Heaney, clerk of the court, announced that he had received a letter from Mr. O'Connell, stating that he had been engaged on behalf of the prisoner, but asked that the case be adjourned. Mr. Gillman, Crown Solicitor, said he could not object to the postponement in such a very serious case, and in order that the prisoner might be given every facility to prepare his defence. It was, he continued, a case that would require thorough investigation, and he would ask for a week's postponement.

Captain Seymour said he hoped that any documentary evidence that might be given should be put in the hands of the proper parties, so that it might be translated.

Mr Gillman agreed by saying that one of the objects he had
in view was to have the documents translated and read to the
prisoner.

Mr Beamish commented : "As the Bench don't understand
Greek, we will want anything else translated into common
English. Any of us then acquainted with Greek can compare
the documents afterwards with the English."

Captain Seymour added that in order to facilitate business at
the next court, a proper interpreter "who was not in any way
connected with the case" should be procured. " One could be
procured easily in Cork", he added confidently. Mr Beamish
quickly responded: "That is for the Crown altogether." Mr
Yourdi, the Greek Consul, then said that if necessary he or
his brother would act as interpreter.

With that, it was generally agreed that the business should be
adnourned until the following Monday. But Mr O'Brien, Solicitor,
who appeared for the owners of the ship, while instructed to assist
the Crown as far as possible, was nevertheless anxious about the
Caswell itself. He applied to have it released to continue its journey
to Bristol, otherwise it's detention was a matter of great expense.
To sweeten his application he added: "All the parties connected
with the ship would be discharged so that they might be at the service
service of the Crown."

The *Caswell* itself had a capital value of £10,000 and its cargo
was estimated to be worth a further £10,000. The owner's anxiety
to have it released was understandably commercial, but a valid
concern nevertheless. And Mr Gillman said that the Crown had
no desire to detain it one hour, were it not for the fact that he had
been informed that it would be utterly impossible to investigate
the case in the absence of the ship.

Now this was enough to turn the Queenstown Magistrates' heads.
They were only warming to their task. And now that they had
their hands on such a beautiful ship, they were not prepared to
part with her so readily. On the contrary, justice had to be seen to
be done. It was therefore with some circumspection that Captain
Seymour thought that "evidence might be brought forward that
would render an investigation of every part of the ship necessary."

Counter Mutiny

Mr Beamish added: "It would be as well if they also had a plan of
the ship."

The case was remanded for a week and the *Caswell* was held in
shore. It was, perhaps, during this period that an unknown pier-
head artist decided to leave us his impressions of the *Caswell*, of
Queenstown harbour 1875, the courthouse, the local Bridewell,
and etchings of Bombos in custody, James Carrick and even the
Goshawk. All these impresions were neatly packed into one frame,
and first appeared in *The Illustrated News* on May 27, 1876. The
sketch was reproduced in a magazine entitled 'Swansea Cape
Horners Remember', and the Swansea City Council Maritime
& Industrial Museum.

Salonica

A week later, on Tuesday May 23, the *Constitution* noted that
Bombos looked very well; his 'dress was more decent than on
previous occasions'. But the time could not be worse for a trial
of its kind. It wasn't that the Queenstown magistrates were fools,
or that they would allow themselves to be swayed by anti-Turk
or anti-Greek sentiment generated by the affairs in the Levant.
Nonetheless, the world knew that the Turks were at war with
Servia/Herzogovina, and the Turks, right down to the second half
of the twentieth century were sometimes interchangeable with
Greeks and Greek Cypriots. Suddenly these low-burning antagonisms were ignited by events in Salonica.

On Saturday, May 6, a week before the *Caswell* was towed into
Queenstown, a fanatical Mussulman-mob attacked and murdered
the German and French consuls, Mr Henry Abbott and his broth-
in-law, M. Paul Moulin. The victims shared a concern with the
American consul in taking charge of a young Christian girl, who
had been removed from her home for conversion to the Moham-
medan religion. At the time of their murder they had taken refuge
in a Mosque.

The German Consul, Mr H. Abbott, was a British subject, born at
Salonica and married to a Greek lady; he was also connected by
marriage with the American Consul, Hadji Lazaro.

The Turkish Government at once promised to inquire into the matter and where necessary to punish the murderers. Six suspects were

73

eventually condemned and publicly executed, and another fifty
were arrested for taking part in the riot.

A joint foreign Commission of inquiry proceeded to Salonica,
which -- next to Constantinople -- was the most important town
in 'European' Turkey. This Aegean town, known to the ancients
as Thessalonica, had a wonderful history. To the ancients the old
Macedonian city gave rise to great commercial activity, especially during the days of the Roman Empire. It was known intimately
by both St. Paul and Cicero.

In the mid and late1870s Salonica carried on a busy trade in
silk, corn, wine, tobacco, wool and timber. Its domes and
minarets, rising intermittently between cypress gardens and
religious and official buildings, gave shelter to a population not
exceeding 75,000. A third of these was Jewish, a further third
belonged to the Greek Orthodox Church, and a further third to
other religions, which included circa 10,000 Mohammedans, The
murder of both Consuls, had an unmistakable nine-eleven effect.
British, French, Russian, Austrian, and German ships of war were
instantly trained defensively on the beautiful bay of Salonica.
This was the largest fleet of foreign ships ever assembled in
Turkish waters. Russia dispatched the frigate Svetna, commanded by Grand Duke Alexis. The Italians ordered three of their
ironclads, the Venesia, the Palestro, and the Maria Pia - under the
command of Rear-Admiral Viry. Another vessel, the Messagiero,
followed. The Austrian ironclad Radetsky also arrived, and was
also followed by two or three more vessels. The French sent three
ironclads and one dispatch-vessel with Admiral Jaures in comm.-
and. These were followed by two Greek ironclads, the Salamis,
and the Georgos. And still they came.The German squadron,
not to be left out of the scramble, consisted of the Nautilus gunboat; the Kaiser, the Deutschland, the Kreonprinz and the Fried-
rich Karl, all ironclads, plus the dispatch vessel, Pomerania,
representing a force of 2570 men, with sixty-nine guns – all
sped to Salonica under the command of Admiral Batsch.

It was against this military background that the trial of Bombos
was to be conducted. Either on the facts or from the long shadow
of a possible *jihad*, the outcome for Bombos looked grim.

The Lennie

Counter Mutiny

In due course Bombos was sent forward for trial at the Cork Summer Assizes. In the meantime he was transferred in custody to the Cork County Gaol. It was just his bad luck that military tensions in the Levant blew up. And on the same day as his adjournment was sought, the Lennie also came back in the news. These two items are of more than passing relevance to Bombos' trial. Indeed, the murders aboard the *Lennie* and the findings of the trial were reported on the same page as the *Caswell*, the one was headed "The *Lennie* Murders " and the other "The *Caswell* Mutiny" And lest anyone should fail to associate the two mutinies the *Constitution* reminded the general public that:

> "Mr Joseph Cartwright of London who acted as interpreter
> on the trial of the *Lennie* mutineers, was sworn as interpreter
> in this case, and it was arranged the evidence should be first
> written out by the clerk of the court, and then read to the
> prisoner..."

=======

Chapter 5

The Trials Of
Bombos

The Senate House

First Sen. My lord, you have my voice to it; the fault's
Bloody; 'tis necessary he should die;
Nothing emboldens sin so much as mercy.
Second Sen. Most true; the law shall bruise him.

Shakespeare /Timon of Athens/Act 111. Scene V.

It was Thursday (July 27 1876), and a beautiful summer's morning in the
city was unfolding. Down in the County Court agrarian crime was still
on the menu, and the terrorist Thomas Crowe was getting ready to be
processed through what is popularly called 'the criminal justice system.'
Even though it was the talk of the country, the common fare of 'agrarian
outrage' would have to play second fiddle to something more colourful --
murder on the high seas! This was rare, exotic, and full of unpredictable
incident. In a word, it was a kind of barrister's caviar, the kind of case
that counsel knew would capture the attention of the press and rivet the
people to their local newspaper throughout the hearing. And what a meal

the lawyers were to make of it! The first trial was destined to
end in a disagreement by the Jury. This meant, in effect, a retrial,
thereby giving the Crown a second bite of the cherry as it were.

His Lordship, Mr Justice Lawson entered court at ten o'clock and proceeded with Bombos' case. As was his wont, he scanned the front bench
before him. It was laden, no doubt, with familiar 'silks', some fingering
their briefs, some striking poses and others sipping water. Like penguins
ready to pop up at any time, they waited upon his Lordship's 'Good
morning', before the starch left their faces.

There were three Q.C.s for the Crown and only one for the defence. There
was nothing unusual about this sense of balance: it was based on the
avoirdupois principle of justice -- a principle that has prevailed since time
began and yet not one Jurist has ever expounded upon its merits. According to the avoirdupois principle three Crown silks will outweigh, in
wiggery, drollery, piety, patience, volume, and smarm any single silk in
the realm. This has been the case since the time of Christ or, before him,
Socrates - neither of whom, unfortunately, bothered themselves with a
'brief.' Needless to say, if they had, the State would have engaged three
prosecutors for every defender hired. The three-against-one-rule was
not a principle of law that had to be acted upon: it was more like a law
of gravity – it just wasn't sufficient to prove justice, it also had to be seen
to be proved. Over time and what with the march of justice it had become
the custom, at least down to the enlightened twenty first century, to mod-
ify the principle and allow a two-against-one-rule to suffice.

Failing that, there was the secondary principle of costs. The Crown,
accordingly, had a long-standing habit of allocating more silks than any
defence could afford, except, that is, for the most obscenely wealthy or
the most notoriously criminal. The only alternative weight that might
counterbalance such a corpulent mass is, of course, that of the people,
who were represented in the jury. The jury, it will be observed, is hardly
ever allowed to open its mouth: for the jury— the criminal justice system's
last sop to democracy—is invariably held to one decision only, 'Guilty'
or 'Not Guilty.' Moreover, it has always been common practice in Ireland
to discretely rig the jury one way or another when the 'exigencies' of
justice so required. Protestant Ireland, for example, always had recourse
to the 'packed jury', in order to galvanise itself against the worst errors of
democracy. Catholic Ireland didn't bother about 'packing juries': it simply
abolished them, and gave its more controversial work to a Special Criminal Court, which has now been sitting in a 'declared emergency' condition
almost as long as the Irish Republic itself has existed. What makes this

arrangement unmistakably Irish is the added fact that the Special Criminal Court still sits even after the Good Friday Agreement released the very
terrorists (the IRA and UVF included) that the Court intended to incar-
cerate.

However much this very unbalanced scale of justice has historically
informed the Crown's concept of propriety, not to mention its sense of
aesthetics, it would be quite wrong to impute any impropriety to the trial
of Christos Emmanuel Bombos. On the contrary, nothing could have
been done with greater courtesy, openness, and fairness.

In a culture where the structural imbalances have predictable and obvious
effects on outcome, concerns for fairness and openness can be liberally
proffered. Counsel for the Crown were - Sergeant Sir Colman O'Loghlen, M.P.m Messrs Murphy, Q.C., Green, Q.C. and O'Hea, instructed by
Mr. Gillman, Crown Solicitor, and all of them quite obviously appearing
for the prosecution. The prisoner at the Bar was defended by Mr Heron,
Q.C., and Mr Peter O'Brien, instructed by Mr J.T. O'Connell, solicitor.

In due course Bombos was moved from the relaxed, sleepy seaside of
Queenstown to the bustle of the city, from the magistrates' court to the
County Court, and from the eyes of a parochial press to that of the city
press. Characteristic of the move was the new, more penetrating description of Bombos. According to the *Cork Examiner* the 24-year-old was

> "... About five feet six in height, dark in complexion and in hair. He has
> very well cut features, and only for having one blind eye, he would be
> considered a handsome man. The left eye has a cataract over it, and it gives
> his face, when one looks at it from that side, a very nervous appearance. The
> most remarkable thing about him is, if we might say, the omnipresence of
> his gaze. He seemed to feel when an eye was fixed on him, for immediately
> he looked in that direction. When before the Queenstown magistrates the
> same thing was more noticeable. No one could even steal a glance at him,
> but directly he met the piercing black eye of the prisoner. For the greater
> portion of yesterday he appeared to have but a very hazy notion, if any at
> all, of what was being sworn against him; for though Mr. Cartwright, the
> Interpreter in the Lennie cases in London, was sworn, he had only translated
> portion of the first witness's testimony by word of mouth as it was being
> given, when the prisoner's Counsel requested that no more should be
> translated. In consequence of this arrangement Baumbos seemed to be
> utterly ignorant of the evidence, except, occasionally when what was called
> 'ship's language' was used."

The facts of the case have in large measure been recited already. Except
for some points of contrast and contradiction, it is futile to repeat them

here as they are invariably repeated ad nauseam in a court of law. In opening the case to the jury counsel for the Crown referred to the case, to the *Caswell*, its cargo, and its 73-day outward-bound voyage. He then referred to the crew and their life-chances. " When the vessel sailed from from Glasgow", he said, "there were nineteen persons (16 according to the Cambrian) on board and of these only three, including two apprentices returned home alive."

Now nobody mentioned this fact before, simply because no one knew about it. The only people who might have known about it were the captain and the crew, and they were either dead or scattered. Of course the owners and the insurers knew, but they were not interested in telling the world about either their investments or such tragedies as might affect their fortunes. Moreover, what precisely did counsel for the Crown mean when he said that "... only three...(out of nineteen) returned home alive?" It could hardly have meant that sixteen of the crew were dead or had some other mishap? Apart from the fact that they refused to work the *Caswell* and that they went elsewhere for work, no great import could be attributed to the words used. It was the stark terms in which counsel chose to couch his language that deepened rather than clarified the mystery. Neither was it intended to endear the dead captain to the jury. So why should Crown counsel do that for the defence?

Perhaps the prosecutor knew that no matter what captain Best had done to the outgoing crew, no matter how cruel the defence could paint him, it was irrelevant to the facts of the instant case. Crown counsel knew that the minds of the jury, as with the minds of all citizens of the Empire, would be directed over and over again to the sole consideration of the facts before it, especially to the testimony dealing with the mutiny and the murder of the captain and his men. No antecedents would excuse Bombos once the Crown demonstrated his part in the mutiny. And this it did laboriously; for the witnesses, one by one, testified to the following facts, namely, that the prisoner at the bar --

i stabbed the captain while he was lying wounded.
ii held the first mate while he was being murdered.
iii stabbed the second mate.
iv might well have killed the young apprentices, were it not for the intervention of the arch-murderer Giuseppe Pistoria.
v helped to dump the bodies overboard, and
vi obliterated the name of the *Caswell* from the ship.

The Trials Of Bombos

The first witness was Peter MacGregor, the carpenter. The *Caswell* was his first ship, and the trip, incidentally, was his second voyage, his first being the outbound trip. It was of some significance that he testified to hearing Giuseppe Pistoria fire three shots (In the second trial he only heard two). All in all, however, he averred the above six points against Bombos, but not before he gave the court an unexpected belly laugh:

> "We left Buenos Aires for Valparaiso on the 23rd October. After 33 days passage we got no cargo there, and left for Antofogasta where the Irishman deserted (laughter). No one was shipped instead of him. At Antofogasta in the middle of December the German cook then deserted and no one was got in his place..."

With irrefutable certainty he went on to say, "I saw the prisoner stab him (the second mate) twice in the back." Or, again, "I saw Baumbos come across to where the captain was lying and plunge the knife twice into his breast. The captain had life in him at the time, but his bowels were protruding. This was after he stabbed the second mate..."

Bombos could not follow the trial. He was put at the severest of disabilities. He hardly understood a word of what was being recited before him. If he had, it would soon have became apparent that there was no escape from the barrage of first-class testimony. His real enemy was the criminal trial itself, not least because it took no cognisance of the milieu of fear in which the mutiny occurred. Never in the history of the world was a mutiny justified in a court of law. And Counsel for the Crown - three of them - were there to see that it wasn't going to happen by way of exception in the Cork County Court.

"The steward was a coloured man ", resumed MacGregor, " about nineteen or twenty years of age. While washing down the poop I saw the steward's heart lying where he had been murdered."

And what defence could erase the following imagery?

> "The prisoner and all the others took part in throwing the bodies overboard. When I was at the captain's head I saw him putting his hand on his entrails to drag them, as I thought to kill himself."

As to the counter-mutiny, MacGregor stated:

> "I went forward to where Carrick and McDonald were off watch. Carrick was in his bunk and when I went down he got up and took an adze from my locker. I got an axe myself. This was at two o'clock in the morning. We proceeded to the poop where we met Big George. He had a knife in his

hand, and as he approached me I struck him with my axe, once, on the head, and he fell. Carrick and I ran to the cabin where Nicholas and Baumbos were. As I entered the cabin a shot was fired. Before this I made a blow of an axe at him, but missed him. I then closed on him and caught him by the arms. I cried to Carrick for help and he struck Nicholas and stumbled him. I came on deck and saw Big George trying to rise. Dunne took the adze from Carrick and struck Big George about the head. Baumbos was in the cabin when I went there, and the next place I saw him, he was wounded on the poop. Two hours afterwards Carrick brought Baumbos forward to the Galley where Dunne sewed up and dressed his wounds. We gave him all the care we could and he recovered in a week. Then we kept him in irons for the remainder of the voyage. "

MacGregor was asked several direct questions and responded as follows:

Counsel - On your oath who killed Big George?
MacGregor - I struck him and Dunne struck him, and he died two hours after.

Counsel - On your oath who killed Nicholas?
MacGregor - Carrick gave him a lick and I gave him a lick. I disabled him at the cabin door, last stroke

Counsel - Who finished him?
MacGregor- Dunne gave him the heaviest lick on the head

Counsel - Now, I ask you on your oath, did you not kill Big George while he was asleep on the deck drunk?
MacGregor- No, sir.

Counsel- Did you strike him while asleep?
MacGregor- No, sir.

Regarding the captain, MacGregor admitted that at Buenos Aires he had put Carrick, Rook (probably Rourke), and Dunne in irons and kept them there for days. He recalled that the captain had also struck Dunne and knocked him insensible to the ground with a baton. He also struck Carrick. But for all that he did not think that the captain had a violent temper. Neither had he ever seen the captain with a revolver. As far as he was concerned the Greeks and the Maltese "wanted us to make a stand so that they might shoot us down."

Then Carrick took the stand and was examined by Mr Green Q.C. He testified to being an able seaman who joined the *Caswell* at Buenos Aires on the 28th September. Generally speaking Carrick's evidence confirmed

The Trials Of Bombos

MacGregor's. When the mutiny broke out he went into the galley and hid himself in the coalbunker. He said:

> "After Joseph shot the captain the mate was then abreast of me before rigging. He ran the same time as I did - but he was at the starboard side and I was at the other. I heard him singing out 'Not me, Joseph'. I saw the second mate running towards the poop on the quarterdeck. As the second mate was going there I saw the prisoner stab him in the shoulder. He was then at the booby hatch, and when the second mate came to the corner of the house, Peno stabbed him and Gaspari shot him. Baumbos was standing by them. Peno had his arm around the second mate stabbing him and singing a song and Gaspari was shooting him in the leg. Soon after that I saw the steward come on deck form the cabin; all the foreigners flew at him stabbing him; after Gaspari stabbed him, then the prisoner was there, too. I saw on the deck portion of the heart of the steward. He was carried down to the deck and fastened to an anchor. I went into the galley and hid myself in the coal bunker..."

When he came out Joseph Pistoria told him to get the stream anchor. He never explained how he remained unscathed by the mutineers.

According to Carrick's testimony he did not intend to kill Big George when he struck him. He claimed that he and the others killed George and Nicholas in self-defence. Nicholas gave a sort of scream when Carrick struck him, but he could not say how many blows were struck. The third witness was John Dunne who was sworn and examined byColman O' Loghlen, Q.C.

Again Dunne confirmed the evidence of the previous witnesses. In cross-examination he said that the captain was a fine able man of about 43 or 44 years of age. He recalled that, when they were in Buenos Aires, captain Best struck Dunne and the blow knocked him down. He also recalled that the captain put him in irons, that he also struck Carrick, and had put him in irons also. But further than these admissions he had nothing to say by way of elaboration. He had witnessed the mutiny, his account tallying with the previous witnesses. In his original Information Dunne swore that Bombos stabbed the second mate once. Now he changed his evidence somewhat and swore that he stabbed him twice.

In the counter-mutiny he said that he went down and into the cabin (on the morning of March 12th), where he made an attempt to strike Bombos, but missed him. Bombos, he said, offered no resistance, and came up very quietly on deck. He was wounded and bleeding; It was then resolved that Bombos' life would be spared.

He then recalled how he took the adze out of Carrick's hand and struck Big George on the head with it. When he struck him, George was crawling towards him with a knife in his hand.

In re-examination by Sir Colman O'Loglen, Dunne reiterated that the reason they were put in irons in Buenos Aires was because they did not want to go to sea with Greeks. And when they made application to go ashore to see the British Consul, captain Best would not allow them. On the contrary, he kept them in irons while the vessel was in the harbour in order to prevent them from going ashore.

The testimony of the apprentices corroborated that of the previous witnesses, and was not without originality. McDonald, for example, caught in a few words the status of both Bombos and Joseph Pistoria vis-à-vis each other:

> "After the chief mate was stabbed Ferguson and I ran to the break of the poop to the apprentice's house. We found the door locked, and while there, the prisoner Bombos rushed towards us with a knife in his hand. As he did so, Joseph called out:" No machata", which means 'no boys.' Joseph then said to me, "go to wheel, boy, you all right, you spared." There was nobody at the wheel then. The second mate called to me "put the ship back" and went down the fore companion. Joseph came to the fore companion and called up the second mate, who immediately came up. Joseph shot him in the arm, and as the second mate ran off the poop, the prisoner stabbed him twice on the back; all the foreigners rushed after him, and when they got close to him they stabbed and shot at him. He ran round the house a couple of times and fell near where the body of the captain was lying…"

In defence of Bombos Mr Heron, Q.C. told the jury that, if indeed there had ever been a conspiracy, the prisoner should not to be regarded as part of it. Why? Because Big George and Nicholas Morellos were both natives of Turkey and, in any event, were in no way connected with Bombos, who belonged to a most respectable Athenian family.That Bombos' father was a retired Greek captain was again mentioned; and that he enjoyed a pensi0on from the Greek Government. Despite the evidence against him, Bombos persisted in his denial of any wrongdoing. Whatever happened during the mutiny, it was due to the coercion exerted by Big George, and for no other reason short of protecting himself from certain and immanent death. As to the counter-mutiny, it was Bombos's case that it had not only been brutal but, in effect, it happened when the deceased were either asleep or drunk. But McDonald's evidence contradicted this and described the counter-mutiny as follows:

> "I saw the prisoner go forward three times. Suspecting him I followed the prisoner into the forecastle, where Dunne, the carpenter and Ferguson were. I saw him lying in a chest in the forecastle. Bombos had been sleeping in the cabin at this time. I afterwards went below, and about two o'clock in the morning, while lying awake in the forecastle, the carpenter came into the forecastle and said, "Now, boys, for your lives," or some words to that effect. In a short time I heard a great roar aft, and on getting on deck I saw the big Greek lying on the poop with a knife in his hand. I saw him crawl towards the companion, when Dunne seized the adze and struck him on the head. I heard a great noise in the cabin also, and saw Bombos led up captive. He came on deck with Carrick and the carpenter after him. He was put in irons by Carrick and Dunne, and was removed to the deckhouse. He was wounded, and his wounds were dressed and attended to…"

But no matter how the counter-mutiny was executed, it remained weak and could never amount to a defence of the mutiny. In effect there was very little the defence could do, but pick holes in the testimony of the Crown witnesses.

One witness for the defence was William Clibbett, a naval architect. Examined by Mr. Peter O' Brien, Clibbett referred to certain marks that were found near the captain's berth and which were examined by him. O'Brien had hoped to demonstrate -- from the two marks left in the bunks -- the savagery of the English in dispatching Big George and Nicholas Morellos. Such testimony, if cogent enough, might have discredited that of the British. The British, it will be remembered, claimed that their dismissal of the Greeks occurred on deck, and that they had no real wish to kill either Big George or Nicholas Morellos.

The marks, in so far as marks can demonstrate such things, supported the view that great violence had been used, if not to dispatch the Greeks then in the struggle to subdue them. The unseen point of this evidence lay in the fact that if the British were capable of such violence, why wasn't it evident when it came to defending their captain? Such inconsistencies were perfectly in accord with Bombos' account. Under cross-examination, however, Clibbett had to concede that he could not say what caused the marks or, indeed " if those strokes were aimed at the beds."

Finally, Nicholas George Yourdi, the Greek Consul, testified that he had been in communication with the prisoner's father. He then volunteered that he knew the prisoner's father well. He also confirmed that Bombos' father was a retired captain in what he called "the navy of the Independence," that he was receiving a pension, and that he was living at the Pirseus, in Athens. But this character reference was abruptly qualified.

To his Lordship he said: " I know nothing of the prisoner's father except by letter."

Mr Peter O' Brien intimated to his Lordship that he would require a little time before he could address the jury on behalf of the prisoner as he felt himself physically 'incapacitated.'

His Lordship ordered the jury to be conducted to Varian's Hotel, and adjourned the hearing until 10 o'clock the following morning, when the trial resumed. The jury, which had been chaperoned overnight by both Police and Bailiff, were made answer to their names on their return. Mr Joseph Cartwright, the interpreter, was briefly called by the Crown to interpret the words *tutte morti*, which were used by the Greeks after the massacre. Not unsurprisingly he said they meant "all dead".

Mr Peter O'Brien then proceeded to sum up the case for the prisoner. Reviewing the proceedings on the 4th of January he dismantled the Crown's theory that the massacre was the result of a concerted conspiracy. If that were so, he said, would Big George be on the rig working, or would the foreigners have done it either in broad daylight or when the watch was changing? They knew that the change of watch brought all hands, including Englishmen, on deck. So why choose it to enact the conspiracy? He would ask them to believe that it was by no means a preconceived plan, but rather the result of a sudden outburst -- a sudden affray arising from some original violence by the captain. If this, indeed, was how it happened, they were entitled to bring in a verdict of guilt in respect of manslaughter rather than murder.

Mr. Murphy Q.C. replied on the part of the Crown. He wanted them to discharge their duty "manfully and boldly." He asked the jury not to be distracted by the happenings of March 1st or March 11th or, for that matter, by theories of conspiracies. They were irrelevant to the evidence. The evidence was all that was important...

His Lordship's Summary

When it came to his Lordship's summary, he was sharp and to the point, and he left the Jury in no doubt as to what its business was. "It was a charge of murder," he said.

> "It was not a charge, as may be supposed from both the speeches of the prisoner's counsel, of conspiracy to murder. It was a charge of actual murder and he should, therefore, tell them to discard that from their minds as entirely irrelevant to the case...The charge against the prisoner was that he was guilty of the willful murder of four persons upon the 4th January 1876.... He was bound to tell them that if a man stood by, aiding and assisting another in committing murder, although he dealt no blow himself, he was guilty of murder. However that did not arise here because if they believed the evidence of the five witnesses who had been produced, the prisoner Christos Baumbos took a very active and prominent part in the affair."

His Lordship then proceeded to read the evidence of the witnesses in detail, reminding the jury that the enquiry was to be confined to the 4th of January. That morning, within the supposed space of five minutes, these four men -- the captain, the chief mate, the second mate, and the steward were weltering on deck in their own blood, and each was fastened to an anchor and thrown overboard.

Perhaps the most important question in the trial hinged on the vacillation between Murder and Manslaughter. Could the jury, in law, bring in a verdict of Manslaughter when the accused was charged with Murder. The Judge was adamant. He felt he was bound to say that on the evidence it was utterly impossible to find a verdict of manslaughter. According to his Lordship the killings amounted to a "deliberate and wilful murder." He then proceeded to chastise Defence counsel for even mentioning it to the jury. The Judge then declared that he was never more startled "by any proposition in a court of justice than when he heard a counsel of eminence say, that this case may be reduced to the offence of manslaughter."

So, what essentially this meant was that, even if the jury on the facts decided that Bombos had been coerced by Big George, or brutalised by captain Best, he was nevertheless culpable in the same manner as if he had never been coerced or brutalised. Surely after this dogmatic ruling there could be little doubt as to to the outcome of the case!

The Jury

At twenty-six minutes past twelve the jury retired. At twenty to three they sent a message to say that they wanted to speak to the judge. When they came back to court his Lordship, an academic, was as ever direct.

His Lordship - Do you wish to say anything to me?
The Foreman- There is no possibility of agreeing to a verdict.

His Lordship - Is that all?
The Foreman – yes

His Lordship - Can I give you any assistance?
The Foreman- I didn't think so.
Another Juror - We are all agreed except me?
The Foreman - And that juror says he won't agree to a verdict.

His Lordship - It is not usual in a case of this very serious kind to discharge a jury so soon. You had better remain a longer time in deliberation. You may be able, Gentlemen, to bring around your brother juror. I hope he will consider the responsibility of his oath and his duty. You had better retire now.

The jury retired again and reappeared in court at a quarter past five.

The Clerk of the Court - How say you Gentlemen, have you agreed to your verdict?
Foreman - No

His Lordship - Is there any probability of you agreeing, Gentlemen, if I were to detain you longer?
Foreman - No, my lord, not the least.

His Lordship - I regret such a result very much, but I would not be justified in detaining you any longer. I will discharge you now, Gentlemen.

The jury was then discharged for the remainder of the assizes. But no sooner was Trial One over than the Crown was championing at the bit for Trial Two to commence.

Sir Colman O'Loghlen - Now, my lord, I wish to state that on the part of the Crown, it is their intention to put the prisoner on trial again on Monday morning, and I ask you to direct the sheriff to notify that the long panel will be recalled then.

His Lordship - I don't know, Sir Colman, if we can do that.

Mr. Murphy Q.C. - it would be utterly impossible, my lord, to have this case postponed until the next assizes in consequence of the nature of the evidence, for the witnesses might not be available hereafter. As your lordship sees, the trial is conducted at enormous expense, and it is one that should be tried here.

Sir Colman O' Loghlen - And your lordship remembers the statement made by the foreman of the jury.

His Lordship - the jury panel is of such a character and is so exhausted by the trial-taking place, it seems to me a question whether the other trial ought to take place. However, as you make the application I will consider it.

Mr Murphy Q.C. - Let the jury attend on Monday. If the announcement is made on the paper that they will be called on heavy fines they will attend.

His Lordship - A great many jurors have been allowed to go home.

Mr. Johnson (Sub-Sheriff) - A great many jurors have been excused.

Mr Peter O'Brien submitted for the prisoner that as the case had been one that excited a great deal of comment amongst jurors who had remained, it should not be retried at the present assizes. Predictably, the Judge of trial had the last word:

His Lordship - I cannot agree with you at all. That would be an excuse for any dishonest juryman.

Mr Murphy Q.C. - It would be a most lamentable failure of justice if the case were not tried at this assizes. It would be a deplorable thing if it were put off until next assizes; and I think from the character of the witnesses, as they may be in any part of the world, the case should be proceeded with. Otherwise it would be a triumphant defeat of justice.

Mr Peter O' Brien said some of the prisoner's witnesses had left.

His Lordship - I don' t care about that. You did not produce a witness that proved anything.

Mr O'Brien - Oh, I think the naval officer proved a good deal.

By direction of his lordship the County long-panel was ordered to be resumed on Monday morning, when the prisoner would be re-tried.

***

Trial 2

At 10 o'clock the following Monday (July 31), Mr Justice Lawson
again entered the County Crown Court and began anew what he had
just completed. No one mentioned the fathomless tedium of listening
to hours of evidence already heard - a little like Sisyphus pushing his
ball of justice up a hill without another side. Tedium notwithstanding,
a throng of people packed the courtroom again and buoyed the case
with their presence throughout the hearing.

Bombos was put on his election again. He pleaded 'Not Guilty' and much
the same teams of lawyers and witnesses lined up for the parties. When
the long panel was called over, seventy-three answered to their names.

Mr. Heron, Q.C. sought his opportunity to make an application for a
postponement on behalf of Bombos. A long postponement would have
been good for Bombos; for an immediate retrial would allow the Crown
to 'correct' its errors and attend to those areas in the concatenation of
proofs, which appeared weakest at the first trial.

Moreover, people generally remember that which is shocking and sensational for a much longer period than they remember matters about
which they are in doubt. Those who had read about Bombos' first trial
would remember the details of the massacre and Bombos' part in it much
more firmly than they would recall the coercion of Big George Peno.
Peno's coercion is nowhere to be envisaged or simply related. It was
contained in body language, forgotten threats, stares and gestures. Fear
isn't chiselled into specific and colourful incidents, and none of them in
any event was directly applicable to Bombos. Before such things are
recalled with sufficient vitality to convince a jury, they have to be recalled at length, and this depends totally on the passion and conviction
of the witnesses and, of course, their ability and desire to describe and
vivify such events. At its best, therefore, it is a description, which however factually based, is difficult to communicate to others or to rely upon
as a defence. In a word, it takes much more time and skill to communicate
the idea of fear by way of evidence. The savagery of the mutineers, in contrast is captured in pictures, in facts, and in the managed recollection of the
missing bodies. In this sense, a retrial is an unfair procedure, and a retrial
immediately after a disagreement of the jury, amounted to a prejudice against the accused. But Heron Q.C. advanced none of these reasons for a postponement; he had his own more relevant concerns to think about.

The Trials Of Bombos

Bombos' Counsel stated that William Clibbett was unavailable and that he was " a material and necessary witness" for the defence. He also reminded the Judge that at the first trial Clibbett deposed to having examined the two cuts which might have been inflicted with a hatchet or an adze in the cabin, where Nicholas Morellos and Big George were alleged to have been sleeping on the night they were killed. He had carefully examined the berth of the prisoner, and alleged, inter alia, that the British had attacked the Greeks as they slept. This evidence, therefore, would tend to discredit the testimony of the British. The problem was that Mr Clibbett had left for Bristol, and despite the numerous telegrams sent him, the fact remained that he could not catch the Holyhead-boat, and, therefore, could not make it back to Cork until Tuesday evening.

His Lordship - I have all the notes of his evidence before me.

Mr Heron respectfully submitted that they could not be read at this trial.

Sir Colman O' Loghlen, on behalf of the Crown said that he would be the last person to make any objection if he thought the evidence material. He certainly thought that the evidence was 'not immaterial' and if they wished they could produce the Sub Inspector instead of Clibbett, and he could just as easily prove the cuts.

His Lordship decided to proceed with the trial and the prisoner was given in charge to a new jury. The jury was duly sworn and the trial began.

The same witnesses were examined as on the first trial and they more or less repeated the same evidence they had previously given.

The Jury

The jury retired , and after an absence of an hour they returned. At about a quarter to six they handed down the issue paper, and answered respectively to their names.

Mr Donovan, the Clerk of the Peace, told the prisoner to stand up. He then addressed the jury. He said: "Gentlemen of the jury, have you agreed to your verdict?"

> Foreman - We have
> Mr Donovan - And you each and all say that Christos Emmanuel Bombos is guilty of the charges laid in the indictment?
> Foreman – We do.

The Trials Of Bombos

His Lordship – Ask him if he has anything to say why sentence of death should not be passed upon him.

Mr Donovan, through the interpreter, Mr Cartwright, then said –

"Christos Emmanuel Bombos, you have been indicted for murder, and upon that indictment have been tried and found guilty, and you have put yourself upon our God and our country, and that country has found you guilty. Have you anything to say why sentence of death and execution should not be passed upon you?"

The prisoner had the question translated, and then replied in Greek, which was also translated –

"Yes, I have. Before my God and my country I declare that I am innocent of the crime imputed to me. At the time that I held one of the mates against the rail, I did it from fear and compulsion of "George", who threatened my life with a knife. I deny that I committed crime on the vessel. On the contrary I did my best to save the English crew, the cargo, and the ship. That is all I have to say, and I declare that before my God, my Saviour and Redeemer. I did not strike any one with my knife at all."

His lordship then addressed the prisoner, and said –

"You have been convicted of the murder upon the clearest evidence. You cannot understand any observations I may address to you, and, therefore, merely say that every one who heard the case must have been convinced that you committed murder upon this occasion. It only remains for me now to pronounce this sentence of the law upon you. His lordship here assumed the black cap, and pronounced sentence of death in the usual manner, the execution to take place on the 25th of August."

The prisoner, who appeared quite unmoved, was then removed, and afterwards talked very freely with Mr Yourdi, the Consul, who throughout the proceedings watched with great interest and attention.

======

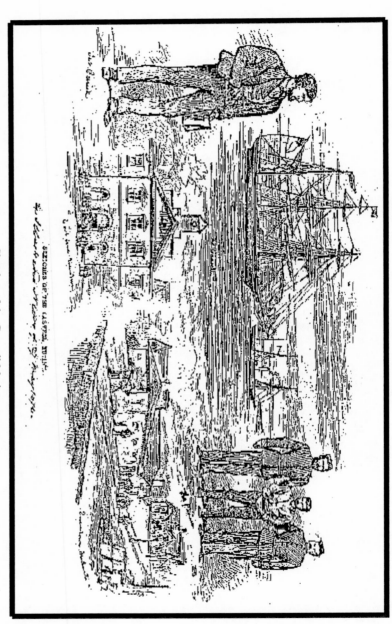

Queenstown Harbour

Sketches of the Caswell Mutiny

The Illustrated News of 27 August 1876

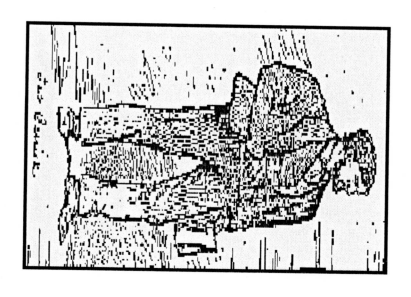

James Carrick

Christos E. Bombos

August 8th 1879
Church Lane
Horncastle
Lincolnshire

Governor
of Stell Prison
Cork
ireland

Sir

Pleas this is to inform you that i received
your Kind Letter conserning a Prisoner now
now under the Sentence of Death at Stell Prison
Cork ireland - i Sent you a Telegraph Message
Stating that i Would Send you a Letter this Day
to arainge for the Time

Sir - Pleas this is to inform
you that Monday and Tuesday the 25th and 26th Days
of this Month August is ingaged in England if
you will be so Kind as to arainge Yor Time
i will Come over to Cork and Execute the
Prisoner Sir - i hope it will not make any
Diferance to you in Regard to the Time Pleas i
Should be very glad if you would be so Kind as
to arainge to apoint Friday the 22 or 29 Day
of August for the Time for the Execution to take
Place at Cork - Pleas if you will arainge for
the Time you may Depend on me to Attend at the
Time apointed and i will Bring all things that
is Wanted for the Execution Rope and things and
Cap

Please let me have your Reply as i shall
leave Home on Tuesday next from Exeter
the 12 Day of August i shall be very glad to have
from you in the Matter in Question

& i Remain your Humble Servant
Wm Marwood
Church Lane
Horncastle
Lincolnshire
England

To The Governor
of H. M. Prison
Cork
Ireland

William Marwood

The Rt. Hon. Charles R. Barry

August 20 1879

To The Governor
of HM Prison
Cork
ireland

Dear Sir
Pleas i feel very Sorrey that i
ham not able to atend at Cork on Monday
to Execute the Prisoner as i ham ingaged
to Execute tow Prisoners in London on th
Day and Tusday to Execute a Prisoner at
Warewick then i will Com Direct to
Cork ireland Pleas to Let the Sheriff now
that he as the Power to arainge the Time
for my coming over thear will not any
Truble acor in araingin the Time i thank
the Sheriff for is kindness but cannot
Execute the Prisoner on Monday the 25 Day
but will on Friday the 29 Day Pleas let m
have a Letter by the Return of Post
Remain your Humble Servant
Wm Marwood
Church Lane
Horncastle
Lencalnshire

To The Governor
of HM Prison
Cork

Chapter 6

Letters And Petitions

No pardon for default - this must be done.
One iron rule at sea binds everyone.
Till now he had been treated with contempt
As neither man nor thing, a creature borne
On the ship's articles, but left exempt
From all the seamen's life except their scorn.
But he would rank as seaman off the Horn,
Work as a seaman, and be kept or cast
By standards set for men before the mast.

John Masefield / Dauber [1912]

Letters

After the trial of Bombos a new awareness of what had happened began
to emerge. Maybe it was just a feeling of widespread and inescapable
sadness at the realization of being committed to execute a fellow creature
-- albeit a killer -- in the most premeditated way imaginable. Then again,
it may have been that the public mind flinched at the notion of a 'double
hanging'; for hangings had an exponential quality about them, such that
their dramatic effect grew disproportionately with their number, as if the
effect of hanging a multiple of persons simultaneously had a much greater effect on the public mind than the sum of hanging their number individ-
ually.The whole, it appeared, was greater than the sum of its parts.

In that respect it was ironic that what the State intended to suppress by the
use of capital punishment -- namely, premeditated murder -- it most promoted by its own example: for what could be more premeditated than the
State's policy of capital punishment? Nothing could be more 'cold bloo-
ded', more public, more calculating and more reprehensible. The State
cannot claim a life-and-death engagement with the prisoner. Between the
State and the citizen there is no such relation. The State does not weep,

or laugh or feel. It has no personal moral sense. We saw this under the Vichy government during the second world war, when, on one occasion , the captive French State executed 50 of its citizens for one executed German soldier. We hear it again with the Americans in Afghanistan and Iraq, the implication being that "one of ours is more important than one of theirs." And by their silence, the Churches acquiesce.

Only humans can immolate themselves for their fellows; they alone can give themselves in selfless sacrifice, because they alone can do it voluntarily. The State could not conceive of such morality; in its punishments it merely imitates its alter ego, the individual. Indeed, what is the loss of a life more or less to any State? It is as nothing -- but the loss of a loved one has the power to destroy an individual, a family, a selection of friends, who, by definition mourne the deceased on the basis of a higher order that the State knows nothing of -- personal love!

Between the parties, the State and the citizen, then, there can be no excusing or exculpatory factors. When the State kills, it is perfectly wicked, and when it calls upon the world to see its wickedness, we should all attend only to protest at the reduction of the whole community to the basest conceivable level. What makes execution inhuman is the fact that between these parties there is no human intercourse, no preliminary taunts, no augmented stages of antagonism, no personal animosity, no anger, spite, sweat, fear, jealousy, preferment, no sense of touch, of taste, of love , of hatred; no heat of battle or struggle for power. Between the parties there is no fairness, no balance, no equity, no feeling...

Thus when the State kills it does so with the greatest imaginable indifference. Its killings are cruel and, like all cruel actions, dumb and stupid. Since reason is rather personal in nature, when we think about it, we see that the State really kills for no reason at all. No living healthy creature ever or anywhere kills as cold-bloodedly as the State. It is to compliment the State to say that it kills as a soldier kills, even when done on the foreign soil of another's problems; it doesn't even have to know its quarry, or what its quarry looks like. It is *ab initio* a *contract* killing, of the type perpetrated by the modern mob, by terrorists, and by reprobates.

It was only after 1843, when Daniel McNaughton in a botched assassination-attempt shot and killed Prime Minister Peel's private secretary, that the notion of mental illness entered the equation. But mental illness aside, the State never cared who was left behind after a murderer was executed, or what affect it had on wives, children or the extended family. Its main purpose is to attack and intimidate society as

a whole: for its sole interest is society as a whole. If the individual was
to kill as the State kills, then he would be unquestionably deranged.

Further, in the 1870s it could not be claimed that the public was not
used to hangings or that the frequency of hanging did not change.
Within ever decreasing margins, the public was quite used both to the
fact of hanging and to its public spectacle. In this its frequency tended
to diminish as the public's sensibilities became more refined. This diminution was pronounced in England and Wales, but was retarded by fearful factors in Ireland. While there was a great and constant tendency
toward diminution over the century, the immediate effect between the
1860s and the 1880s was one of vacillation upwards, as the following
rule-of-thumb figures will demonstrate.

Roughly speaking executions in Ireland ran at an annual rate of 1.5
throughout the 1870s. This compared favourably with a rate of two
annual executions in the sixties, but was eclipsed in the eighties when
the annual average actually increased to three. For youth and age there
was no escaping the inevitability of the local execution. Moreover,
while averages convey but a general impression, a contour; they could
never call up the same outrage which particular events evoked. The
memory of hangings and their received wisdoms in the folk memory is
hardly comparable to the personal experience of a hanging.

In 1870, for example, a woman, Margaret Sheil, was hanged. She was
the first in years and the last of the century. And if the decade seemed
mild on executions, 1876, was unusually harsh in that it saw four
executions as against the annual average of 1.5 for the decade. In
particular there was the case of John Daly, who was hanged in Antrim
by Baron Fitzgerald. That was in April, just four months before Bombos was sentenced to be hanged. Additionally, just days before Bombos' execution there was the widely reported case of Stephen McKeown
who was hanged for feuding in Armagh. That was on August 21st. As
part of the feud McKeown killed Mary McShane by fracturing her
skull 'with some rough cutting instrument, probably a stone'.

Hanging in the 1870s, therefore, if not regarded as an ordinary part of
everyday life, was nevertheless quite familiar to the nineteenth century
citizen. Maybe sadness and remorse were present either before or after
a hanging -- or perhaps both were inscribed before and after an execution in the day-to-day rhythms of life in the 1870s. Whatever the reason,
in Bombos' case the public appetite for hanging was dulled. The brutality of captain 'Bully' Best had been subdued in the evidence of the Brit-

ish, who quite understandably did not want to appear to harbour a hatred for their dead captain. In their evidence they admitted that the captain personally assaulted them and put them in irons. But, regardless of such admissions, the slow process of saying 'yes' and saying 'no' to the questions put, did not constitute "the truth, the whole truth and nothing but the truth." Far from it! In the exchanges between the witnesses and opposing counsel nothing of the fear of either Peno or captain Best could be exhibited between the lines of the responses. This was only to be expected when one considers that the witnesses were somewhat constrained to protect the memory of their dead captain. And the audience in the courtroom -- including the Judge, the Jury and the Gallery -- did not especially want to hear otherwise.

Was there anyone who could make up for this deficit? Was there an independent voice anywhere to be had? Even one of the crew who left Glasgow?

The only crewmembers who sailed out of Glasgow, and who were still alive on board, were MacGregor and the apprentice-teenager from Skye, Charles McDonald. As senior man MacGregor vouched for the good behaviour of his dead captain; but then again, he was caught up in the business of prosecuting the mutineers, and in that sense was not impartial or independent. Was there anyone else?

As it happened Edward Warner had served under captain Best some eleven years earlier. Moved by the accounts published of Bombos' impending trial, he wrote to an MP concerned with the trial, a Mr Sheridan, to whom he gave a courageous and independent account of his experiences while serving under captain George Best. In a word he accused the dead captain of having turned the *William Leckie* into a "floating hell." The full text of the letter is given below, but suffice it at this juncture to point out that, however persuasive the contents of the letter appeared, it did not constitute 'evidence', and -- arguably-- if it did, it would not have changed the minds of the Jurors. Nor would it for that matter have influenced them sufficiently to acquit Bombos. What, of course, it could have done -- and might have done had it not been for the dogmatism of the Judge of Trial -- was to reduce the finding of murder to one of manslaughter.

There was much sympathy for the convicted Greek. He had appeared most reasonable, and even if the evidence against him was compelling, it was widely felt that he had been caught up in a compromising situation, which was not of his own making. He was caught between a proverbial rock and a hard place, between the Scylla of Big George Peno and the Charybdis of captain George Best. On the *Caswell* there was no hidting place from either George Best or George Peno – a mitigating circumstance that could not be conveyed to either Judge or jury.

Having said that, of course, we must admit that in 1876 people were not, as we have already noted, unsympathetic to the harsh conditions under which ordinary seaman lived, particularly seamen on British vessels. Moreover, in Ireland (or in the Americas a hundred years earlier, or contemporaneously, if one was an Indian) one hardly needed to be reminded of the preconditions and incidents of oppressive government, whether that government was on land or sea. From this it appeared that sympathy for Bombos was an extension of sympathies earmarked for other offenders, notably agrarian ones. And from the manner in which Irish rebels were treated, the Victorian public knew full well that once they were convicted, all hope could be abandoned. Counsel for Bombos, Mr Peter O' Brien, could not have made it plainer than when he reflected on his own role. To the jury, he said:

> "Counsel was often relieved of much of this responsibility in a case of murder where even though the jury returned a verdict of guilty the Crown interposed, and, exercising its prerogative of mercy, commuted the sentence to penal servitude for life: but in this case if they recorded a verdict of guilty there was no hope of commutation. As sure as night followed day, and day followed night, the prerogative of mercy would not be interposed between the prisoner and the gallows, and death and burial in the precincts of the Gaol would be the prisoner's inevitable doom. " (The *Cork Constitution*, July 29, 1876)

Furthermore, Bombos' trial was widely reported in the *Cork Constitution*, the *Cork Examiner*, the *Times* and other interested and reliable newspapers, national and provincial. The predominant feeling -- and not just in the local papers -- was one of sympathy.

The *Times*, which followed the mutinies on the *Lennie* and the *Caswell*, suggested that the first lesson to be learned was that ship-owners (rather than sea-captains) should recruit better seamen, even if they had to pay them better salaries.

As for the captain of the *Caswell*, the *Times* didn't know whether to laugh or cry. "Poor Captain Best seems to have had his own opinion of his new sailors", stated the *Times*. "He would not venture to go among them without his revolver, although perhaps he was not very wise in telling them so". These sympathies echoed Corkonian sentiments as much as they were echoed in Wales. (See *The Cambrian*, May 19, 1876) and elsewhere, but these, unhappily, were not action-orientated . The trial also gave rise to an assortment of opinions, some of the most interesting of which delineated unusual aspects of the case, and all of which argued for mercy.

'Humanitas', for example, a very informed nom-de-plume, wrote to the editor of the *Cork Examiner* and referred 'to the case of this unfortunate man, who now awaits his doom...' 'Humanitas' was upset because the Chief Secretary had called attention to the fact that there had been no Petition to date signed on Bombos' behalf. More than anything else this exchange reflected both the widespread feeling that the sentence was unfair and, at the same time, the public's paralysis and inability to alter it.

"I am sure there are many impartial persons who will agree with me that there are sufficient grounds for having a memorial forwarded for a commutation of the sentence of death in this case. Seldom there are such extenuating circumstances present to warrant the hands of the executioner being stayed.

I was pleased to learn that it was brought under the notice of the House of Commons, when, in reply to Mr. H. B. Sheridan, the Chief Secretary for Ireland, stated that no memorial has been presented on the convict's behalf. Certainly, this might be construed as against him, but is it not owing to the apathy of his friends or from the fact of his being a foreigner and a Greek?

Perhaps he has got no friends in this country, in which a strong feeling exists against the class of criminals I write about, and particularly so at present against the nationality to which the condemned man belongs. His friends, if any he has, may consider it would be hoping against hope that exertion on their part could affect anything.

The Chief Secretary also stated he believed one jury refused to find him guilty of murder because a single juryman, being adverse to capital punishment, stood out for a verdict of manslaughter.

Now, I have ascertained that for a considerable time eight of the jury was for manslaughter. And after much consideration, all were brought over to consider it murder except one, and he stood out for manslaughter, not as alleged - because he was adverse to capital punishment - but, as I learned from him, he considered the evidence disclosed only the lesser crime of manslaughter.

As one of those who was liable to be on this jury and had to attend court each day, I had an opportunity of hearing the evidence for and against, as well as others, from which it can be easily deduced and equally well sustained, as so ably put by counsel for the defense. That the irascible temper and most irritating conduct of that tyrant of a captain, was the sole cause of that sudden outburst of passion, which terminated as it did.

At the preliminary enquiry before the Local Bench at Queenstown, did it not transpire that shortly after when the Greeks were brought on board at Buenos Aires, the captain went on deck unusually well armed with revolvers, and when one of the crew asked him why he came so armed among them he replied, sharp enough, ' why not; is it not foolish to come amongst a pack of Greeks unarmed; and, if necessary, I will use them too.'

Was there nothing in this language to provoke a breach of the peace? As an Irishman, if such were said to anyone of us by one of a different nationality, there would be every excuse for any serious consequences, which may ensue. There, again, were exhibited further signs of the uncontrollable temper of this man, as deposed to by witnesses for the Crown.

When some of the English crew wanted to go ashore to see the English Consul at Buenos Aires, they were forthwith put in irons. If they were less than eager to protect their captain when he was being assailed, there was some excuse. They may have been petrified by "Big George." By the same token maybe the "Greeks" were equally petrified. And how could Bombos, acting, under compulsion, do otherwise than obey through fear of being stabbed. Even the English crew did not render the assistance they might have. It is remarkable that Baumbos had no revolver on this occasion, though he usually carried one, merely a knife that was necessary for his work, proving he premeditated nothing. Under all the circumstances it is to be hoped his relatives will lose no time in presenting a prayer for a commutation of his sentence, and trusting it will receive the needful consideration it deserves at the hands of the Executive.

I am, Mr. Editor, yours,

HUMANITAS.

P.S - It is almost needless for me to add, I am no acquaintance of him about whom I penned these few words. I give my name and address not for publication.

***

Another letter entitled *The Condemned Christos Baumbos*, recounted how an appeal had come into the possession of Mr. H.B. Sheridan MP. Its import demonstrated in what regard -- or lack of it -- the memory of captain George Best was held:

103

Letters And Petitions

"I put a question in the House to the Chief Secretary for Ireland to the effect that, considering that the companions of the Greek had been all killed, and that there was no evidence possible for the defence, and considering that one jury had refused to find the man guilty, etc. whether there was to be any alteration of sentence recommended. The reply gave no hope of an alteration of sentence. But, whether the man is executed or not, I think the enclosed letter, which is genuine and impartial is worth placing before your readers, particularly if it draws the attention of owners of ships to the importance of selecting considerate and humane captains for the position they are to occupy, remembering that while our laws recognize no provocation as sufficient to justify mutiny, human forbearance has some limits.

The following are the contents of the letter to which Mr. Sheridan referred.

64, Hurst-street, Birmingham,
August 15, 1876

Mr. Sheridan, - Sir,

Seeing through the papers that you have taken the case of Christos Baumbos in hand, I take the liberty of writing these few lines; and, if any good can come to the poor fellow, you are at liberty to make what use of them as you think proper. The truth of them I can swear to.

In the beginning of the year 1864 I sailed from Sunderland in the bark 'William Leckie', for Calders, South America. Captain George Edward Best was the captain and I was an apprentice on board. There was a mixed crew of 17 hands, only four or five being English. The steward, a young Scotshman, had never been on board a ship before, and of course, did not know his duty; he was most inhumanly and brutally treated by the above captain and the mate who was as bad.

On one occasion, the steward not having breakfast ready in the cabin at the proper time, the mate went forward to the galley and pushed him out and struck him. The steward returned the blow. The mate then ran aft and called the captain, and told him the steward had struck him. The captain who was a big, powerful man, went to the steward, caught him by the neck, and, with the foretopsail clew-line – a rope as thick as a man's thumb - beat the poor fellow about the face till his face was all of a jelly, the flesh was cut through, and the blood ran down on to the deck. He was then, although half dead and suffering from the terrible punishment he had undergone, kept on deck the whole of the day.

Another time one of the water-casks had been broached, the steward was sent for into the cabin, and was accused by the captain of doing it. He denied it. The captain then ordered me to bring the irons, and made him get down into the store-room, where he put the irons on him –

hands and feet – and lashed him up to a beam, and here let him swing for about 20 minutes.

On another occasion the mate struck him on the head with a broom-handle and broke it in two; and every day there was always quarreling going on between the officers and men. It was a common thing for the captain to go up to the men, shake a loaded revolver in their faces, and yell at them if it was not for the laws of this country, he would put a hole through them.

Five of us ran away in Calders, but had to return to the port, having lost our way, and nearly our lives, on a sandy desert. We were caught and put in Gaol. Three wanted their discharges, for they were terrified at the thought of going home in the William Leckie, or the 'floating hell' as they called her.

The English consul refused to let them leave, and the captain said he would take them if he took them limb-by-limb. Now, Sir, I expect the captain has been carrying on the same game on board the *Caswell*, and driven the men in desperation to commit the dreadful murders for which one has got to pay with his life. It seems as if he picked a mixed crew that he could marry on his game, knowing he would be safer than if they were all English, or of one country.

I have been about 14 years at sea, and have been in a good many vessels; but I never in all my time have seen such practices since. Hoping you will excuse me taking the liberty of addressing you, and hoping to do the poor fellow who now awaits his doom justice by letting it be known what sort of a man captain George Edward Best was.

I remain Sir, your obedient servant

Edward Warner

Here, then, for the first time was an independent account of what it was like to serve under captain George Best. Not unlike Dana's experiences aboard the Pilgrim, Best and his first mate created the same moral dilemma for the crew of the *Caswell*, as was created for the crew of the Pilgrim. The worst fears of thinking men were beginning to be realised. However one spelled it out, it meant the same thing: lawful authority had been put in the hands of a tyrant. However much Warner's account obtained aboard the *Caswell*, the witnesses called upon to prosecute Bombos could not testify to it, simply because in the trial there was no room for them to tell "the whole truth..." It was now the responsibility of lawful authority to judge of itself; for the tyranny on the *Caswell* sprung , arguably, from the same line of authority as that of the court. Maybe this explains the ambivalence shown to Bombos, not just in the muted testimony of more involved witnesses like Dunne and Carrick, but also in the opinions expressed in the Press generally.

Another correspondent, Edwin Freshfield, an authority on maritime affairs and one who was familiar with the case, wrote the following letter:

19th August 1876

SIR,

" I am intimately connected with the East and have myself lived some time there, and it is a matter of great astonishment to me how it comes to pass that while such a crime as mutiny is almost - I believe I may say, entirely - unknown on board Greek ships, it has happened so frequently here, particularly lately. I think it is to be attributed in a great measure to the manner in which Greek sailors employed on English ships are treated by the English Captains, which is essentially different to that which they are accustomed to on board their own ships.

There still remains among the Greeks the old idea of the sailors partic-ipating in the adventure, and a Greek ship is conducted more upon the principles of a Republic than an English ship, where the old notion has long since exploded. The Greek sailors in consequence talk to each other and treat each other quite differently to the manner in which an English captain breaks his crew. And so the Greek Sailors who find themselves on board an English ship occasionally receive a very different, and it seems clear that they found this difference very marked in the case of *the Caswell.*

I would refer to an extract from the *Times* newspaper, which I enclose as bearing on the subject:

"In the particular case there were on board the *Caswell* several Greek sailors, two Maltese and some English – when the mutiny took place the foreign Sailors got the best of it, murdered the captain and Officers, and took charge of the vessel themselves. The two Maltese left the vessel and escaped, and are now being sought after by the English Government.

Subsequently the English turned upon the Greeks and killed them all with the exception of the particular man Christos Baumbos and severely woun-ded him, and brought him into Queenstown.

There is no doubt that the prisoner took part in the mutiny, but he states, and there is some internal evidence to show that his statement is correct, that it was done under the threat of one of the leaders of the mutiny whose name was George Pinos or Bulgario. The prisoner himself had always stated this and he stated it at the trial, and he stated that anything he did then he did under fear for his life. The English admitted that during the time that the mutineers were in possession of the ship, the prisoner Baumbos had always treated them kindly, and it should be remembered that he himself was severely punished by the wound that was inflicted upon him."

Upon this point also I beg to enclose letter from the Greek Consul at Corinth addressed to the Consul General here. There is no doubt that the English Sailors, in killing Pinos, killed one of the ringleaders. The Maltese had escaped. I have already referred to the fact that the English government is seeking the Maltese sailors, and it must be assumed that sooner or later, as they are English subjects, they will get them. I would therefore venture to submit that it would not be proper that Christos Baumbos should be executed until they have been apprehended and the result of their trial is known, and for this reason, at present the only parties before the court are the English sailors and Baumbos. Baumbos has stated that he acted under compulsion – and his treatment of the English Sailors shows that he was not actuated by any feeling against them, and it may well be that the Maltese who were also ringleaders, and who, by their leaving the ship seem to have been perfectly aware of the effect of the crime they had committed, may on apprehension, confess that they themselves had been the ringleaders, and that this man had acted upon compulsion.

The information that I have upon the subject is mainly derived from Mr. Joseph Cartwright who acted as Interpreter at the trial. He lives in London, and would - I am sure - be willing to give you any further information upon the subject. He is well acquainted with the Greek language, as his father held the post of Collector of Customs under the government of the Ionian Islands, and he was born there. I do not for a moment say that Christos Baumbos' execution will not be strictly legal and unimpeachable, but I venture to say that he was not a ringleader, that one of the ringleaders has been killed and that two others are being sought by the government and that the government might without any public detriment commute the sentence of this man to imprisonment for life. It is not as if this was a light sentence, and it would ensure a witness when the Maltese are tried.

Edwin Freshfield

***

Letters And Petitions

Petitions

A petition in Greek , dignified by its simplicity, and signed by Bombos' parents was translated and forwarded to the Lord Lieutenant. It affirmed modestly :

> That upon the first trial of the Greek convict Christos Emmanuel Bombos now under sentence of death, the Jury was unable to agree upon a verdict.

> That upon the second trial of said Christos Emmanuel Bombos the evidence went to show that he was rather an accessory than a principal, and acted rather under compulsion than voluntarily.

> That the undersigned Consul for his Hellenic Majesty at Queenstown declares his belief that if time had permitted, additional evidence might have been adduced which would have tended to mitigate his punishment: that the convicts' inability to understand the English language and his utter friendlessness placed him at a terrible disadvantage while on his trial

> That his conduct while imprisoned has made a favourable impression on the undersigned Chaplain, on the very Rev. Dean Daunt, on the Rev. John Connolly as well as on the Prison Officials.

> That for these reasons, the case appears to the undersigned a suitable one for exercising the clemency of the Crown

At least 28 people added their signatures to this memorial.

A further letter on Bombos' behalf, hopeful in its tone if difficult in its construction, was signed by Mr. Yourdi and was received by the Under Secretary to the Lord Lieutenant on the 19th August.

> "I heard yesterday from our police that the English Government in London is making enquiries respecting the addresses of the witnesses of the *Caswell*. Possibly to institute an enquiry previous to the carrying out of the sentence of Bombos on the 25th inst.. The protestant priest I.G. Connolly, who from the commencement has shown sympathy with the prisoner whilst visiting him, has asked him to give a statement of the *Caswell* affair, which he has done -- and I have translated it into English, and delivered it to him.

> In his statement, it is said, that when the Maltese sailors took a boat to go to Monte Video, Bombos also wished to go; he intended to inform ... the English Consul of the tragic event, but Big George did not permit him. Then the knowledge of the English sailor James Carrick, with whom he was on friendly terms, wrote a letter addressed to his cousin in

Monte Video to be delivered to him at the Coffee house which Bomb-os' cousin frequented. In that letter he wrote to inform immediately the English Consul – to send a man-of -war to arrest George and Nicolas and to liberate the ship, and that the Maltese will land and to arrest them. Bombos declares that this letter was presented to him by James Carrick when the ship arrived at Queenstown. At that time Carrick also told Bombos - 'the Maltese are arrested'.

This circumstance came to my knowledge only lately. I have made enquiries respecting this letter at the Police, but they refused to give me any explanations. They only told me that they had found in the Post Office a letter addressed (to) Giuseppe Gaspari from his family, which they sent to the Government in London to give a clue to the address of the Maltese.

Bombos insists that he had seen the letter, he recognized it as his letter. He says let them produce it and they will then see what I wrote in it.

This letter is a proof of sentiments, facts, and ideas for what happened on that day.

Should you think that this circumstance can bear upon the sentence in favour of Bombos bring it forward."

I remain

Signed N.G Yourdi

It is hard to evaluate the evidential value of such a lost letter. Even if it had been found, it would not wipe out the statements already put into evidence by the surviving crewmembers. What is puzzling -- though not unimaginable -- is why Bombos should make such a claim, if no such letter existed. The Civil Servants annotated Yourdi's letter with the following reminder: "The Irish Government made enquiry about the addresses of these men (witnesses) so as to be able to tell them in the event of the Maltese Sailors being arrested..."

In a moving and circumlocutory Memorial stamped August 23 and which failed to reveal any address, some 70 women prayed for mercy for Bombos, the first to sign was a lady named Kathleen Myran. It read:

"That your memorialists having learned with a feeling of profound sorrow and regret that up to the present time the prayer of the different memorialists forwarded to your grace on behalf of the unfortunate Greek sailor Christos E. Bombos now under sentence of death has not been granted, beg leave to approach your grace and supplicate mercy for him.

That there are good grounds for doubt that the prisoner is morally responsible for the shedding of the blood of any of the unfortunate officers of the *Caswell* we should not be found interceding on his behalf.

That the opinion we entertain is shared almost universally by persons of all classes and creeds of the Country and great and grievous will be the disappointment experienced if this unfortunate foreigner should be executed.

That, feeling that as women, a duty devolves on us and on others in this dread crisis, we on the eve of the day fixed for the death of this unfortunate man, feel impelled before all time for hope has past in all earnestness and humility, to invoke your Grace's clemency in his regard and beseech of your mercy to spare his life and your memorialists will as in duty bound ever pray."

***

If Bombos waited patiently for a response from the Lord Lieutenant, he did not wait alone. Another man, Thomas Crowe, a 63-year-old Fenian also waited for a response to the petitions sent on his behalf. What was between these two condemned men somehow flared the imagination of the local press. In death, as in life's struggle, they were destined to be somehow intertwined. The forces that brought them together were extraordinary when viewed in the overall context of the British Empire.

Already the Judge's Report -- submitted in August -- had reached the Lord Lieutenant. The brunt of the Judge's message, sanitised by cliché, signified that in his opinion there weren't "any mitigating circumstances, which would render the prisoner a proper object of mercy." The dye was cast, the prisoners could only await their fate.

On Friday morning August 25, the following notification and account appeared on the *Cork Examiner:*

The Condemned Men in the County Gaol

The sentence of the law in the cases of the two men, Thomas Crowe and Christos Baumbos, will be carried out this morning in the County Gaol. In reference to the efforts made to procure a reprieve in the case of the Greek, Mr N. Murphy, the senior member for the city, yesterday morning received the following reply: -

110

"Dublin Castle, 23rd August, 1876

Sir, I am directed by the Lord Lieutenant to acknowledge the receipt of the memorial signed by you and other gentlemen on behalf of Christos Emmanuel Baumbos, now lying in the County Cork Gaol under sentence of death; and I am to state for your information and that of the other memorialists, that, after a full consideration of all the circumstances of the case, his Grace has felt it to be his painful duty to decide that the law must take its course.

I have the honour to be, Sir, your obedient servant

Henry Robinson

"The result of the efforts on his behalf were conveyed to the unfortunate criminal yesterday afternoon. He received the intelligence calmly, but still protested that he took no willful part in the massacre on board the *Caswell*. He has been most attentive to the ministration of the Greek priest who has been in constant attendance upon him. Crowe, in whose favour an appeal has also been made and rejected, is perfectly resigned to his fate. He has observed a strict silence as regards his crime, and has made no complaint of the dreadful sentence, which he has to undergo. Marwood, the Executioner, arrived in Cork on Wednesday morning and immediately proceeded to the County Gaol where he occupied the quarters provided for him."

======

Chapter 7

The Case of
Thomas Crowe

At Slievenamon I met a man
Who axt, "Is Scully dead?"
I cannot give you that account,
But I hear he's bad in bed.
He turned my mother out of doors,
But I may meet him still.
We're bold Tipperary mountaineers,
Says Rory of the Hill.

(Contemporary Ballad)

In 1868,William Scully, assisted by a sheriff's posse, tried to evict a
family at Ballycohey, Co. Tipperary. An assassination-attempt was made
on his life. The incident was widely believed to have begun the rent agit-
ations, which in turn led on to the formation of the Land League and the
passing of the Land Act of 1870. Scully's brother, Vincent, an MP for
County Cork up to 1865, attracted a universal hatred comparable to that
engendered by the infamous Lord Leitrim a decade later. The revolt against the increased rents initially extended to Mayo in '79, to Galway in
the '80s, and thereafter it became nationwide. Quite often these and similar revolts were characterised by the assassination or attempted assassination of the Landlord in question or his agent. They also led -- almost

112

The Case Of Thomas Crowe

invariably -- to the execution of the culprits. If hanging assassins was any index of social agitation, then Tipperary was the most consistently agitated county since the Tithe War of the 1830s.

It is with reference to this tradition of revolt that the case of Thomas Crowe is best understood. Most of the more immediate influences on him were unmistakably pro-rebellion. The Fenian Brotherhood (founded in New York in 1858 with some military expertise drawn from Union and Confederate armies alike) was not short on ambition: it even made two abortive attempts at invading British Canada. And the home rebellion in 1867 was also put down by the British occupattion. In the same year an attempt to rescue three Manchester Fenians -- Allen, Larkin and O'Brien -- resulted in the death of thirteen innocent civilians. In a second rescue attempt a police sergeant was shot dead, and the three Fenians were hanged for his murder. It was with this unrelenting resistance that old Thomas Crowe would have identified. In much the same vein the Home Rule Confederation of Great Britain was founded in Manchester in January 1873, and was augmented in November when the Home Rule League was founded in Dublin. The Fenian movement reconstituted itself and declared that war with England should await the endorsement of a majority of the 'Irish nation'. More importantly, however, Charles Kickham's popular *Knocknagow*, (or *The Homes of Tipperary*) was published in Dublin in 1873, while in 1875 John Mitchell, a fanatical rebel with the conviction of a John Brown, even on his death bed was elected and re-elected MP for Tipperary. Resistance ran through the warp and weft of Tipperary.

The case of Thomas Crowe if not uncomplicated is nevertheless lengthy and is, perhaps, best understood if recited in a systematic way. Towards this end it is convenient if his story is narrated with respect to the following six areas of concern:

1. The Murder
2. The Who's Who of Billarue
3. Weighing in at Court
4. Rewarding the Good and Punishing the Wicked
5. Threatening Letters
6. "Crime does not pay"

1. The Murder

At eleven o'clock on the morning of the 30th of March, Mr Patten Smight Bridge drove into Mitchelstown to collect rents. He remained there doing business until about a quarter to five in the evening. He then left Mitchelstown to return home to his residence at Galtee Castle, situated on the Tipperary side of the Cork/Tipperary border. Mr Bridge rarely travelled alone, and on this occasion four other persons accompanied him on his jaunting car. As he himself later testified:

"It was daylight. I sat at the left hand side of the car with constable Nugent. I was next the horse. John Hyland, a servant of mine, was driving the car. Patrick O'Loughlen, my bailiff, and Sub-constable Jones were at the other side of the car. When coming on to a part of the road two miles from Mitchelstown, where there is an incline on the road, a shot was fired. I was looking towards the fence at the left side then. Previous to the shot I saw no one, but after it the horse gave a few strides and inside that fence I saw the prisoner Crowe. I saw nothing in his hand. From that shot I got nine wounds. The horse stopped up and I said "Nugent, there's the man that shot at us." Nugent fired at him. He jumped over the fence and arrested the prisoner. I kept my eye on the prisoner till he was arrested; the moment the prisoner was arrested I turned around to see what was going on at the other side, and I saw Hyland lying over on the car. I got a second wound under the left eye. Hyland fell off the car.

I drove on as quickly as I could to the police barrack at Kilbenny, leaving the two constables after me. The next time I saw the prisoner was when he was brought into Kilbenny village. I was not speaking to him. I saw him the following day when I was in bed, and when he was brought before me in the presence of Mr Eaton, the magistrate. In his presence I swore that the prisoner to the best of my belief was the man who wounded me and killed Hyland. When my information was read over to the prisoner by Mr Eaton, the prisoner said, "I cannot contradict him." I had never known the prisoner before this occasion, and had nothing to do with him as far as I am aware. Neither had Hyland as far as I know."

Cross-examined by defence Counsel, Mr Blackall, Mr Bridge elaborat-
further:

" I never knew the prisoner before this. I suppose he knew me. I am land agent over a considerable property in the neighbourhood. The prisoner is not one of the tenants. The policemen Nugent and Jones have been living in an iron barrack in the yard attached to my house for four or five months, and they have, of course, been in constant communication with me. I had a loaded revolver in my right hand pocket this day, with six chambers loaded. I did not fire it, as my hand was badly smashed; the first shot struck me in the hand; there was a distance of seven or eight yards between the firing of the shot from the field and the shot fired by Nugent; I am sure there was no other man but the prisoner where the shot was fired. I didn't see any man in white flannel. I will undertake to swear that there was no other person in that part of the field, but the prisoner. If anyone swore it, I would not believe him."

The Case Of Thomas Crowe

Even though Mr Bridge saw no one else in the same field as Thomas Crowe, his constables testified that there were two others present, one wearing a white 'flannel' waistcoat and another who had his face blackened. Moreover, before the banditti fled, they discharged their firearms. These sightings had some bearing on Thomas Crowe's hitherto non-existing defence: for if no less than three persons shot at John Hyland, who could say that Thomas Crowe's shot was the fatal one? In the meantime the more pressing question concerning Thomas Crowe, a total stranger, remained unanswered. Why did he shoot and kill John Hyland? Practically everyone in the courtroom knew the answer, but it was Defence Counsel's job to make it explicit.

Mr Blackall - Do you know any reason why the prisoner should fire at the driver?
Mr Bridge - I don't

Mr Blackall - On your oath do you believe he fired at the driver?
Mr Bridge - I believe the shot he fired killed Hyland

Mr Blackall - That is not an answer
His Lordship - It is an answer.

Mr Blackall (to witness) - Don't you believe the shot was fired at you?
Mr Bridge - I do; I have no doubt about it.

Mr Blackall - And not at Hyland?
Mr Bridge - I won't say that; I never had any dispute with Crowe. I had no disputes with any other people in the neighbourhood except John Ryan.

Mr Blackall -. Do you swear you had no disputes with the tenantry?
Mr Bridge - I had a good many *Notices to Quit* served, because I am getting the rents revalued. I don't call these 'disputes'.

Mr Blackall - You had been fired at before?
Mr Bridge - Yes, by John Ryan

Mr Blackall - Where is John Ryan?
Mr Bridge - If you could tell, you would get £100.

The Case Of Thomas Crowe

***

2. The Who's Who of Billarue

For some time prior to these events Mr Bridge had been the land agent to Mr Nathaniel Buckley, a Lancashire cotton-spinner, who had only recently become the owner of part of an estate in Limerick, Tipperary and Cork. The Land Company of Ireland had formerly owned the estate. Then in 1873, under its new ownership, the estate underwent a revaluation, which signalled an increase in rents to be paid by the tenants. Altogether there were 527 tenants on the estate in question. The rent yield from the estate grossed £5,550, £180 of which accrued to the small holdings at Billarue on the Tipperary/Cork border. Of these tenants about 450 had their rents raised, and about 130 had *Notices to Quit* served on them. Roughly speaking, about 410 of the tenants settled: - "a good many at once and several since they had been served with *Notices to Quit*." Notwithstanding these settlements at least 60 tenants had failed or refused to settle. It should be said that *a Notice to Quit* served on a nineteenth century Irish peasant was tantamount to reducing him and his family to a Dickensian fatality, the only difference being that Dickens' poor begged until they died in central London, whereas the evicted Irish begged until they starved on the side of an Irish countryside. Those who didn't die were dealt with by the criminal justice system – which more often than not meant the Gallows prior to the 1830s and transportation to Australia and elsewhere afterwards.

One of these tenants, a man named John Ryan, who had held under an old lease at Billarue, Co. Cork, refused to accede to the new agreement, and was consequently pursued by way of ejectment proceedings. In January 1875, at Clonmel Sessions, a decree for possession of his farm was duly obtained. It became apparent that no settlement or compromise was possible or likely, and the Sheriff fixed March 23 for the execution of the decree.

On the evening before the execution of the decree, John Ryan tried to assassinate Mr Bridge. Mr Bridge at the time was strolling in the avenue of his home at Galtee Castle. The assassination attempt failed, but Bridge was wounded, and Ryan immediately fled the scene. Protected by neighbours and well-wishers, invariably at great risk to themselves and their families, Ryan evaded detection and arrest. Thereafter Bridge applied to the Grand Jury of the county of Limerick for compensation

116

The Case Of Thomas Crowe

under the Peace Preservation Act, and received the substantial award of £200.

A week later, on March 30, Thomas Crowe also made an attempt on Mr Bridge's life. The shooting of John Hyland, albeit with a careless disregard for Highland's life, was not intended. Several further questions attended upon this second attempted assassination. How many people were involved? How unpopular was Mr Patten Smight Bridge amongst the tenantry? Why did Thomas Crowe try to assassinate him? Was there any particular reason for choosing Mitchelstown as the venue for the assassination? And how much compensation was due on foot of the murder of John Hyland?

A satisfactory answer to these questions is nowhere to be found in the criminal trial alone. On the contrary, by skilful manipulation the criminal court was turned into a social prism, which only allowed certain, well-chosen and almost rehearsed chinks of light to penetrate the court chamber. It also prohibited certain other data from entering the punitive arena, the theory behind this occurrence being that the greater the likelihood of public punishment the greater the need for strict and constantly defined rules of evidence. This is not to say that an injustice was done to Thomas Crowe or that he was innocent of the charges laid against him. If, however, we want a fuller social picture, not just of people's status across the criminal divide, but of the amelioration made by the State to those offended, then we must also look at the type of evidence given to the Grand Jury when an application for compensation was made by Mr Smight Bridge. In other words, by looking at the court and the compensation tribunal together we get a a more complete account of how the felt needs of justice were met.

What would maximise Mr Patten Smight Bridge's interest was, on the one hand, to prove or have proved the murder charge in the criminal case, and, on the other hand, to prove or have proved that it was an 'Agrarian Outrage' for which he and others were entitled to lawful compensation under the Peace Preservation Acts. Generally speaking ideal proof in the murder case is best served if events are kept very simple, that is, by proving that there was only one man, one shot, one dead body, and plenty of witnesses who saw it etc. Such items gave rise to little scrutiny and are most difficult to contest. It was also preferable that as little as possible of the Landlord and Tenant relationship or the history thereof should be introduced into the murder trial, lest the jury sympathise unduly with the defendant. On the other hand the ideal case for claimants for compensation was otherwise framed.

The Case Of Thomas Crowe

Here it was more significant to magnify the outrage, to demonstrate a conspiracy of others, and to show that they recklessly damaged persons and property. Such a case fared much better if it could be proved that every peasant in Ireland had a hand in it or, alternatively, that they sympathised with the wrongdoer, and even aided and abetted him.

Both cases were dealt with expeditiously. The trial and sentence of Thomas Crowe at Cork County Court took place on Tuesday 25th July 1876, and the compensation claim was heard before the Grand Jury the following day. Both these cases are dealt with separately.

***

3. Weighing in at Court

At ten o' clock on Tuesday morning July 25th, two days before the *Caswell* hearing, the right Honourable Mr Justice Lawson took his seat at the Cork City Crown Court and resumed the hearing of criminal business. Next on his list was *The Mitchelstown Murder*. 'Thomas Crowe was put forward and indicted for having on the 30th March past, at Garryleigh, in the county of Cork, feloniously killed and murdered one John Hyland. It was apparent from the outset how serious the Crown was treating the case. Two items indicated the Crown's determination to secure a conviction: the first was 'the line out' for the Crown, the second was the number of objections made in selecting a jury.

As in Bombos' case the lineout was impressive in favour of the "avoirdupois principle'. Sergeant Sir Colman O'Loghlen, MP, Messrs Murphy, Q.C., Exham, Q.C.; Green Q.C. and J. O'Hea, instructed by Mr Sylvester Gillman, appeared on the part of the Crown. Gillman, incidentally, was the "Castle solicitor' who instructed prosecuting counsel in Bombos' case and appeared at Queenstown back in May.

Messrs N.G.Blackall, and G. Lawrence, instructed by Mr .J T O'Connell, appeared for the defence. O'Connell, it will be noted, was the solicitor who defended Bombos at the Queenstown Petty Sessions.

The long panel of possible jurors was called over and one hundred and forty persons answered to their names. No less than 55 objections were made on behalf of the Crown and a further 20 on behalf of the prisoner. That is, over half the long panel was objected to. By twenty first-

The Case Of Thomas Crowe

century standards this is an enormous number and, given the increased annual number of murder trials, an unmanageable one as well. Prosececution counsel led off with the claim that the case was "the clearest one that was ever submitted to a court of justice." By this he meant Thomas Crowe was obviously guilty of the murder. Counsel for the defence later countered:

> "...If that were so, what was the necessity of such an array of court counsel ...They had here an array of the greatest ability the bar could produce in order to demonstrate that the man was guilty. ... As many as fifty five of their fellow jurors of the county of Cork had been compelled by the crown to abstain from taking a part in this case. "

Because the Defence knew that evidence would be given of three persons being seen at the scene of the murder, they built their defence on the uncertainty as to who fired the fatal shot. And since two of those persons escaped the constabulary, Mr Blackall applied for a postponement of the trial. The prisoner swore the affidavit grounding the application, deposing, inter alia, that he was entirely unprepared to stand his trial at the present assize because two of his " most material and necessary witnesses" were absent.

These witnesses, he stated, could give such evidence as would establish his innocence. Moreover, because he had been in custody since his arrest, he had been unable personally to contact them. Because of these circumstances, he had instructed his solicitor to get his friends to search for the witnesses. Despite the fact that they had made exertions on his behalf, up to the present time, that is, they were unable to find the witnesses to subpoena them. Further, he believed that if his trial was now postponed, he would not be able to produce these witnesses at the next assizes.

This application seemed perfectly reasonable. Blackall confirmed that the prisoner had been in custody ever since he was arrested, and, as he would continue to remain in custody-- so that there could be "no injury to justice"-- his defence would be impaired if the trial went ahead.

His Lordship - I suppose the Crown opposes this application?
Sergeant Colman O'Loghlen - I oppose it my lord.

His Lordship - Of course, it is the most untenable application I ever heard
        ...without naming witnesses or saying who they are.
Mr Blackall - The prisoner can't name them. That's his difficulty.
His Lordship - Go on with the case.

The Case Of Thomas Crowe

After his Lordship put his peremptory boot down, the case proceeded. In his opening statement to the jury Counsel for the Crown referred to the unusualness of the murder:

> " This murder was committed in the open day, it was committed by a person without any disguise, and it was committed in the presence of police, who were actually on the spot when the murder was committed."

Equally unusual was the refusal of the defence to appear to defend himself. When Thomas Crowe said, " I don't want to ask Mr Bridge any question. I hear what he says and I cannot contradict him", the "I-cannot-contradict-him" part interested the prosecutors. Much was made of the fact that by these words he was implicitly admitting that it was he who fired the fatal shot at Hyland. And while motive need never be proved in a murder trial, throughout the trial it provoked the question 'why' -- why had he shot and killed a man whose acquaintance he had never known?

According to Dr Edward M'Craith, a post mortem examination showed that a pellet had passed through Hyland's heart, lodged in his backbone, and had to be sawed out. Dr O Neill, who observed that the shot killed him almost instantaneously, confirmed these findings

On this evidence, coupled with a map prepared by the County surveyor, Smight Bridge's account, together with that of his two constables, was ample to prove the case.

And even if Mr Bridge saw no one but Thomas Crowe, the question was manipulable as between the trial and the compensation claim. In any event constables Mathew Nugent and Sub constable William Jones gave evidence of the murder, some of which was not without its Gilbertian aspects. Constable Mathew Nugent, for example, deposed that when Thomas Crowe shot from the left,

> "Mr Bridge said, "Oh, there's a shot", and added, "Sergeant there's the man who fired the shot." I looked and saw a great deal of smoke, and got a glimpse of a man behind the bush; I fired into the bush believing the man was taking shelter there; I saw the man's head over the ditch near the bush, and I immediately jumped off the car, went back over the ditch where the man was. I saw him stooping down hiding behind the ditch. When he saw me he stood up straight. That man is the prisoner. He had then a loaded pistol - and capped in his hand. At his feet this blunderbuss (produced) was on the ground. It was not loaded. The next thing I did was

The Case Of Thomas Crowe

I said to the prisoner, "ho, ho, come, I said, I call upon you in the Queen's name to surrender." The prisoner said, "I do surrender." He had the pistol in his hand. I said: "Lay down your arms." He threw down the pistol. I then went up and handcuffed him. After that I examined the pistol. I found it full cocked and took the cap off. I then examined the blunderbuss and found an exploded cap on the nipple, which was blue from being recently discharged. The pistol was loaded; there were six pellets in it. While I was in the act of handcuffing the prisoner there were several shots fired from the opposite side of the road at Mr Bridge. I likewise saw Mr Bridge bleeding in the face.

After securing the prisoner I said 'Oh, you wretch with one foot in the grave and the other out of it -- to be guilty of such an act!" He made no reply but shook his head; I told the prisoner to remain there for a while. I went out on the road to see what had occurred. The car was gone. I saw Hyland's body lying on the road. I went back to where I left the prisoner and found that he was running away. I closed on him and called on him to stand. He had not the handcuffs on and I asked where they were. He said he did not know. I arrested him again and put Sub constable Jones' handcuffs on him. I cautioned the prisoner then, telling him that he was charged with murder. He said he would say nothing. When I arrested prisoner I saw no one in the field. I afterwards found the handcuffs in the same field."

When cross-examined, he said: -

" I have been stationed at Galtee Castle from the 19th October '75 to the 30th March '76 as guard to Mr Bridge. I came here from the depot, and had no previous knowledge of the place. I won't swear positively that I never saw the prisoner before, but I think I saw him in Mitchelstown. It was while I was taking the pistol from the prisoner and examining the blunder-buss that I heard the shot from the other side. I did not mention in my infor-mation as to the prisoner having one foot in the grave, because I didn't think it necessary to mention it.

His Lordship - I suppose, as a remark made by yourself to the prisoner you didn't think it necessary to mention it?

Witness – Yes"

In his testimony sub constable William Jones said:

"I was stationed in March last in the iron barrack, Galtee Castle. I had been in Mitchelstown with Mr Bridge on the 30th March, and we returned from there in the evening. I sat on the right hand side of the car, sitting beside O'Loghlen, who was nearest the horse. When we reached Garryleigh I heard a shot from the left hand side of the road and I looked up and saw the prisoner in the act of dropping a blunderbuss. I had never seen him before. Constable Nugent returned the fire and jumped off the

The Case Of Thomas Crowe

car. He went on a bit and John Hyland fell back in the car, dead. He was dead before the second shot was fired. I got off the car to go in the direction where the first shot was fired, when I heard a rustling in the hedge at right hand side, and I saw a gun projecting. Seeing the gun, I got ready my rifle and fired in the direction, and immediately afterwards a shot came from the hedge and shot Mr Bridge near the eye. A shot also came from the same side of the road from the Mitchelstown direction. Mr Bridge was putting up his hand and he was shot in the hand. I tried to get in through the hedge, but it was too high, and ran to a gap thirty yards down where I got in. I saw a man near a hayrick behind O 'Brien's house with a gun or blunderbuss in each hand. I fired and he stumbled and dropped the gun. He picked them up and got away at this time.

I saw a man in the corner of O'Brien's haggard with a blackened face. He fired two shots at me, but missed me. He escaped through the gap in the corner of the haggard. I did not follow them, but returned towards the right hand side of the road. I saw the prisoner running away and the constable in pursuit of him. I joined in the pursuit, and we captured and handcuffed him."

Q. - Were you frightened that evening of the attack?
A. - Not the least was I frightened.
Q. - You saw at the right side of the road a man with a blunderbuss?
A - Yes.
Q. - And you saw the muzzle of a gun pointing through the hedge at the other side? - Not at me - at Mr Bridge. The man with his face blackened fired at me after I went into the field. The other man did not fire at me when I went into the field. Both of these men were active men. I saw the prisoner running away from Constable Nugent.

Questions dealing with why the murder took place, what precisely provoked or inspired it, never featured beyond the fact of the crime. Indeed, lest the jury sympathise unduly with the cause of the prisoner, such considerations were deliberately played down. In his summation counsel for the Crown said to the jury:

"On all this evidence the jury can only come to a verdict establishing the prisoner's guilt. What could be the origin of that transaction? What brought the three men there on that occasion in ambush? To shoot some person in the car, they knew not and they cared not. It was not their (the court's) business to enquire into the origin of the affair at all, for the jury, counsel and his lordship were there as ministers of justice. An outrage of a most unexampled character had been committed in their county, a man against whom there was not malice or ill will, a man who was only doing his duty as a servant driving a car, was foully murdered in the month of March last and the Crown had simply brought this case to vindicate the law and convict the murderer as he stood in the dock."

***

The Case Of Thomas Crowe

4. Rewarding the Good and Punishing the Wicked

The differences between a criminal and a civil matter are not easy to
unearth. Indisputably they originated in some black forest or other of
the common law. When we look at them closely we find them bewild-
eringly apposite (rather than opposite), the one being punitive in nature and the other being restorative. In Crowe's case these distinctions
became very pronounced.

On Tuesday July 25 Thomas Crowe had been tried and sentenced.
At 11 o'clock the following day the Grand Jury assembled for a
remarkably different purpose. It now appeared opportune for the
restorative principle of justice to take effect, and already the business
of the assembly had palpably changed. There was a radical change in
the teams of lawyers employed . The applications before the Grand
Jury, however, were not of a criminal nature, but rather of a civil
dimension. Consequently, without a hint of indecency the mood and
disposition of the proceedings shifted from a punitive to a compensatory
orientation. Under the Peace Preservation Act 1875, compensation was
available to all those parties who sustained injuries arising out of certain
types of outrage.

In the instant case, Mr Patten Smight Bridge claimed £2,000 for injuries sustained, Mrs Hyland claimed £1,000 for the loss of her husband,
and Constables Nugent and Patrick O'Loghlen claimed £500 each for
injuries sustained by them.

These were not modest sums of money in 1876; even the least sum
claimed, that of £500 would have been regarded as a considerable
prize by most Irish citizens, who, incidentally, still lived under the fear
of famine.

Regarding the legal representatives, three parties were present: the
claimants, the tenants and the ratepayers. While the claimants called
for compensation to be paid out of the State's coffers - such claims and
payment being in perfect harmony with the State's underlying values -
in the instant case the "State" meant the taxpayers of County Cork -- a
fact regarding which Thomas Crowe was ever mindful.

The claimants instructed Messrs Heron QC and Peter O'Brien. Messrs
Murphy, QC, O'Brien, QC. Messrs O'Riordan, and Fitzgerald instructed
by S.O'Grady represented the tenantry of the Kingdom Estate, and Mr. J

The Case Of Thomas Crowe

Roche, instructed by Mr B. Cronin, represented the ratepayers of Mitchelstown.

In order to prove the claimants' case, elaborate maps of the scene of the murder were prepared by Mr. James J. Haycroft, B.E., assistant County Surveyor, Co. Tipperary, and laid on the table before the Grand Jury with copies all round for the respective parties.

The details of the attack and the murder were again recited. The history of the attacks and the claims made on Mr Bridge by Mr Ryan and Mr Crowe were also recited. The main concern of the business was not one of murder, but of 'outrage.' It now behoved the claimants to magnify things, particularly the causes of the murder, the involvement of the community, and the enormity of the conspiracy. Toward these ends the language changed somewhat. Counsel now described matters thus:

> "In this dreadful affray, which resembled an act of warfare more than any former murder he had heard of in Ireland, six shots in all were fired by the attacking party. With unexampled daring two of the assassins returned the fire of the constabulary and escaped, and there was no probability whatever of these two assassins being brought to justice. There were many houses around, and a number of people were known to be looking on, who, upon Crowe's trial gave evidence in his favour and who, in every way the ingenuity of an Irish tenant could devise, had since baffled the officers of Justice. He asked them to remember the words of the learned judge in reference to this case, who said that this crime would have been impossible without the sympathy of the district."

Some days after the murder two guns were found at the place where the two men had fled in the direction of Mitchelstown. Counsel said that he never before heard of so many persons looking on at a murder since 'Mrs Terry's murder' when, he alleged, seventeen persons were proved to have witnessed it. He then contrasted the instant case and claimed that no less than

> " Six stands of arms were brought to the scene of the murder, and it was supposed (though this was mere conjecture) that three of the intended assassins missed the appointment, and that only three were ultimately there to use the six stand of arms. It could not be supposed that a man with a blackened face could go along a public road in the broad daylight without being seen, nor could firearms be carried along the public highway without considerable danger of detection. It was therefore supposed - there were many ways of accounting for it - that the six stands of arms was brought there by night and concealed there. The nearest house to the scene of the murder was that of O'Brien's, and

124

The Case Of Thomas Crowe

there were several others a little farther off, but all adjacent to the road. A large number of people lived in these houses and must have known what was going on, but in reply to the inquiries of the police there invariable answer was that they heard the firing, but they thought it was fowling."

Now it seemed to be a virtue to prove what was denied in the criminal trial, namely, that Mr Bridge was a notoriously unpopular person and that the community totally conspired illegally and unfairly against him. Letters were liberally exhibited : and even Thomas Crowe's defence was now used to further the applicants' claims:

"In the trial the previous day some of these people were examined on the part of the prisoner, and the case they endeavored to make out was that the shot was not fired by the prisoner, but by some man with a white waistcoat whom they saw running away from the scene of the outrage. Immediately after the occurrence when the police were making inquiries they gave no information, and not one ever said anything about a man wearing a white waistcoat. Unhappily, they know there was a conspiracy against property in several parts of Ireland, and the story told by Mr Trench was not untrue - that in Ireland if a man went into a house and said he was pursued by the police for murder he would get protection. Thomas Crowe, the unfortunate man who was convicted of this murder and sentenced to death, was staying in the house of a man named Mackesy in Mitchelstown immediately before the murder. They had endeavoured to bring Makesy there and they were informed that he was in Cork that morning, but left in company with a young man named Ryan, a brother of Ryan who fired at Mr Bridge on a previous occasion, and who was now on the run."

***

5. Threatening Letters

Having heard that Thomas Crowe had lived in Mackesy's house, the house was duly searched and several letters were found. The first letter produced was from a 'Well-wisher' :

"April 5th, 1876
Dear Sir - please be a little cautious about your house for this time to come, as I am told from good authority there is a strict watch on your place. There was a report that strangers were seen about your place these days past. Do not allow any person, no matter who it may be, that any person may have any suspicion on them, for you know some of the people are bad, and, moreover, are poor. Tom was stopping at your house - I remain yours
"A Friend and a Well-wisher"
To Mr John Makesy, Mitchelstown"

The Case Of Thomas Crowe

This letter linked Thomas Crowe to a series of threatening letters sent to Mr Patten Smight Bridge after the murder of Hyland. Why he did not receive such letters before the murder was never questioned. Nevertheless, they tended to define the agrarian nature of the murder-attempt, which, when followed up with supportive evidence of the actual attempt itself, compounded the case for compensation.

The first letter Mr Bridge received was posted in Tipperary on the 29th of April 1876. It stated: -

> "Bridge - LEAVE, LEAVE, LEAVE, or if you don't we'll face you and your bodyguard, in the face of God and man - if it was in the chambers of Galtee Castle, in the noonday, and will not leave until your body will be old and your soul in hell with John Sadlier, your master. Hyland got the same warning and ridiculed it. Let you ridicule this if you value life, it is the last, and if rejected will prove fatal
> "Your Attempted Assassin"

A second letter, this time from "A Peacemaker and Truth teller" was posted in Dublin on the 13th May, '76 and recited the following: -

> "You, for the second time, have escaped being shot, and your private and public driver, Hyland, the ignorant, despoiling tool, suffered loss of life through your means. Had you shown common humanity towards the miserable tenants under your iron, tyrannical sway - ever rented poor serfs, recipients of outdoor relief to meet the rent gale - you'd not be at present under the doctor's care, nor protected by an auxiliary barrack and police at your castle. Let me assure you, sir, if you change not your policy towards the tenantry in exercising justice, instead of rack-renting the wretched toilers, your life insurance would bear a very heavy premium. And in defiance of all your lifeguards you'll be still in imminent danger, kept a prisoner amongst your outraged, legally plundered race, by right owners of the soil, whom you have been grinding down to utter ruin. Then, for the sake of peace, your own respect, and that of Mr Buckley's, relent timely, and cease from spreading the name of discontent between landlord and tenant through the land, and give a bright public example to other agents to do likewise.
>
> The time is approaching, Sir, when the English and Irish reformers may cause the millions of acres to be taken from the fee landed proprietors turning the island into a bullock pasture, while evicting men, for just compensation by the government, and divided amongst the cultivators. If you and Mr Buckley would timely and seriously reflect on this contemplated reformation, as in Belgium and France &, you might prudently be inspired to abate, instead of raising or doubling, the rent on your immense tract of country, which generous act would be hailed by the poor occupants with joy, and you'd be then released from your house

The Case Of Thomas Crowe

prison, no longer requiring any guard but a contented and grateful tenantry. You must know now that they murder tenants by wholesale. In driving them from the homes of their assessors for high rents, is not the way to win their affections, but on the contrary increase their vengeance.

Another word of advice from the stranger - show noble revenge towards Crowe. Bear in mind if he has fired at you, he never would have done so without great cause. Ask yourself the question, have you been a good kind, considerate agent, and hear the reply of your conscience! A jury may acquit or find him guilty. Should he be transported or hanged another may take his place. 'Twill but increase the rancorous relations between landowners and tenants, causing the smoldering embers to burst forth in a volcano, and can do you no good, while increasing your danger in Ireland. Begging for your recovery if this distant strange counsel be carried out ere the twelfth hour (when it may be too late), in a manly Christian spirit as a thanksgiving offering to God for your escape.

"A Peacemaker and Truth teller
Mr Bridge, Agent &etc"

A long rambling letter posted in Skibbereen went as follows:

"Southern Seaside
June 19th, 1876

Bridge YOU VILLIAN - you infernal devil, I will in spite of all your tricks, come up with you in a few days. You will never see the day you will prosecute Mr Casey. Saturday week will never dawn on you if God spares me strength and health. I have got my plans from a French fisherman here. You, perhaps, think I am not in existence, but you are well mistaken. I will, with God's help, send your body to atoms and your soul to hell in a few days, if you had so much more police and a regiment of soldiers. I will do for you in spite of the devil and all the police in Ireland. I would have done so long before now, only I did not wish to come in danger of a musket shot of yours; but now, thank God, I have got a very nice plan of sending you to hell. How I long for the hour when I shall be satisfied in my burning heart that heart burning fever shall then stop, when you are done for, and blazing in hell, perhaps you think you can avoid me, but no. I sware as I am here, and sware by all this world I shall give you Casey in the heart, if you have takings in the heart, the truth is told of you in the Cork Examiner. Thanks to the able fisherman, who has shown and planned for me how I will send you blazing for I know God will bless him. I suppose you will send this letter to your attorney, to the devil with him and the police too I care as much for the police as I care for a straw, and I have the thoughts of you as much as God hated the thoughts of the renegade, Judge Keogh. You think perhaps you will avoid my plot, no not if you were the devil of hell. No one ever knew of such a fine game before. Put out a reward for me. You may try and catch me if you can, but I am here in a nutshell safe ever till I be certain to be not out of my aim. You will never see Casey punished.

127

The Case Of Thomas Crowe

You will soon get the contents of his French preparation, which will make
riddles of your house and iron barrack and peelers also

Your Certain Assassin."

The reference to Casey was to one Sarsfield Casey, a Fenian; whose
letters signed "Galtee Boy" first exposed the Galtee evictions on the
Buckley estate. Mr Bridge sued Casey for defamation. Reports of the
case were widely and enthusiastically followed. At the time of the
compensation claim, however, as counsel rightly pointed out, the case
was still pending. Large subscriptions were being raised for Casey's
defence. Eventually the jury (in the libel case), after a substantial trial,
and despite the murder of Hyland and the fact that Mr Bridge had been
shot at and wounded, found for Casey rather than for Mr Bridge. In
April 1878, the question of the Galtee evictions was raised in the
House of Commons by Lancashire-born Mitchell Henry, M.P. for
Galway.

Finally , counsel for the claimants called upon the Grand Jury to
award substantial compensation to the parties "so grievously injured
by the barbarous and bloody outrage, which was so successfully, perpetrated on this occasion."

***

6. "Crime does not pay"

After much time was given to reading out the letters, evidence was
then taken, and Mr Johnson, Q.C. examined Mr Patten Bridge –

> "I am one of the claimants. I am agent of Mr Buckley's estate, situate in
> Tipperary, Limerick, and Cork, since 1859. There were some disputes with
> the tenantry owing to a revaluation of the rents. I was fired at by Ryan, one
> of the tenants and received £200 compensation for that from the County
> Limerick Grand Jury. I was shot at on the 30th March last; there were then
> notices to quit pending against some of the tenantry. On that day I was in
> Mitchelstown receiving rents."

The witness then detailed the circumstances of the affray at Garryleigh. Mr Murphy said there was no question but that this was an agrarian murder. The only question was whether the county of Cork was to
pay for it.

The Case Of Thomas Crowe

Mr Patten Bridge said that he received nine wounds on the occasion of the murder of Hyland. He was attended by Dr Porter of Dublin, Dr O' Neill and Dr McCraith. He paid Dr Porter £100, Dr O'Neill £15, and Dr McCraith £2. He was ten days in bed and it was six weeks before he could go about the estate. One finger was broken, and he had permanently lost the hearing of one ear.

> Mr Murphy - You know this outrage and the previous one occurred by people plotting with Ryan?
> Mr Bridge - Yes.
> Mr Murphy - And you know no other person who would have any pretext for this murderous attack on your life?
> Mr Bridge - No other.
> Mr Murphy - And it is not that Crowe is an uncle of Ryan?
> Mr Bridge - No.
> Mr Murphy - Are you not in error in saying that the property is situated in the counties of Cork, Tipperary and Limerick?
> Mr Bridge - No.
> Mr Murphy - Is there an acre of it in the county of Cork?
> Mr Bridge - Yes, the town land of Billarue, in the Fermoy Union, in the direction of Kilworth. The extent of that property is about a couple of hundred a year. There is not an acre of the property between Kilbenny bridge and Mitchelstown. I don't know that Ryan has any relatives in the county Cork, but I believe his wife had. The entire of the property between Kilbenny Bridge and Mitchelstown is the property of Lord Kingston.
> Mr Murphy - As far as you know Mr Farrer is the agent of that?
> Mr Bridge - Yes.
> Mr Murphy - And is there a single dispute between Mr Farrer and his tenantry?
> Mr Bridge - I think not. I left the property in too good order for that.
> Mr Murphy - Has he not kept it in good order?
> Mr Bridge - I hope so.

In respect of the 527 tenants and the 410 of whom had purportedly settled, the question eventually arose as to how many had been served with *Notices to Quit*, and why the attack came from Billarue.

> Mr Murphy Q.C. - Out of all these *Notices to Quit* you had not the slightest suspicion that the attack proceeded from the Billarue part of the property?
> Mr Bridge - I think not.
> Mr Murphy Q.C. - Were all the tenants served with Notices to Quit?
> Mr Bridge - No, because some of them held by lease. The greatest number served with *Notices to Quit* at one time was 124
> About a dozen or a dozen-and-a-half held by lease.
> Mr Murphy Q.C. - Were there five hundred of the tenantry on whom the

The Case Of Thomas Crowe

rents were raised?

Mr Bridge - About that … No, say, 450.

Mr Murphy Q.C. - Of these, on how many were Notices to Quit served?

Mr Bridge - At the outsize 130 was the highest number I had out.

Mr Murphy Q.C. - And all these were on the property in Limerick and Tipperary ?

Mr Bridge - Yes, and at Billarue.

Mr Murphy Q.C. - But you said you had no suspicion of any one on the latter property?

Mr Bridge - Yes.

Mr Murphy Q.C. - Ryan was the only one you suspected?

Mr Bridge - Yes.

(To the Foreman) - The rents I was receiving were from Mr Buckley's property in the first counties.

(To Mr Murphy, QC) - the gross rental is £5,550 and £180 of this is Billarue.

Mr Welsted - When this revaluation was made, who did it?

Mr Bridge - Mr Walker, of the King's County -- a most upright and honorable man. It was made in '73 and '74.

(To Mr Johnson, Q.C.) - He is no relation of Mr Buckley's or mine

(To Mr Welsted) - I took no part in the valuation.

Mr Macay - How much over the Ordinance Valuation was it?

Mr Bridge - In some cases up to 1/4. In some cases very little over it. The Ordinance valuation was not very correct on that estate.

Sub-constable Jones and Constable Nugent were then examined and repeated the testimony given by them at the murder trial. Jones said a strange woman appeared to take charge of Hyland's body while the police were going to Kilbenny. Nugent claimed that two women came up when Hyland's body was lying on the road, and one of them refused to take charge of it unless she was paid. The other said she was a passing stranger.

Constable Deviron, of Kilbenny deposed to finding two guns (produced) the next day at a thick hedge, about 150 yards from where the first shot was fired.

Head constable Doyle deposed that, up to within ten days of the murder, Crowe had lived with Mackesy in Mitchelstown. The people in the neighbourhood of Garryleigh all said they thought that fowlers fired the shots. That was all the information they would give. Although he made every inquiry he got no information from the people. According to head constable Doyle "the people who would talk to me before used make away when I came near them. I think they were afraid to be seen talking to me."

The Case Of Thomas Crowe

Evidence was then given to show that the outrage was of an agrarian character, and that the police had found great unwillingness amongst the people to assist them in tracing the assassins. On the part of the ratepayer it was submitted that strangers committed the outrage and that the people of the locality really knew nothing about it or the persons by whom it was perpetrated, and had no information to give. The Grand Jury, however, came to the conclusion that material evidence had been withheld, and they determined to grant compensation in all the cases.

Mr. Bridge was awarded £1,000, Hyland's widow £700, the constable £100, and O'Loghlen £10. It was decided that the amount should be levied off the parish of Brigown in three installments.

When Thomas Crowe planned to kill Mr Patten Smight Bridge, he planned to do so in Co. Cork, and not in Co. Tipperary. The burthen of the compensation, therefore, under the Peace Preservation Act of 1875 fell on Cork. Had he shot at him in Tipperary, he would have had a Tipperary Jury, but the cess would have had to be paid locally. Apparently Crowe chose to inflict the burden of the Cess on Cork. After his conviction, it was reported that when he was asked if he had anything to say why sentence of death should not be passed on him, he said :
"I knew I had no chance when I didn't fire at him in Tipperary."

======

Chapter 8

A Double
Execution

Do not go gentle into that good night,
Old age should burn and rave at close of day;
Rage, rage against the dying of the light...
Wild men who caught and sang the sun in flight
And learn, too late, they grieved it on its way.
Do not go gentle into that good night.

(Dylan Thomas (1914–1953))

In accordance with his sentence, Bombos was due to die on the morning of August 25. Under the Prison Rules this meant that the execution
would take place at 8 o'clock in the morning. Perhaps he was consoled
by the fact that he would not die alone!

Thomas Crowe was also scheduled to be executed at the same time, on
the same day, and at the same place. There was going to be a 'double
hanging' in Cork's County Gaol! Twenty years earlier - even ten –
they would have made a public spectacle of it, the intention at that
time being to deter Irishmen (usually Catholics) from killing other
Irishmen (usually Protestants), trying to regain land that was lost in wars
that no one could remember or forget. Behind the theory of deterrence
lay the theory of martyrdom and resurrection. More explicitly, it meant
that if you terrorise people enough, by hanging them in public, you
will deter them from committing murder in private. This Ashes-and
Brimstone-theory of deterrence had not moved an inch from its biblical
formulation for almost two thousand years. Now enshrined in a legal
and Protestant formalism that made every Catholic cringe, it was hardly
likely to be reformed in the Holy Roman Empire's most desolated outpost.

Nevertheless, when a penal enquiry demonstrated that people were not

A Double Execution

so outraged by public executions as hitherto presumed, the authorities moved the spectacle back into the prison. Of course there were other reasons why public executions were abolished, but these are too numerous to mention. Suffice it to say that the same penal enquiries, which suggested the cessation of public executions, also suggested that indoor executions be attended by at least those who should certify the procedure (the Sheriff), prepare the place and apparatus of execution and dispose of the body (the Prison Governor), execute the hanging and provide the requisite paraphernalia (the Executioner), certify the death (the Prison Surgeon), and prove the death (the Coroner). Others like the Chaplain, the warders and general dogs' bodies were also present.

In the instant case, however, the circumstances were quite unusual. The complement (or attendants' list) was specially augmented when the Sheriff invited interested people -- mostly doctors and journalists -- to attend and witness the execution for themselves. To this can be added the buzz of professional curiosity, the public's interest in two unusual murders, several devastating trials, and now a double hanging.

The same old spectacle was repeated with a difference that -- it was left to society's mediators to spread the gospel of deterrence to the common people. With the spread of literacy, the telegraph, and the popularity of newspapers, news of the hangings were no longer aimed at the attending public but at a national and international audience.

The double (and multiple) execution had its uncelebrated niche in the penological history of Ireland. It crept in from the valorised shadows of martyrology and the religious wars, through the battlefields of pike-ridden encampments from time immemorial, from the crossroads of unmentionable and forgotten places through gates of nearly every walled town and Castle, through the portals of places with names like Kilmainham, Lanyon, Belfast, Spike Island, Crumlin, Mountjoy, and every circuit town with a gaol delivery from Cork to Carrickfergus.

And this event did not escape the attention of observers like the fluent T.M.Healy, Parnell's bitterest enemy, who managed a memoir:

> "On the day of his execution there was led with him to the gallows a Greek youth named Bombos. The late William O'Brien, a young reporter on the *Cork Herald* (afterwards M.P.), thrilled Munster by an account of the executions. O'Brien had previously won renown by his Christmas in the Galtees, describing the mountain holdings where Patten Bridge wrought havoc. Bombos was a youth of good family, who left Attica through a love affair, and shipped aboard the *Caswell*. On his first trial the jury

A Double Execution

disagreed. The dissenting juror was J. O' Mara, then owner of the Royal

> Hotel, Mallow, who did not believe the seamen's evidence. On the
> second arraignment O'Mara was set aside by the Crown, i.e., not
> allowed to serve, and Bombos was convicted. Then for his soul's health
> an Archimandrite of the Oriental rite was brought from Liverpool to
> Cork to speed the way to heaven. The death-scene was described by
> O'Brien with telling artistry. He drew a picture of the Greek pope in
> gorgeous robes intoning canticles in the tongue of Sophocles and lead-
> ing his coreligionist to the trap door, to the swaying of a thurible, while
> Bombos puffed a cigarette. Behind him came a grey-haired Munster
> peasant in his shirtsleeves telling his beads in response to the "Hail
> Marys" of a plainly surpliced priest. Neither quavered. As the 'drop' fell,
> the representatives of the Greek and Latin rites saluted. Thus flew the
> souls of Bombos and Crowe into eternity. Their bodies were quick-limed
> in a common grave in the jail yard, and East and West were in death
> united."

> (See T. M. Healy, K. C. / Vol 1. Letters and Leaders of my
> Day/Thornton Butterworth, Ltd. 15 Bedford Street,
> London, W.C)

The curious minded must surely have wondered how and why within
the same County Gaol a Tipperary terrorist and a Greek sailor should
receive the law's most terrible sanction. Bombos was 24 years old.
Thomas Crowe was 63. Not that life was any sweeter to the one than
to the other, but it was difficult to avoid the contrast between youth
and age. Obviously Bombos had more living to do, more to contribute
to society, and therefore had more to lose than Thomas Crowe. That's
the high-minded view, or the blasé view, or the view given to stun you
out of thinking that at 63 life -- not least because it is so fragile and
contingent - is somehow less precious than at 24. On this reasoning
Thomas Crowe had more to lose. No one doubted that he had a tuned
body -- tuned enough to escape the constable after his capture -- and a
principled mind. He experienced sensuality -- of smell, of touch, of
taste, of love, of life -- all made precious by long reflection and the
testimony of finite things. His sensibility was unique by virtue of the
failing power of his senses and the recall of former vigour; it was made
mellow by the loss of friends, the memory of pain, and the constant
witness of want in self and in others. It takes a poet to appreciate
that,

> An aged man is but a paltry thing,
> A tattered coat upon a stick, unless

134

A Double Execution

Soul claps its hands and sing, and louder sing
For every tatter in its mortal dress.

But Thomas Crowe - no less than Osama Bin Laden - was a terrorist.
In his heart he was like his Afghan counterpart. Their tattered coats,
once the pride of saints, were embroidered with the terror that comes
of caring; for they, perhaps more than others, heard the awful cries of
their kind, the hunger and privation of prospective generations, brutalised and starved by clever economic policies -- strategies that raise the
rents, tear up the earth, and whether such strategies be about spuds,
gas or gold, they invariably lead on to fortune for some and incurable
famine for others. All our universities produce such men; they are
clever men, democratic, pious, powerful, and a long way from the
personal priorities of terrorists like Thomas Crowe and Osama Bin
Laden. It is these terrorists who live on the personal and passionate
level, unschooled in strategies and the middle range diplomacies of
indifference. Bin Laden was a witness to the struggle in the Arab
basin, where, as yet no High King had emerged. And the Christian
west and Jewish/American alliance was going to make sure that no
such High King would emerge; for with High Kingship came *Sinn
Fein*, self-knowledge, pride, oil control and the big gun itself -- nuclear power! How could the medieval mind be trusted with it?

In the same way Thomas Crowe had been assessed and had been found
wanting. He was still a *betagh*, one of the *Hibernici*, whose land and
labour the Roman Church and the English at one time craved and
actually possessed for at least a Reich and a half. Like an American
Indian, an Inca, or an Aztec, he was merely a remaining embarrassment to the fifteen-hundred-year-old Christian conquest over pagan
Gaelic culture. These two terrorists can only be understood as holy
men. All military men are at bottom holy, for all violence is at bottom
a purgation. They are, as the saints of old were, faithful and fanatical.

Properly understood, they belong to a period of history that few
countries remember, least of all America; they belong to the time of
the Martyrs, when faith in one's tribe was synonymous with faith in
God, when both, as one, were one's religion, one's identity, one's
sacred and personal integrity, so much so, in fact, that its loss was
synonymous with self-immolation. Herein lies the secret about
terrorists: they are essentially saintly men for whom all sufferings and

A Double Execution

privations are borne for their faith, for their God, for their community. These are men who live at the end of all streets, in the cul-de-sac not of meglomania but of nationalism and self-worth, *Sinn Fein*. They merely revisit that street, when their country, their kith, their kin, or their culture is threatened, and whether that threat is real or imagined.

Alongside this, was the laughter and the indifference of the powerful and the privileged, the awful smugness behind the technological gifts that made matter for one and misery for the other, the insipid and insincere language that makes a religion of injustice and an injustice of religion. There is a moral, famed by Christian preachers, which begins, 'Consider the lilies...' and ends with words of reassurance and splendour of the almighty Father of the universe. These words, like so many others, not only make a promise but also with their rhetoric bewilder the world. It is as if religion is the excuse for human misery and greed, particularly within its own provenance.

Who ever cared for the weak and the poor and the inadequate of this world? Ask any Greenpeace worker and he will tell you all about America's great love of our world. Go to Rome and see how the Pope cares for the poor whose pennies have built his ugly palaces. Go to Brussels and they'll tell you how marvelous humanism is in helping the third world. Go into any university and witness how much time is spent in the making of economists, accountants and lawyers - Why? To protect property and privilege. Ask any of your friends what they spend most of their lives doing, and why they do it. Look in the mirror and analyze the structure of self and judge Thomas Crowe!

It is not simply because of the fate of others that these men forfeit life; it is to give their own lives some dignity and meaning that they pursue their actions. And, as they perceive it, -- without action, terrorist action -- there is no dignity or meaning possible. It is as if all else has failed, and action which goes to the root of their masculine existence, is called forth as a primary and necessary consequence of that existence.

Yes, Thomas Crowe was just like Osama Bin Laden, or an Asian monk who would be consumed by fire rather than live an undignified life. He was a tottering, old terrorist. He struck back in terror, recklessly and carelessly. He had to reciprocate in kind, to hit back; somehow, sometime, somewhere; he had to land a punch for all the beatings he had taken in his life. Just as Bin Laden aimed at Israel by killing the innocent in New York, so, too, did Thomas Crowe aim at Patten Smight Bridge by shooting John Hyland: and both of them hated Landlordism. It was

136

A Double Execution

time for him to refuse to turn the other cheek, and to deliver something of what he and his kind were all the time receiving. He could not live with himself further without striking back. No animal on earth can watch "self" being destroyed without some defence. Only dispossessed Christians were taught how to turn the other cheek. In effect it permitted Christian Princes to punish their subjects with impunity. Religion was all a lie. Only might is right; George Bush and Tony Blair said so.

Even though Christos Bombos and Thomas Crowe had perpetrated their crimes at a distance approximating half the circumference of the earth apart, they nevertheless managed in their crimes to assert momentarily the primacy of might. One was a mutineer and the other was a terrorist, but what was unforgiveable was that their crimes, the most startling and sensational, actually affirmed the principle that might was right. As Christians, they now forgave their accusers and admitted their errors -- errors which both Church and State would suitably correct!

The facts of both 'the Mitchelstown Murder' and 'the *Caswell* mutiny' had been widely disseminated by the time the cases came on for hearing. The perpetrators had everything and nothing in common, and on their way to the scaffold, they would inevitably, fatefully meet for the the first and last time. The occasion of the meeting, like that of the execution itself, was solemn, impressive and full of fancifiable coincidence.

Since the sentence of death had been passed on them, both Bombos and Crowe had conducted themselves in a most edifying manner.From the first, they attended to the rights of their respective Churches and and followed their canons reverentially. Crowe received instructions from the Roman Catholic clergymen, who were placed in attendance on him – the Rev. Messrs McNamara and O'Keefe. He had an appearance of penitence and resignation. He seemed thoroughly prepared to die, and the effort that was made on his behalf did not seem to make him hope for any reprieve. He attended confession, received communion, and was prepared to meet his maker, whom he awaited with firmness and an exhibition of true sorrow for his crime.

Bombos was equally resigned to his fate. Since his sentence he was being attended to by the Rev. John Q. Connolly. He also received visits from the Dean of Cork and others who took a great interest in him. Their exertions to save him, and the pressure of waiting for an answer to the Petitions, eventually bore a result -- one which was announced to him on Thursday. The news did not disturb him notice-

A Double Execution

ably. Since Sunday past Dr. Constantine Stratuli, Archimandrite of
the Greek Church, Liverpool, who was assisted in his ministrations
by Mr. Nicholas B. Vidiano, and Mr. Nicholas Stratuli, his nephew,
attended him constantly. To the last he proclaimed his innocence and
confided that he was prepared for death. Indeed, he confessed, he
would die 'without malice in his heart'.

Both convicts now had clergymen in their death cells day and night.
The cells, placed in a schoolroom, were comfortable and commodious.
Each of the prisoners was very strict in the observance of the rules of
his church -- Bombos fasting on every Wednesday and Friday as
required by the Greek Church, and Crowe fasted every Friday .The
clergymen had been with the condemned men almost continually and
they were now prepared for the execution. They had comforted them
with all that religion could offer. M. Vidiano had spent Thursday night
with the Greek, who prayed until half past eleven at night before returning to bed. He fell asleep at a quarter to twelve and slept for four hours.
When he awoke he again joined in prayer until the arrival of the
Archimandrite, when the Lessons and Gospels were read for him. He
also received the service of the Holy Communion.

He received the sacrament as he had done on Wednesday. The mass
in accordance with the Greek ritual could not be celebrated in a Greek
Church. He smoked during the morning but took no breakfast. Crowe
went to bed at ten o'clock on Thursday night and slept for about five
hours, but, unlike Bombos, his sleep was calm and without any sign of
nervous excitement: for while Bombos was starting continually in his
sleep, Crowe, the old agrarian bandit, slept the slumber of a child. He,
too, was visited soon after five o' clock on Friday morning by the Rev.
Messrs MacNamara and O'Keefe, and with them he proceeded to the
chapel, where mass was said and the communion administered to him.
A reporter from the *Cork Constitution* took up the story of the actual
procession and the following executions. Apart from some minor corr-
ections the reporter's account is faithfully reproduced:

> At a quarter to eight the gaol bell began to toll, and outside the building
> about 80 people assembled. At ten minutes to the hour the procession to
> the scaffold began. Before Bombos left the room in which he had been
> confined he turned to the Rev. J. Q. Connolly and gave him an apple,
> saying it was the only thing he could give in this world. He had given
> another to Warder Oxford who had been with him daily since being
> sentenced.

> The Gallows was erected in a corner of the airing yard. To reach it the

A Double Execution

criminals had to walk first into an open space a considerable distance off, and by a passage 300 yards in length to the yard where they were to die. At the end of the wall, which leads to the southern extremity of the gaol, there was a small gateway opening into the airing yard, forming a complete square, two sides of which were bounded by the prison buildings, and the other two by walls. In the furthest corner of the yard a scaffold was erected. This yard was reserved for hanging.

The scaffold was so situated that the culprit could not see it until he entered the doorway leading into the yard. It consisted of an iron frame which, when not in use, could be lowered by means of a windlass to lie horizontally upon the ground. It was the same iron frame, which was formerly used in front of the gaol for public executions before the 1860s. When required for use, the iron frame was raised up and the top crossbar, equipped with two hooks for the rope, then stands about 15 feet from the level of the yard. A rudely constructed platform with wooden supports was also constructed around this, and a flight of wooden steps led up to the drop. The two hooks still remained at the top crossbar and from one of these the rope and noose was attached. From a side in the yard the executioner and his assistant emerged.

Crowe was accompanied by two clergymen in white surplices and two warders. They first appeared from the chapel. And immediately afterwards came Bombos, the Archimandrite, his two assistants, the Rev. J. Q. Connolly and the two warders. All came from the entrance to the house of correction, and then the two murderers, meeting for the first time since their sentence.

In what we may call the executioner's yard there were at this time seven reporters, two doctors and three warders. In this small crowd there was intense excitement. Then the warder, who was stationed on the central tower - and whose duty it was to hoist the black flag when the men were dropped - was seen to remove his hat. This was the sign that the procession was approaching.

Soon the deeply intoned prayers of the Catholic clergymen were heard.! Crowe's loud and fervent response, "Lord have mercy on me" was repeated unceasingly. And from the rear of the procession a loud, pathetic cry of "Kyrie Elison" from the Greek priest contrasted with the soft, deep, responsive! "Kyrie Elison", voiced by Bombos. As they walked in the procession Crowe clasped a rosary and a crucifix, and with the two clergymen beside him, he appeared first at the entrance to the yard. He stood perfectly alert, and his well-cut features and his brilliant eyes gave him an aspect of great firmness.

Then Marwood, the executioner, suddenly appeared before him. In its suddenness it was shocking. It made one think that he had either sprung from the ground or dropped from the sky. He surveyed his victim, and clinically unloosed Crowe's black scarf in order that he might have the neck more completely at his disposal. The old man gave him a piercing glance, and whispered something to the Rev. Mr Mac Namara, who was

A Double Execution

heard replying: "In two minutes you will be before a merciful god, and I hope, enjoying the happiness of Heaven. Let us only pray." And then Crowe kissed the crucifix, and holding it and a rosary beads in his hand submitted to be pinioned quietly, calling out meantime with great fervour, "Lord, have mercy on me".

A short delay ensued, but to the onlooker it seemed insufferable while Bombos was being pinioned. After a minute Crowe stepped into the yard and looked at the scaffold. Praying loudly, he walked directly to it, with the two priests beside him and the two warders behind him. He walked up the dozen steps without flinching and stood with greater calmness than any of the onlookers on the trap. Bombos walked six paces behind him. On entering the yard he bowed to the reporters, and walked in that military stride towards the scaffold.

At his left side was Dr. Stratuli who was robed in the full costumes of Archpriest of his church. He is an old man, with a long flowing grey beard. He wore a black velvet cloak, called a 'felony', with white satin crosses worked into it; his headdress was symbolical of his order in the church, and was called " the Epanokalumaigon". It is a leafless hat broadening towards the crown. In his hand the Archimandrite held a large crucifix set with precious stones, and he wore a smaller one on his breast. The large crucifix he held before the eyes of the convict and the ringing voices of both, as they repeated the Kyrie Elison on that dread walk to the scaffold, caused the small group of onlookers to join fervently in the responses.

When Bombos reached the stairs leading to the scaffold he shrank back for a moment. He stared at the dread apparatus of death. Momentarily he recovered his self-possession and immediately stiffened his resolve. Before him went Dr Stratuli, who had to be helped to the platform by his two assistants, and if anything could have added new terror to the scene it was the bravery of this old ecclesiastic tottering up the steps of the scaffold and still crying for Christ's mercy for the culprit - the culprit all the time ejaculating prayers for mercy on his own behalf.

The two men stood erect on the drop. Marwood was dressed in a black body coat and light tweed trouser. He fixed each man under his rope - an exercise that was set in relief to the constant prayers of the three clergymen and the two condemned men. The Rev. Mr McNamara made the sign of the Cross over Crowe's head, and performed absolution according to the rite of the Roman Catholic Church. The Archimandrite kissed Bombos, who turned afterwards and kissed his hand. The dreadful spectacle of adjusting the rope was then gone through by Marwood, and caps were thrown over their faces. Both were praying loudly in response to the three clergymen, and while the name of the Saviour was on their lips the bolt was drawn. The convicts fell.

The drop was 8 feet, and it killed Crowe instantaneously. He had in his hand a red handkerchief when the bolt was drawn, and the rapidity with

A Double Execution

which he met his death may be gathered from the fact that he hadn't time to clutch the handkerchief in a firm grasp before he was killed. He remainned hanging for an hour and the handkerchief still held in his hand, but hardly enough pressure to hold it.

The suddenness of the drop knocked the white cap from off his head.! The executioner had put it on in order to conceal the features, so before the features could now be noticed Marwood ran down the stairs and placed it over his head again. Although Crowe died as quickly as if he had been shot through the heart it was not so with Bombos - he showed signs of life for 4 minutes at least. When it was thought he was dead he was seen to lift his shoulders 4 or 5 times, and a spasmodic jerk of his knees showed that he still had life in him, even though he was probably unconscious. He shook and wriggled in this way for about 4 minutes.

It all happened so fast. Both men had expressed the wish to make a final statement. Bombos made a declaration the night before, and it is printed hereafter. Thomas Crowe was anxious to make his statement on the scaffold, but he was unfortunately dissuaded from so doing by the clergymen who attended him. They impressed upon him the absolute priority of considering his eternal welfare, such that even in death the great revolutionary could not speak his mind. The arrangements for the execution were otherwise very well arranged and carried out by the governor of the gaol, captain Roberts, the Sub-Sheriff, Mr. Johnson, and the prison staff.

Even though a number of distinguished medical men in the city were given passes to attend, only two witnessed the execution - Dr Denis Donovan and Dr. F. H. Smith. The former was present as the representative of Dr. F B Beamish, medical officer to the Gaol, and Dr. Smith attended for scientific purposes, and as a correspondent for a medical journal. After the bodies had hung for an hour two coffins were brought out by prisoners and placed underneath. Marwood very carefully lowered the bodies into the coffins peviously prepared. Some blood dripped about Crowe's face, which gave him a livid appearance. Bombos' mouth, on the other hand, was much distorted. Dr. F.H. Smith has kindly supplied us with the following remarkable observations of the execution. Though brief the report is very much to the point : -

" The convulsions which I saw in the case of the Greek are common. For it is observed that in those who are criminally executed there are often violent convulsions of the limbs and trunk. There is no reason, however, to believe that the individual suffers pain any more than he would if in the convulsion of an epileptic fit, as, on recovery, there is an entire loss of consciousness of pain in both cases; however, in my judgment the rope was placed too high in the Greek's case, or else his wearing a beard

A Double Execution

and being short and stout -necked it slipped above the cricord cartilage whereas in Crowe's instance it pressed on the windpipe itself. In his case also the body swung round thereby tending to produce compression of the spinal chord, and therefore were rapid deaths as first noticed..."

An inquest before a jury was held on the bodies by Mr M. J. Horgan, Coroner. Evidence was first given in Bombos' case. Timothy Byrne, the Chief Warder of the County Cork Prison, swore that he was present at 8 o'clock and that he saw that the sentence was duly carried out on the deceased, who was 24 years of age.

Denis D. Donovan, M.D., acting surgeon for Dr Beamish, the surgeon at the County Gaol, swore that he was present at the execution, that after the execution he found Bombos dead, and that a subsequent post-mortem examination revealed that 'death was caused by strangulation consequent on pressure on the windpipe'. He also testified that 'Death was painless'.

The jury found that the deceased came to his death by strangulation effected by hanging. This procedure was repeated almost verbatim in respect of Thomas Crowe. Death, in his case, having been " caused by pressure on the spinal chord consequent on the fracture." The jury returned a verdict in accordance with the medical evidence. Bombos had made the following dying statement translated from the Greek: -

"Cork County Gaol, 12 o'clock
25th August 1876

Mr Dear Brothers –

I, Christos Emmanuel Bombos, having two brothers living, Cyriac and Alexander, a father and a mother, an unmarried sister, Catherine, and a married one, Irene, living at Ibraila, and also many paternal and maternal relations, hereby affirm to all Greeks and Irishmen that I, the said C. E. Bombos embarked on board the *Caswell* at Buenos Aires for Valparaiso. I emphatically proclaim that I am innocent of the crimes for which I have been convicted and took no part in the perpetration of the murders. At the moment which I depart this life, I express my deep gratitude to the Dean of Cork and the two Protestant clergymen, Mr. Connolly and his son, who took such a kind and humane interest in me; to Mr Yourdi, and to all those Greeks and Britons who have tried to save me from the gallows; to the two ladies of the city who have given my spiritual father, the Rev. Archimandrite Constantine Stratuli, a silver crucifix, which according to their desire, is to be forwarded to my mother after my death; and to all those who signed the memorials on my behalf to the governor of the gaol, Mr Joyce, captain Robert, and the officials who have showed me so much consideration and sympathy. Finally, I forgive those who have been witnesses against me, as I hope to be forgiven by God and received into His holy Kingdom.

Signed: Christos Emmanuel Bombos.

The following day, in a guarded Editorial, the Examiner portrayed the city's confused feelings after the double hanging:

The Cork Examiner,
Saturday Morning,
August 26th, 1876

"YESTERDAY morning the black flag was flying for the second time within the space of two years over the tower of the County Gaol in token that capital punishment had been executed upon Christos Baumbos and Thomas Crowe, the unhappy men who were sentenced to death at the last Assizes. The recurrence of an execution after so short an interval was, we rejoice to say, an event of a very unusual character in Cork. Before capital punishment was inflicted upon William Tobin in 1875, there had been no occasion for the services of the hangman in this county or city for a period of more than ten years. And in the present instance it was owing to circumstances of a purely adventitious character that the execution took place in Cork. The crime for which Baumbos suffered was committed upon the High Seas, almost within sight of the shores of South America, and of the second tragedy the cause and the actors belonged to a neighbour county.

In each instance we are happy to think this great county of Cork has been guiltless of the blood that has been shed and has had to bear the onus of carrying the dread sentence of the law into effect for offences not properly its own.

Acting upon what we must describe as a wise reconsideration of his decision in the case of Tobin, the Sheriff on this occasion permitted the representatives of the Press to be spectators of the awful scene when the law claimed its victims, and the painful incidents of the morning are described elsewhere. We shall not abuse the confidence the authorities have thus reposed in the discretion of the Press by indulging in any reflections of a sensational or unbecoming character upon the sad and terrible scene. Neither shall we venture to discuss the justice of the sentence pronounced by high tribunal acting under the most awful sanctions to which human beings can be submitted.

But there was one feature in both these crimes, which, now that the exigencies of the law have been satisfied, forces itself upon our attention.

143

A Double Execution

The Greek, who died with strange protestations of innocence upon his lips, was one of a party of foreign seamen who rose upon their officers and slaughtered them one after another with a relentless fury that seemed to be the sign of natures insensible to ruth or pity.

At the trial the explanation suggested for the crime was that the men were common pirates whose object was to seize and plunder the ship. Since then suggestions have been made that derive some probability from what we know to be in too many instances the relations of seamen and their officers in the merchant service. It has been asserted, with what degree of truth we shall not pretend to say, that captain Best was a man of cruel and violent temper as well as great physical strength, who choose to rule by terror, and frequently indulged in acts of great brutality to the members of his crew.

One writer whose letter was admitted into the columns of the *Times*, alleged that not many years ago a ship, commanded by this captain, was known as "the floating hell", and that her crew deserted *en masse* in South America sooner than return with him to England.

It is due to the memory of the murdered seamen to add that nothing appeared in the course of the trial to suggest that the Greek and his companions had been driven by ill treatment into their sanguinary mutiny. But yet many things which do not enter into the scope of a criminal trial may exist and affect the complexion of the crime when regarded from a higher point of view than that which the law, for sufficient reasons, thinks it proper to take. And cruelty, oppression, and violence are only too certain to result in acts of retaliation, in which men not naturally prone to deeds of blood too often become insensible to the common dictates of humanity and religion.

The case of Thomas Crowe was assuredly a peculiar one. He was an old man, almost on the brink of the grave, and there was nothing in his character or antecedents to account for his having, in the clear light of a spring afternoon, come down to the side of a public road to do murder in full view of five persons.

From the moment of his condemnation his demeanour was not that of a desperado. He listened with attention to the ministrations of his clergyman, and laboured assiduously to make his peace with Heaven. When the prayer of the memorial presented on his behalf was refused, he received the intelligence with resignation and fortitude. While his fellow prisoner clung to the last to the hope that mercy would be extended to him, THOMAS CROWE quietly reconciled himself to his fate and sought only the consolations of religion. And he died in the firm spirit of a Christian, without a trace either of fear or defiance.

How has it come to pass that this man in the last decade of his life closed his ears to the awful mandate, "Thou shalt not 'kill'", and braved the doom of a felon?

144

A Double Execution

Unfortunately we have the key to the whole mystery in the fact that the crime was one of an agrarian character. The Land Code, which has stained our annals with many an act of oppression, and many a deed of blood, must still, it seems, have its victim. But now that two more lives have been sacrificed, now that justice has had her due, and the curtain has fallen upon the last act of the tragedy, may we not ask our rulers whether it is not worth their while to inquire into the sources of these abnormal outbursts of murderous rage?

To the statesman crimes such as that of Thomas Crowe and his associates must ever have a different aspect from that in which they are viewed from the Judicial Bench. The function of the Judge is simply to punish the deed of blood. It is the duty of the Legislator to probe to their sources the causes from which it has arisen, and ascertain whether there is aught in the relations of privileges of various classes which puts great masses of the people in conflict with the laws, and renders many of them deaf even to the mandates of religion."

======

Chapter 9

Hue And Cry
The *Caswell*

We make ourselves a place apart
Behind light words that tease and flout,
But oh, the agitated heart
Till someone find us really out.

'Tis pity if the case require
(Or so we say) that in the end
We speak the literal to inspire
The understanding of a friend.

But so with all, from babes that play
At hide-and-seek to God afar,
So all who hide too well away
Must speak and tell us where they are.

Robert Frost (1874–1963). A Boy's Will. 1915.

Administrative Problems:

It was inevitable that the *Caswell* would generate some legal and administrative problems. The first concern was whether to get on with the trial of Bombos or to delay matters in the hope that the Pistorias would be picked up in Buenos Aires or, indeed, somewhere else more extradition-friendly. The ideal, of course, would be to have both Bombos and the Pistoria-brothers tried together. That way justice would have been simpler as well as being obviously safer. For one thing, there would be no loose ends in the testimony of the witnesses and, secondly, the process would be drawn to a close within a reasonably expeditious period.

The immediate problem was the trial of Bombos – whether to wait or whether to proceed. It made little sense, particularly to those who held up the rule of law as society's first virtue, if one of the mutineers was tried and executed while two others escaped with impunity. Under the circumstances, proceeding with the Bombos execution was thought by some to be foolhardy. It meant that whatever evidence the Pistorias might offer when captured, would, for the purposes of Bombos' trial, be ignored. If such evidence was in Bombos' favour, then he was entitled to it; he was, after all fighting for his life. And if the evidence was against him, then at least he would have the opportunity of cross-examining them. The same reasoning prevailed when applied to the Pistorias. For if after some years they got caught, and, if at that stage Bombos was either hanged (or freed), how could his evidence be used in favour of (or against) the Pistorias? The obvious consequences of going ahead with the trial were significant for both the Pistorias as well as for Bombos, and showed, perhaps, the establishment's preference for administrative exegencies over their pursuit of truth or their regard for the integrity of any of the defendants.

On further consideration it became apparent that the capture of the Pistorias had to remain something of a pious aspiration rather than a realistic expectation. Indeed, where were they? Could they be located at all? Or, more to the point, could they be located expeditiously enough to have them tried with Bombos? It was like looking for a needle in a proverbial haystack.

As it happened, the Cork constabulary discovered that there was a letter in the local Post Office awaiting collection by Gaspari Pistoria. Gaspari's wife, unaware of the mutiny when writing to her husband, addressed it for collection at Queenstown. The letter contained the couple's Buenos Aires address and the Ships' Agents released it forthwith to the police who sent it post haste to Dublin Castle for the information of the Home Office. As one might have expected, it came to naught. The Pistorias were not going to be hoisted on their own petard. All the letter did was concentrate the attention of detectives around Buenos Aires.

Even if the Pistorias could have been readily located, there would still be other administrative problems either to do with jurisdiction, extradition, or the general administrative machinery of Empire. Already the question was raised whether the Resident Magistrate at Queenstown could issue two warrants for their arrest. Because the case was so important and because the Magistrates were hamstrung by the existing law (more particularly, Section 10 of the 14th and 15th of Vic cap. 93), they wanted another opinion. Under the law a Resident Irish Magistrate could not issue arrest warrants as he pleased, even on the sworn information of James Carrick. On the contrary, he could only issue where the crime was committed within his jurisdiction, or where the person to be arrested is or was suspected of being within his jurisdiction. In the instant case it was evident that the crime was committed on the 'high seas' and the Pistorias had never come within the jurisdiction of Queenstown. So, who could issue the warrants? Who would execute them? And what was the point, if, supposing for a moment that the Pistorias were arrested in Buenos Aires, Britain had no extradition arrangements with the Republic of Argentina?

According to legal opinion at the time, a Secretary of State could lawfully issue an arrest Warrant, his jurisdiction being regarded as co-extensive with the limits of the English Admiralty. When the two warrants were issued the Undersecretary of State requested that a 'quiet enquiry' be made to determine the whereabouts of the Pistorias, after which (on the 9th of June) instructions were sent by mail to Her Majesty's *Charge d'Aff-aires* at Buenos Aires to "take such steps as he thinks best" to return the fugitives to justice.

Spreading the News

It should be borne in mind that the *Caswell* was still on the high seas when the news of the mutiny first broke in Rio de Janeiro. Her Majesty's Consul in Rio notified the Board of Trade (on May 8th) that all the officers on board the *Caswell* "had been murdered by mutineers." In a stream of letters written in longhand, the words were relayed to the Foreign Office, the Home Office, and thence through the Consuls to every port in the sprawling Empire. Like some massive oak the roots of which had been touched with fire or arsenic, it sent its felt displeasure to every bow, branch and twig on its cascading commonwealth.

The first to be notified were those on the Coast of Europe and on the East Coast of South America. The Foreign Office made special mention of offices at Pernambuco, Bahia and Madeira, the Canary Islands and Cape de Verdes. Similar letters were sent to the Earl of Carnarvon, the Under Secretary of State at the Colonial Office, the Earl of Derby at the Home Office, and thence to the authorities in Her Majesty's possessions on the

West Coast of Africa and at Gibraltar. More letters were sent to rouse the
sea dogs in Admiralty to greater effort.

"In order that every effort may be made to bring the murderers to justice,
the Board of trade would be glad if their Lordships would cause such
instructions as may appear to them desirable, to be issued without delay
to Commanders of Her Majesty's ships"

The Commissioners of Customs were also to instruct their officers. They
were to report the arrival of the vessel "at any port in the United Kingdom," and to obtain the assistance of the police for the apprehension of
the mutineers.

Three days later, Dublin Castle had no sooner assured the Home Office
of its vigilance than a telegram from the Deputy Receiver of Wrecks at
Queenstown informed them of the *Caswell*'s disposition. The mutinous
vessel, it said, was "… shorthanded (and) in charge of a young man who
would give no information until he arrives in Queenstown." The young
man was Carrick and he meant what he said. A further missive claimed
that the "*Caswell* (was) towed into this harbour at 8.20 am by gunboat
'Orwell'. As it happened this missive was incorrect. The man-of-war was
not the 'Orwell' but the "Goshawk" -- a fact confirmed by the Rear
Admiral Commanding Queenstown, who succinctly recapitulated the
saga to date:

"Goshawk arrived this morning with barque *Caswell* in tow. Three Greeks
and two Maltese, part of crew on 4th January last, rose and murdered the
Captain, first and second mates, and steward. The Maltese left the ship in
neighbourhood of River Plate. Subsequently English portion of crew
overpowered the Greeks two of whom were killed and the other made
prisoner who is now on board. The *Caswell* has been handed over to the
civil power."

Apart from the coverage of the Bombos trial, the *Caswell* story has never
been told. The trial preoccupied the *Times* (London), the *Cork Examiner*, and the *Cork Constitution*. And with the death of Bombos, so died the
press' interest as well. In Wales, where it had a rapidly diminishing impact,
the *Cambrian* of Swansea first reported the matter on the 12th May 1876,
and again on the 19th. It was under this initial widespread news coverage
that the search for the Pistorias proceeded.

For three years between 1876 and 1879 the search for the Pistorias span-
ed the shipping world with false starts and comic suspicions. All in all
only three suspicious episodes emerged from the worldwide vigil. At first
there was the Pinatel/Mazeres case, which ran roughly from June 23 until

mid-July, 1876. This period , arguably the most intensive term of the search, lasted throughout the Bombos trial. Then for 8 months -- up to April '77 -- there was a total lack of any feedback whatsoever. Then a suspect named Clayton made a brief appearance in the Home Office files, following which -- for over a year and a half -- there was nothing. From April '77 until late August '78 it was as if the Pistorias never existed. All knowledge and memory of them had practically evaporated, that is, as far as the surveillance of the Consuls of the empire was concerned. It was at this juncture that the Kelsoes made their entry into the world of British espionage. How these respective suspects arose and were sustained in the files gives us some conceivable idea of the unwieldy ways of imperial under-cover work in the age of the telegraph. Let us look at these suspects separately and briefly.

The Charleston Suspect

The first suspect was a Frenchman named E. Pinatel, who on Friday 23 June 1876, made his singular way aboard a Steamer, *The Pilot Boy*, from Buenos Aires to Charleston, South Carolina. Pinatel was broke, and the Captain gave him free board and lodging as far as Charleston. On arrival, and with only thirty cents to his name, he slept on a Charleston wharf. In search of relief he then called upon H. Pinckney Walker at the Charleston Consulate. Walker told him to make application to the French Consul. Pinatel, who was without papers, told Walker that he had already done so -- but without success.

Walker then posed a pre-eminently intelligent question. He asked Pinatel what induced him in the first place to come to him for relief. With that Pinatel set out the circumstances of his arrival in Charleston. This wasn't the first time he found himself explaining his antecedents. The following evening he had to repeat his story to a Masonic Committee, who apparently didn't believe a word he said. Neither for that matter did H.Pinckney Walker; for no sooner had he finished with Pinatel than he sent a message to the Home Office entitled suggestively: "Re *Caswell*: An arrival from Buenos Aires excites suspicion. Is Giuseppe at large?"

Pinatel was a 52 year-old widower with two children living in Marseilles. He was regarded as intelligent but with a slightly nervous disposition. He stood 5' 11" in height, had closely cropped white hair and a beard that was full but not long. Without a full and detailed description it was somewhat futile trying to guess what the Pistorias looked like. Moreover, in mid-'76 the press (as well as the authorities) was at this juncture more interested in trying the bird in hand - as opposed to catching the two in the bushes of Buenos Aires.

Pinatel told one and all that he was a miner by occupation. He was in the employ of a mining company in London called Parodi Mina and Co., a consortium of large Petroleum exporters. His job was to examine mines in South America and elsewhere for their profitability, and he was paid accordingly, ie. in proportion to the profits the mines generated. Should the mines fail to show a profit, then he had his expenses reimbursed.

He had worked in several countries, including Italy and Arabia, and had been recently in the Argentine Republic. While on the La Plata, he was sent in a small Brigantine to a port in Brazil whose name, he claimed, was incomprehensible, and while off the Brazilian coast, the same vessel was capsized by a sudden squall. It was most unfortunate that all hands on bord had been lost at sea. He survived without tools or possessions. He had lost everything, in fact, except some clothes. He managed a small boat until he was very fortunately picked up in April 1876 by an English Barque called the *Glynliffon*. The captain of the "*Glynliffon*," captain Tullock brought him to South Carolina.

This was Pinatel's account of how he came to be down and out and utterly dependent upon charity. The story was frayed at the edges - or perhaps it was his accent! It was in any event his story, and he was sticking to it. In the course of his account he also said that he had been made a Master Mason in 1857 in Marseilles, but that since then he had never returned to his lodge. If this was a lie, it was hardly a good lie to tell, particularly when, still in need of relief, he presented himself before a Masonic Board for examination. By the time the Board was finished with him, not only did he fail "to establish his connection with the Masonic Fraternity," but he also managed to have his application for relief "unanimously dismissed." Before leaving, the secretary noted that "he seemed very much distressed and became very pale, as if about to faint …" The secretary's report did not mention if he was offered refreshment by the fraternity, observing rather that "as soon as he recovered (he) left the Masonic Hall."

Being down and out in Charleston was one thing; but being a *Caswell*-mutineer was quite another. Perhaps any man standing 5'11' with white hair could, technically speaking, be Joseph Pistoria. Without a full description, how could anyone , including embassy-staff , tell? And since there was nothing approaching a reasonable description of the escaped Pistorias, no matter how corny Pinatel's account was, no inferences could be drawn as to his identity. Prior to the use of the telegram it took a ship – as we saw with the *Caswell* --73 days to go from Glasgow to Buenos Aires. But by this time the Telegram had become useful if not popular in the British civil service. So if distance was no object, why did it take so long to provide a description?

This is one of those questions for which it is difficult to assign a convincing answer. While the descriptions had not been known except to the crew of the *Caswell*, perhaps the best answer is that as yet no one thought of asking the crew for a description of the Pistorias, or, alternatively, no one realised the significance of the Telegraph for the purposes of conveying criminal information. More than likely, it was a combination of both the above reasons. A further consideration must be the fact that the availability of the Telegraph did not mean that it was universally so. Obviusly, some places benefitted from its use before others – which might explain why it didn't reach the places in which the suspects were sighted. Furthermore, the home attention was focused on the trial of Bombos, and nowhere in the trial procedure did it call for a description of the escapees. So, even for those who read the papers, there was still no clear description of the escapees available.

To confound matters further, Pinatel had suspiciously changed his hair colouring at least once. In some ways Walker was clever enough to obtain Pitatel's signature for comparison. No doubt he had his misgivings -- which is why he wrote to the Master of the *Glynliffon* for his observations. He also wrote to his authorities seeking instructions. " I may labour under a great mistake," he wrote, " but I suspect the present applicant to be the identical Giuseppe and therefore I have ventured to enquire of you whether Giuseppe is still at large." In fairness to Walker it should be recalled that accounts in the London papers a month earlier suggested that the brothers Pistoria had both been arrested at Buenos Aires, but since there had been no follow up, Walker could not be sure whether or not they were still at large.

Pinatel's story was full of unexplained gaps. While claiming to be French he admitted that he was a native of Sardinia. He said his wife lived in Marseilles, but he also gave people to believe that she lived in Buenos Aires. He said he wanted to go home (to France) and get help, but Captain Tullock would have brought him to England -- and this he refused. Further, when his boat capsized on La Plata, he could not even remember the vessel's name or point to any survivor who could vouch for him. Moreover, like Joseph Pistoria he spoke English. He also managed to tell copious 'porkies', to confound the Masons, and to arouse the suspicions of Captain Tucker, not to mention H.Pinckney Walker. The Masons, who examined him extensively, didn't like the cut of his jib either. And how could the entire committee,which had lined up to cross-examine him in a Masonic Hall in Charleston, be unanimously wrong!

Frantic letters were exchanged in an attempt to have these suspicions confirmed. But even by the end of July Edward Thornton at the Washington consulate could not inform Walker at Charleston whether the Pistorias were still at large or not. In turn he wrote to the Board of Trade through the Foreign Office asking for a description of the Pistorias. His doubts persisted. "Unless Mr Walker knows more than he has communicated to me," he wrote, " there does not seem to be very strong ground for believing that the man in question is Giuseppe of the '*Caswell*,' though there is always a possibility that he is so."

The news did the rounds. The Board of Trade transmitted the information to the Home Office and the Foreign Office. The 'Charleston Suspect', everyone agreed, fitted the available description - all, that is, except 'as to his height and clothing.' Without a 'firm description' there was no hope of correspondence between the communicants. Walker was nevertheless instructed to 'keep his eye' on Pinatel. So also was Her Majesty's Consul General at New York, in the event of his arrival at New York from Charleston.

Everything now hinged on the description of the Pistorias, and this could only be had from the witnesses to be assembled at the trial of Bombos.

After his 'exposure' before the Masons on June 29th no one was surprised when at midnight the following day Pinatel took flight on board the *Sea Gull* bound for Baltimore. Sir Edward Thornton from the Washington Office directed that a detective be employed to follow him, and the following description of Pinatel was forwarded to assist him.

> From 35 to 40 years old
> Five feet 9 or 10 inches high
> Short black beard slightly tinged with grey covers face
> Black hair and eyes
> Large red nose.
> Dressed in old suit of black and black hat very old
> Has a small sized sailor's chest with him

Pinatel had hardly landed when a further report recited that:

> "A Frenchman calling himself Philip Mazeres answering Pinatel's description is a steerage passenger on Steamer "*Sea Gull*" due at Baltimore

on Monday. Pitatel is tall and dark with prominent nose and square-toed shoes."

Immediately upon disembarkation Pinatel "was at once recognized and followed" by James Wood, a detective attached to the firm of Messrs Smith, Pearson and West. According to Wood, Pinatel arrived at daylight on the 3rd of July and now called himself Philip Mazeres. When he landed he made his way with his chest of belongings to the Erickson Line. The Erickson Line had two boats sailing every day at 3 pm for Philadelphia, and Wood was directed to proceed with him to Philadelphia.

It was a Monday evening and the Erickson Steamer was overcrowded. Wood could not secure a berth, which meant that he had to sit up all night without any sleep. When they arrived at Philadelphia his man was 'excited' and 'restless' and, if he was to get any sleep, a second man would have to be employed to watch Mazeres over night.

Unaware of the detectives, Mazeres took refuge in "a broken down kind of French shanty," which sold wines and liquors in " a very common locality." His address was at 526 Locust Street, between 5th and 6th Streets. Wood, on the other hand, boarded at the Arah St Hotel, Delaware Avenue. He told his superiors that he was afraid that the suspect had "become a little uneasy running across me so often."

The following day Mazeres got a job cleaning silver at the West End Hotel. He was trying to save some money to pay his way to New York. Detective Wood in the meantime hired an assistant at $2.50 per day and sought approval for his outlay. "I am sorry that I have had to employ help," he said, "but one man can't follow up this son of a B --." He then forwarded a report to his employers:

James H. Wood to Messrs Smith, Pierson and West
Philadelphia
July 7th 1876

" The man who in Charleston called himself (so I understand) E. Pinatel and took passage in the steamer "Sea Gull" for Baltimore, is, I think, a Frenchman, although he looks more like an Italian. He entered his name on a Steamer as Philip Mazeres.

He is about 5 feet in height and slightly stooping shoulders - Black hair; crisp, curly black beard, very slightly mixed with grey black eyes and large red nose. Glances sneakingly and suspiciously, has a slouching sailor walk, but gets along very rapidly without seeming to do so.

His manner is usually very quiet and he does not apparently appear to be interested in anything that is occurring about him.

If he had a monkey and an organ he would be a perfect picture of an Italian organ grinder. If there are any points that I have omitted, write me and I will furnish them.

It is a very hard matter to keep this man under observation without alarming him, and if ever he does become alarmed he will be off, certain as I can't arrest him and sooner or later he would be able to dodge me. So from the nature of the case there has to be two of us constantly dogging him at long distances

According to your directions, I am managing the matter at as little expense as possible.

Very truly yours

James .H. Wood

He sleeps and has his chest at a disreputable French wine shop, but may be off at any moment.

I forgot in the description to say that Mazares appears to be about 45 years old.

From the dispatches it became evident that something was wrong with the police side of things. The *Glynliffon* had left for Dublin and Walker regretted the fact that he had not interviewed captain Tullock. On July 7th, 1876, he ventured to say:

"...I might have acted more efficiently in this matter, perhaps, had I been furnished with a description of the men who left the "*Caswell*" off the La Plata: which descriptions I presume, the witness John Dunne could have furnished"

The following day (the 8th) no less than three reports emanated from the pen of detective Wood, who was shadowing Mazeres in Philadelphia. On the 10th of July the New York office felt that there was something wrong, particularly when it had been casually learned that Pinatel arrived at New York while he was still purportedly under surveillance in Philadelphia. At this point Thornton decided to re-read Walker's dispatches. That done, he went forthwith to check out the Firm of Parodi Mina and Co., the Petroleum exporters. He soon learned from Mr Parodi, that he knew Pinatel in Genoa and Marseilles, where Mina formerly carried on business. Mr. M. Mina confirmed this. Thornton began to appreciate the regard in which

155

his employers held Pinatel. He was duly informed that Pinatel -- no matter what the Masons chose to think of him - was "a well educated man, who spoke several languages, and was once in good circumstances: but was always an extravagant man."

From all the circumstances it now became evident that Pinatel, however dodgy, could not be one of the Pistorias. The following day (the 11th July, '86) Edward Thornton (K.G.B.) was constrained to admit that "Mr Consul Walker must have been mistaken about the man Philip Mazeres, whom I have caused to be watched at his suggestion, and that the man whom he originally saw and suspected is now in New York under the name he gave at first, E. Pinatel."

With that the detectives watching Mazeres were withdrawn forthwith, even though some suspicion still attached to Pinatel. On July 18th Pinatel boarded a steamer called the *Spaniard* bound for Liverpool, and Thornton at last conceded: "I am confident that he had nothing to do with the *Caswell*." Elsewhere, however, he thought that if Pinatel was Pistoria, he might still have traveled to England: "Such temerity on the part of criminals," he wrote, "is not without precedent." Whatever his stratagems and difficulties, Pinatel was not Joseph Pistoria and the notion that he was eventually floated into that bottomless ocean of "mistaken identities."

A Man Named Clayton

By April '77 the steam had all but gone out of the search for the Pistorias. There was a temptation to grasp at straws and the suspicion that fell on Clayton proved it. Clayton first came under notice when he shipped on the coal Schooner 'J. McManamey'. He had been cleared for Port Johnston and thence to Boston. For some time he stayed in a Sailor's Boarding House on Cherry Street, New York, an establishment run by James Galvin. Clayton was described as follows:

> "He is about 38 or 40 years old, about 5 ft 10 inches in height, medium build very dark swarthy complexion, blackened hair and dark eyes, high cheek bones, thick broad neck. The fleshy part of his cheeks hang down and stick out from the back part of his cheeks very much. Wears short black beard and moustache around the chin, and mouth cheeks shaved clean. He has two teeth out in the upper and lower front of his mouth and one single tooth stands in lower front. He stammers very much in his speech. Has had his left leg broken and walks a little stiff in consequence."

Clayton was also described as somewhat morose and singular in his habits, given to perambulating with his head down and, according to the report, casting "furtive glances at each and everyone who comes near him." Moreover, " His eyes are continually on the move and he has a bad sinister expression -- and seems to be ill at ease."

It was only to be expected that seamen everywhere would have strong opinions on the issues raised in the trial and execution of Bombos. The suspect Clayton entertained strong opinions, or maybe it was more 'how' he said things rather than 'what' he said. Be that as it may, on Sunday April 8th a fellow lodger heard Clayton say that he knew the crew of the *Caswell*. The Captain, he claimed, was a "very hard man." He starved and "worked his men to death", and otherwise treated them very badly. Clayton also claimed that if any captain treated him in that way, he would cut his throat. When asked how he knew about the *Caswell*, he said that he had read about it in the papers. The problem with this reply was that Clayton was known to be unable to read.

Another lodger, Thomas Edwards, asked him more directly if he had ever been on board the *Caswell*. He replied "Yes" instantly, then "No." This response was relayed to the proprietor and it wasn't long before police constable Brown appeared in full regalia. It was a Sunday and when Clayton saw him, he became excited and subsequently urged Mr Galvin to get him a ship as soon as possible, as he wanted "to get away."

On April 10,1877, the British Consul General in New York was the recipient of good news. He received a report from M.D.G. McKelvey, a detective police agent 'of good standing in this city', which directly fingered Clayton ('an Italian or Greek') as Joseph Pistoria. McKelvey followed Clayton everywhere. "I will cause his movements to be watched," he said, " until I shall have received such instructions -- if any -- as the Lord Lieutenant may be pleased to give me in reference to this matter."

It took a month before Clayton's description was sent to the Foreign Office, thence to the Board of Trade, and thence to the Home Office. Things were so unsatisfactory that the Board of Trade timorously sugges-ted to the Under Secretary at the Home Office -- that "it will save time if the Home Office will communicate directly with the Foreign Office." Papers were then sent to the Irish Government to ask Carrick and Dunne if the description of Clayton corresponded to that of the mutineers. On May 3rd Dublin Castle replied: "The man Clayton may be Joseph Pist-oria," although "the resemblance is little more than general." Shortly afterwards -- and on more detailed enquiry-- it was realised that Clayton was a bad prospect, and the matter was dropped as speedily as it had begun. Everything was set at naught, and interest in the Pistorias went into severe decline.

Two Norfolk Men From Wexford.

A year later (in August '78) all eyes were focused on San Martin in the Province of Buenos Aires, and more particularly on the boarding establishment of one John Murphy. The consulate's agents were resolute; two men calling themselves "Jasper Kelsoe and William Kelsoe, Norfolk men," were none other than the Pistoria brothers in disguise. Mr Murphy was proving to be irritatingly difficult, and between May and September of '78 he tried without success to convince Her Majesty's Consulate that he never knew any Kelsoes from Norfolk or elsewhere, and that neither of the Kelsoes, to his knowledge, had ever graced his establishment.

A matter that should have been cleared up on one visit was now being spun out interminably. The set-off extended into July before the penny dropped. Having made every inquiry in the locality, a dispatch confessed:

> " I think ...there must be some mistake about this information as it would
> be quite impossible for two foreigners whose persons were so well-known
> here, and whose knowledge of English so very limited, to pass themselves
> off as Englishmen, and unknowingly adopt the same surname, while mutu-
> ally denying their knowledge of each other. Besides, they would not ventu-
> re to reside in this country, where they would be liable to recognition, their
> lives being at stake."

This made perfect sense. What was confusing was how the suspicion fell on Mr Murphy's inmates in the first place. Upon enquiry it was ascertained that the wild goose chase had apparently begun in Wexford where the resident magistrate E.F. Ryan in responding to an order for information returned the following report.

Wexford
May 4th 1878

> "A respectable young farmer who resided for some time in South America,
> and who has at present friends residing there, informed me that he has
> received positive information from a friend that two of the Maltese men
> who took part in the mutiny and murder ...are now living at Salto on the
> *Entrancia* of Le Martin in the province of Buenos Ayres - that they have
> assumed the names of Jackie Kehoe and William Kehoe - state they are

Wexford men and profess to be strangers to each other, although really brothers.

Informant states that his sole object in giving this information, is in the interests of Justice and humanity, but he declines to give the name of the person from whom he received it. This is of course very vague, but I think it my duty -- such as it is -- to lay it before government in order that it may, should it think proper, instruct its representative in the Argentine Republic to make inquiry into the matter

E.F. Ryan RM

I have written to the Resident Magistrate in Cork, where the offence was tried, on the above subject.

The Government got its bureaucratic hands on this report and relayed it throughout the length and breadth of the relevant consulates and their departments. Unfortunately, these relays were in longhand. And what with dispatches and correspondence floating between Dublin Castle, the intermediary offices, and Buenos Aires, the reference to the suspect mutineers became somewhat blurred. "Jackie Kehoe and William Kehoe, Wexford men" sooner, rather than later, was transcribed into "Jasper Kelsoe and William Kelsoe, Norfolk men."

"Jackie Kehoe and William Kehoe, Wexford men"
"Jasper Kelsoe and William Kelsoe, Norfolk men."

When one looks closely at these words, especially when written in a longhand in which a 'h' looks ambiguously like an 'l' and a 'We' looks like a 'No', and '-ford' looks like '-folk', one can see how similar they are, and how easily mistakes could be made. Unfortunately, these mistakes translated themselves into a nonsense for which Mr Murphy could not be held responsible.

This was the third and last suspect throughout the period. Meanwhile the following descriptions had at long last been circulated of the wanted mutineers.

Joseph Pistoria: aged 40, 5' 7", stout build, dark complexion, black-haired, eyes black with Tattoo marks either on one arm, or on both, with mark in form of a cross under the right ear;
Dressed with a grey silken cap, blue plaid navy coat and brown trousers; Maltese and brought up in Genoa, with top of head very bald and a very large growth of hair on his body

Hue And Cry The *Caswell*

Gasper Pistoria: aged 30, 5 ' 6", medium built, dark complexion and black
hair and eyes black; with tattoo marks on left hand forming a five-pointed
cross;
Dressed in felt "tilly-cock" hat, black coated, grey plaid trousers;
Maltese and brought up in Genoa;
Slightly bald on top of head and a very large growth of hair on his body.

These descriptions were taken from the witnesses who attended the
Bombos trial. And after three long years the hard questions had to be
asked. Would the Pistoria brothers ever surface? Officially the search
had been abandoned. Bombos had been hanged and what good was a
description in parts of the world that weren't even policed! The truth is
that people generally go about their daily business and rarely have time
for local police matters, much less international concerns. Not only that,
but the witnesses in the case of the *Caswell* were inclined to put things
behind them and to get on with their lives. For most if not all of the
witnesses this meant a return to the sea.

In Carrick's case, for example, it meant making his way back to South
America to work a very lucrative contract he had secured in August. As a
Mate on board the *Valetto,* Carrick had seen guano phosphate shipped off
the coast of Patagonia and discharged in Birkenhead. Captain Carlen, the
owner of the *Jorgen Bruhn,* had a great need for such guano and made
Carrick an offer, which he couldn't refuse. Carrick in essence agreed to
pilot the *Jorgen Bruhn* to a little known Patagonian site to fetch and load
a shipful of phosphate. He would then deliver it to a specified destination.
Everything depended upon Carrick's ability to find the inlet in Patagonia,
a Ulyssian task, which to a navigator like the cannie Scot, was child's
play. But he would have to keep his wits about him and he needed both
time and resources to search the Patagonian coastline. The 'consideration'
for this venture meant that Carrick was to be paid £6 sterling per month
from the time of sailing to the time of arrival at the port of discharge, plus
a gratuity of four shillings per ton delivered. Half the monthly payments
were to be paid to Carrick's wife. Obviously, time and tonnage were
important items in the calculus of Carrick's income -- an income, which
incidentally, was no mean achievement for an 'ordinary' seaman.

In the meantime, Carrick was getting on with his life. And even if his
wife and family were at home in Liverpool, it didn't mean that he never
socialized or went out for a meal. On January 21, 1879, he was doing just
that. He was relaxing in a café in Monte Video when for a moment the
sight of stranger suddenly arrested him, someone whom he thought he
knew. For a split second he was riveted to his seat; he was certain he had
seen one of the Pistorias. He continued casually as if nothing had happen-

ed; but before he could look again, the suspect had vanished. However it happened, it shocked and surprised Carrick. Maybe it was no more than a momentary glimpse. Maybe Carrick didn't want to be reminded of other days – days, which thankfully, he had forgotten - days that he would gladly have left in the dormant depths of oblivion. Whatever the reason, he did not pursue the matter further. He carried his shock out of doors, and nothing further came of the incident. It was like some apparition out of Hamlet: a ghost had made its entrance and its exit all at once.

A week later, however, on January 27th, as he was making his way by boat to board a German barque called the Maria, he saw before his eyes -- in the same little boat in fact! -- one Giuseppe Pistoria. Both of them were coincidentally serving on the same ship, but as yet Pistoria, who was a rigger, did not recognise him. Carrick scanned for sight of Gaspari, but he was nowhere to be seen. He managed as best he could to avoid eye contact with Giuseppe and to say as little as possible for fear he might be recognised. He remained 'stumm,' until he had an opportunity to disembark, when he duly summoned the assistance of the consular authorities. Giuseppe was duly arrested. He offered no resistance when confronted, and was quietly taken into custody.

On the 1st of February 1879, Theodore Lemm, acting British Consul at the port of Monte Video, learned that a man called Muschara was confined in the local Prison. He was being accused of causing mutiny on the *Caswell* three years earlier. James Carrick was his accuser. So, too, was Daniel Johnson, the 36-year-old Shipping Master at Buenos Aires, who, incidentally, didn't have to look up his records, for he also recognised Joseph. All he needed from the records was the date, the 19th of September '75 -- the date he enlisted the Pistorias on board the *Caswell*. He double-checked, just to make sure. No; there was no mistake; it was the one and only Joseph Pistoria. In Joseph's presence the Clerk at the Consulate, Mr Sweetland, carefully took down the depositions of Carrick and Johnson. They were then signed and read over to the prisoner by Theodore Lemm. The prisoner was then invited to ask whatever questions he wished, but he wasn't bothered with legalities.

"What became of all the rest on board the *Caswell*?" he asked Carrick casually.

"All the English and one of the Greeks reached home," said Carrick.

The prisoner was then asked if he wanted to ask Daniel Johnson any questions, to which he replied: "No Sir"

Subsistence Allowance

Every telegraph office in Christendom decoded the news. The Foreign Office, the Home Office, the Board of Trade, the Consulates, Customs, Police Stations, and the Admiralty -- all were informed of the capture. It was a time to rejoice, for justice was going to be done. The problem for Carrick -- now that he had a lucrative contract in tow -- was the cost of Justice. He knew he couldn't be in two places at the one time: it was either Queenstown or the coast of Patagonia — it couldn't be both. As a witness he knew he would be detained for months in Cork. He had been there before. Surely he would now have to abandon his contract! Carlen would contract elsewhere. He was beginning to feel lucky that there were no penalty clauses in the contract, no punitive damages for unilaterally reneging on the deal. But would he be sued, and would he be liable for the breach?

Increasingly, Carrick began to doubt. Even if his mind shied away from notions of justice or revenge, he had nothing to reproach himself with. The world knew he had done his duty several times over. He was very active in the counter-mutiny, where he showed leadership and courage; he brought the *Caswell* safely to Queenstown and protected her cargo. He not only saved the lives of the men on board a ship that had only a third of its crew, but he salvaged a cargo valued at £10,000, and reimbursed the owners. He had given evidence against Bombos and was made part of his execution. Here he was again, caught to give evidence that would surely lead to another execution, and this time he was solely responsible for the capture and arrest of Joseph Pistoria. No; he had nothing to reproach himself with. Doubtless, on the question of duty, no man could criticise him. But having said that, the nagging concern persisted: why should justice cost him so much? So much more than anyone else? These losses would affect him,and they would also affect his wife and family in Liverpool. More and more James Carrick began to focus on his first concern -- How was he going to recoup his considerable losses?

On February 5th a transmission from Her Majesty's Minister at Buenos Aires to the Foreign Office stated the dilemma clearly: "Joseph Pistoria has been captured at the instance of James Carrick who refuses to return to England without indemnity. Enquire what answer should we return. Pressing." This was to set the tone to, and define the tensions in, an

interesting correspondence between Carrick and the authorities -- a correspondence which lasted right up to the trial of Giuseppe Pistoria.

The following day the Buenos Aires Office received the following reply:

> "Send Pistoria and Carrick to England -- Promise Carrick expenses and
> indemnity not exceeding £200 in all.... Report name of ship bringing
> prisoner, and port of arrival here. Warrant out"

For the next 10 days there was much ado about extraditing Pistoria. The
Monte Video authorities were reluctant to surrender him. Eventually they
did; but even in the thick of the negotiations there was always room in the
dispatches to seek advice regarding the promise to pay Carrick £200 by
way of indemnity. By April (17th) Pistoria was handed over, the Foreign
Office directing the Home Office to "... express concurrence in proposed
approval" to pay Carrick the £200. The following day Lemm, the Acting
British Consul in Buenos Aires, packed Pistoria and Carrick off to England and assured the Home Office that Carrick "will be indemnified in the
sum of two hundred pounds, after having given his evidence in England."

Carrick, it seems, wasn't very happy and was growing impatient with the
replies. He had been strongly advised to write to Cross at the Home Office
regarding his claims to compensation. He duly wrote the following letters,
sent respectively to the Home Office and the Foreign Office:

12 Bridgewater Street,
Liverpool
22 April '79

Rt. Hon R. A. Cross,
Home Secretary.

Dear Sir,

I beg to call your attention to my position in regard to the *Caswell*
mutiny and ask her Majesty's Government to kindly allow me subsistence
money in addition to the £200, promised by the Marquis of Salisbury on my
leaving my ship at Monte Video. I enclose my agreement with the
Merchant and Captain of said vessel by which you will see, that I was in
receipt of £6 - per month wages and was to receive a bonus of four shillings
a ton of Guano phosphate, on the completion of the voyage. As the vessel

would carry 1200 tons I reckoned my profit on the voyage would have been £240 - besides my wages, as I will be detained until after the July Assizes, and I must eat whether in Ireland or Liverpool. It will be a serious loss to me if I do not obtain the necessary money for subsistence.

I also send you a newspaper report of a presentation made to me at The Town Hall, and hope that you will grant my humble petition

Your obedient servant,

James Carrick

PS I have also written to the Foreign Secretary on this matter.

22nd April '79
To the Marquis of Salisbury,
Foreign Secretary

My Lord

I beg to call your Lordship's attention to my position in the *Caswell* mutiny prosecution, and to ask Her Majesty's Government to kindly allow me subsistence money in addition to the £200 that your Lordship promised on my leaving my ship at Montevideo. I enclose my agreement with the merchant and captain of the vessel by which it will be seen that I was in receipt of £6 per month, and was to receive at the end of the voyage a Bonus of four shillings per ton of Guano phosphate. the vessel carrying 1200 tons would have yielded me £240 profit besides my wages. As I am detained here until after the July Court, it will be a serious loss to me unless I get subsistence money. I have a wife and child to keep. And we must all eat. I have also written to Mr Cross on this matter, as I am not sure whether He or your Lordship will now have to deal with it. I also send you a newspaper report, of a medal presentation to me in the town hall here the other day. Hoping you will grant my humble petition.

I remain your humble servant

James Carrick.

Carrick had been presented with a silver medal for "heroic conduct." The presentation was made at the annual meeting of the Liverpool Mercantile Marine Service Association. And when one thinks about it, it was a medal he richly deserved. He had not only taken part in the counter-mutiny, which freed the *Caswell*, but he was one of those who predicted the fiasco in the first place. The only doubt about his heroism that one could entertain arose from the distinct possibility that he had caused the mutiny or -- by his loose talk amongst the Greeks -- contributed to it. Certainly the owners had good reason to be pleased. Carrick had not only saved their ship but their cargo as well. He returned both ship and cargo to the safety of the *Caswell's* owners. Similarly, the authorities had to be pleased with his evidence, his conduct, and his vigilance. And, needless to say, without Carrick neither Bombos nor Pistoria would ever have been brought to justice. He was, after all, singled out for his heroism and for his reward!

All in all the *Caswell* and its cargo was worth at least £20,000 pounds in the currency of the 1870s; but as Captain Hatfield, who made the presentation, pointed out - Carrick "had only as yet received a paltry £5 note." Initially it was thought that the silver medal, if accompanied with £100.00, would have made a suitable presentation. After a year's haggling between the lawyers and the underwriters, however, the lawyers claimed their fees, and Carrick was left with an unflattering £5.

In presenting the medal the Lord Mayor of Liverpool mentioned how much they all admired the manner in which Carrick had identified Pistoria, and how 'at considerable risk and inconvenience to himself,' he assisted in bringing the foreigners to justice.

> "He trusted that the knowledge of this would spread over the world, and that those who sailed in our ships, whether foreigners or not would learn that, at any rate, as long as some Englishmen were on Board they could not commit these crimes with impunity, and that Englishmen were always prepared to defend, at any risk and at any hazard the lives of themselves and their fellow-subjects."

The press report of the event also mentioned that "great credit" was also due to MacGregor, who struck the first blow (The *Times* April 21st, 1879).

* * *

Towards the end of April (the 28th) it was agreed to pay Carrick 'subsistence money pending the trial of Pistoria'. The Irish Government to whom a similar application for money was made, proposed to pay the hero of the *Caswell* 5/- (shillings) a day 'while detained on shore, (and) for the purpose of giving evidence.' The missive also made it clear that "the money so paid is wholly irrespective of any promise which may have been made to Carrick by the directions of the Secretary of State for Foreign Affairs: that being a matter with which the Irish government has no concern'.

Hue And Cry The *Caswell*

By early May Carrick acknowledged 'with thanks' the 5/- per day, and he trusted that the Government would 'consider that he is entitled also to compensation for loss of wages'.

There was no denying it; matters were getting tacky, so Carrick wrote another letter. This time it was sent to the Crown Solicitor whom, he claimed, did not -- or could not – 'give me a direct answer'. His use of the word 'did' and the word 'could' in the last sentence were crossed through, indicating that he did not know which to use. Between May and August there was much prevarication but little by way of a direct solution to the problem.

Since reaching Ireland he had been paid 5/- per day by the Irish Government. It was now agreed that he would be paid £200 sterling, but this had not been paid as yet, and he still insisted that he should be paid a wage, which up to 31st of July came to £36.16. On August 5th the Foreign Office required an answer: "Shall the treasury be asked to pay him £200 and Carrick be informed that his claim to £36.16 cannot be entertained?"

An irksome reminder from Carrick (on August 9th) stated: "I shall be glad to receive payment for my claim for services in relation to the *Caswell* mutiny case, the particulars of which I delivered to the Marquis of Salisbury (at the Home Office) on the 31st ult…"

In August (14th) Carrick collected the outstanding £200, but there was no reference to the further sum of £36.16. A week later (21st) he wrote another letter to the Home Office. This would be his final throw of the dice as far as his personal losses were concerned.

> 21 August 1879
>
> The Secretary of State,
> Home Department,
> Whitehall,
> London
>
> Sir
>
> ### THE CASWELL MUTINY
>
> I am obliged by your communication bearing date the 19th instant which was delivered only today and already I had received from the Treasury an order for the £200 due to me, but I respectfully beg to urge that I am fairly entitled to the further sum of £36.16.0 as the equivalent of my wages which I have lost by reason of the Consul at Monte Video having compelled me to leave

my ship where I received £6 per month pay independently of a bonus for special services of 4/- per ton on the cargo the vessel was to load and the £200 merely represented the equivalent of the latter. If you think it right that I should be damnified because I was required as a witness I suppose I must submit but if on the other hand you think I should be dealt with equitably I shall place before you unequivocal proof of what my position in the ship was and what I have lost by being taken from my employ and shall be perfectly content then to leave the matter absolutely in your hands.

I am, Sir,

Your obedient servant

James Carrick

12 Bridgewater Street,
Liverpool

One can only surmise that, before giving evidence against Giuseppe Pistoria, the hero of the *Caswell* mutiny received the sum of £36.16 which was due and owing.

======

Chapter 10

The Trial Of
Francesco Moschara
(*Alias* Joseph Pistoria)

GONZALO:

I have great comfort from this fellow: methinks he
hath no drowning mark upon him; his complexion is
perfect gallows. Stand fast, good Fate, to his
hanging: make the rope of his destiny our cable,
for our own doth little advantage. If he be not
born to be hanged, our case is miserable.

Shakespeare | The Tempest | Act 1, Scene 1

The Victorians, always aware of the importance of putting things in
their proper place, reasoned that any person not a British subject who
had committed a crime on board a British ship, had to be tried in the
place at which the ship first arrived after the crime. This meant, in
effect, that jurisdiction was given to the Cork courts to hear the case
in the same way as they would if the offence had been committed in
Cork harbour. Accordingly an application was made in Liverpool for
an order that the prisoner to be handed over to the Irish Constabulary
and that he be conveyed to Cork and put on his trial there.

After three long years of waiting, the process, once begun, was
remarkably fast. First spotted on January 21st 1879, Pistoria was
arrested a week later (on the 27th), and within two months (on

The Trial of Francesco Moschara

March20th) the *Araucania* arrived in Liverpool. bearing both Carrick and Pistoria. A fortnight later (on April fool's day) Pistoria was delivered over to the Irish authorities, and by July 24th he would be tried and convicted. A month later -- almost to the day (August 25th) -- he would be hanged. All these events were accomplished. therefore, within the space of eight months.

In the meantime the *Times* reported the capture of the man 'who was wanted since 1876'. He now had to face the Queenstown magistrates. before whom he was duly charged - as was Bombos - with the murder of George Edward Best. William Wilson, Allan McLean, and Edward Griffiths. He was then returned for trial on July 22nd at a Special Commission before Judge Barry. He was found guilty of the murder of one William Wilson. He was sentenced to be hanged in Cork County Gaol on August 25. his body to be buried within its precincts.

The Times reported:

> "The prisoner now admits he is a Sicilian and that his real name is Francesco Moschera. He is about 42. of short stature, and squarely built. He speaks and understands English. on this account there was no necessity for an interpreter. He paid great attention to the evidence of Carrick and frequently shook his head when references were made to his part in the affair."

The claim to being a Sicilian yet again placed a question mark over the identity of the Pistorias. The matter had to be cleared up. and there were several reasons for doing so. Pistoria would have to dispose of his property. he was likely to make a Petition. and he would need the assistance of the Italian Consul. Accordingly. the Italian Consular Agent. Sir George Milero stated that Joseph Pistoria was none other than Francesco Moschara. He was 37 years old and was born at Acci Castello. which is situated at the foot of Mount Etna, Sicily. His father's name was also Joseph.

The Maltese community had become associated with murder and mutiny wherever the *Caswell* trials were mentioned. Not unreasonably. therefore, those who had the wider interest of the Maltese community at heart wished to redress this publicity by dissociating Malta from the exploits aboard the *Caswell*. In an attempt to redress this widespread slander the following letter was forwarded to the Editor of the Cork Examiner.

The Cork Examiner
Tuesday, July 29, 1879

The Trial of Francesco Moschara

The *Caswell* Mutiny

To the editor of the Cork Examiner

Dear Sir, I notice by your issue of yesterday the condemned prisoner, Francesco Moschara, is mentioned, as being a Maltese sailor, which I beg to state is totally false. Mr Reardon, prisoner's counsel, in addressing the jury on the prisoner's behalf, stated distinctly that the foreigners consisted of two Greeks, and two Sicilians, which was the prisoner and his brother. The prisoner also positively stated, whilst at Queenstown Bridewell, he was an Italian, born in Sicily, near Palermo; he also sent for the Italian Consul to get his advice and protection. His Consul then engaged Mr J.P. O'Connell to defend him.

Also during the trial the Italian Consul was always present to watch the proceedings. Therefore, if the prisoner was a Maltese he would be a British subject, and would not require the Italian authority's protection. And I should think it is the duty of the English Bar to ascertain his true nationality before allowing such reports to circulate. Therefore, I trust the Crown officers will investigate this matter and prove to the public the prisoner is not a Maltese. I have taken up this matter, as there are hundreds of Maltese sailors employed in the British Navy, also, in the mercantile marine service, where men's characters were never stained with such atrocious deeds. Therefore, Mr Editor, in order to remove this impression, I would thank you to give this insertion in your next issue.

I remain, dear Sir, yours respectfully

JUSTITIA

The Trial was intended to be an exact repetition of the Bombos trial, which meant that the same number of witnesses would be required to swear the same evidence. The question was, were the five survivors of the *Caswell* available? And where did they live?

1. James Carrick's family still lived at 12 Bridgewater Street, Liverpool. His availability was assured.

2. Charles McDonald lived at Sardinian Terrace Glasgow in 1876. In 1879 he lived at Cecilia Road, Hill Head, Glasgow. He was also available.

3. Peter MacGregor, the Carpenter, who had lived in 1876 at 13 Back Street, Dumbarton Renton, Dumbarton, now resided at Glasgow Road, Dumbarton. He was found to be working on shore and was

permanently located at the above address. He also made himself available.

4. John Dunne, who in 1876 had lived with his wife at 5 Cleardon Terrace, Kingstown, Bristol, still lived in Bristol but at number 10 Dale Street, St Paul's. On February 1st, 1878, he signed Articles and shipped on the "*La Zengara*" for the West Coast of Africa. He was due back around May of '79.

5. And Walter Ferguson lived at 13 Rockley Terrace, Hill Head, Glasgow. In 1876 he was a young apprentice on board the *Caswell*. In 1879 he was an apprentice on board the ship "*Ben Ledi*," and was expected very shortly to arrive in London from San Francisco.

In Mr Justice Barry, Bombos had drawn perhaps the best Judge on the Irish -- or any other -- Bench. It was said that everybody in Ireland knew 'Charlie' Barry or pretended to know him. He was known alike in London and Dublin, and knew every Derby winner past, present and to come. He had oodles of talents, but none so envied as his unerring ability to inspire affection. Charles Robert Barry had done the rounds for a man in his position. He matriculated in Dublin University in 1840 and was called to the Irish Bar in 1848. He was a Roman ('Castle') Catholic, with a liberal political streak that carried him to Westminster as the representative for Dungarvan. He also served as solicitor-general (1868) and Attorney-General (1870). And by all accounts he was happily married. Now in his mid-fifties, he was fated to outlive the criminal he was to sentence to death by over twenty years.

Throughout the trial Pistoria took up more or less where Bombos had left off. The defence -- apart from denying the worst aspects of the charges against him -- had to rely totally upon the terror created by Big George Peno, in whose presence everyone had to follow orders. As before this was impossible to prove. Failing that, the defence had to fall back upon Pistoria's deeds of mercy -- deeds which had saved the English from further calamity. But again this hardly constituted a defence. The most that it could achieve was by way of mitigation and this was in the hands of the Judge and the Lord Lieutenant.

Cross-examined by counsel for Pistoria, Carrick admitted that some days before Giuseppe and his brother left the vessel, they had warned the English to look out for their lives, as Big George intended to kill them. Carrick also said that it was he who dictated the letter given to the Pistorias in which he tried to give both of them a "good character." Under the circumstances in which it was written, it was always of questionable merit to the defence. But why defence counsel denied that it was ever written, and why he called it a 'fabrication' was never clarified. Perhaps defence counsel thought that by admitting to such a letter in the first place, the Pistorias were seeking to be pardoned for wrongs they had committed. As such the jury would unfortunately see the letter as an admission of guilt, rather than as an explanation of the circumstances that provoked the mutiny.

As a legal document it could be argued that it was written in fear and therefore inadmissible or, at least, that it did not validly represent what it purported to represent. By admitting the letter, however, it would more than likely allow the jury to ponder whether the foreigners actually mutinied against the English or against the captain. By seeking the approval of Carrick and Dunne, the letter might well have made the jury think twice about how and why the mutiny started. The main line of antipathy had at all times been drawn between the English and their Captain. How the Greeks got so caught up in it, was not only at the heart of whatever defence they might muster but was in itself something of a mystery. Was it the case that Carrick and Dunne had stirred up hatred between the 'illiterate' foreigners and the captain? If not, why did the Pistorias seek Carrick's approval when leaving the *Caswell*? Maybe it was an admission that they sought rather than a pardon?

Under cross-examination Carrick was asked what, if anything, the logbook might contain. "In the logbook that is lost ", he replied, "there would have been an account of my being kept in irons." He did not elucidate further, save to say that he had not seen it since the day Big George was killed. But pressed on this, he then said he had not seen it since the day the captain was killed - which is when Bombos claimed that he (Carrick) had thrown it overboard.

Dunne's evidence supported Carrick's. He admitted that he had felt the captain's wrath, and that he had seen the butt of a revolver sticking out of the captain's pocket. When asked why he thought the captain came loaded with a revolver to give orders to his crew, he remembered the captain saying that he was not a man to go among a lot of Greeks without being armed. Was this also an oblique reference to the Lennie mutiny?

When the case for the Crown closed, defence counsel, Mr. Reardon Q.C., addressed the jury on behalf of the prisoner in much the same terms as had been done at Bombos' trial, but with a little more drama. He recalled how the three Englishmen were put in irons by the captain. He commented at length on the fact that the logbook disappeared after the English got possession of the ship, so that no record now remained of the punishment inflicted on the Englishmen before the massacre or the reason why such punishment became necessary. He asked the jury to believe that the letter, alleged to have been given as a certificate to the two Pistorias , was in fact a fabrication concocted by Carrick and Dunne to protect themselves. In the light of Bombos' statement (See Appendix A), this assertion - that the letter(s) was a fabrication - is hardly sustainable. It was the only imponderable in what was, after all, a very simple murder case. Everyone agreed that at least one letter was written, so why did Pistoria's counsel deny it?

In his concluding remarks, counsel for Pistoria asked the jury to accept that there was enough doubt to warrant the acquittal of the prisoner.

In his summation Mr Murphy, Q.C for the prosecution said that he hoped the jury would pay the same attention to him as they had paid to the very able speech advanced 'by his learned friend'. A great deal had been said; and very properly said as to the importance of the case they were investigating. But all the public wanted was justice -- justice for the 'slaughter' done on board the *Caswell*.

Like Bombos, Pistoria now found himself between a rock and a hard place. To take the stand meant that he would have to explain his actions on board the *Caswell* -- not an easy task, even with the best of English at his disposal. His counsel most likely advised him not to take the stand. But was there a price to be paid for such a tactic?

It is true that in English law there is no compunction on a defendant to get into the witness box and defend himself. At least that's the theory. But if an accused person wants the Jury to think well of him, while at the same time refusing to deny his crimes personally before them and his accusers, no matter how couched in the letter of the law, that Jury will think - or be disposed to think - the worst of him.

The prosecution made full use of this in the remarks made by Mr Murphy Q.C., when he said:

The Trial of Francesco Moschara

"The prisoner's mouth was not closed, and it was the great point of
English law that it would not compel him to make his defence, but it
made the public prosecute him; and bring the crime home to him by
evidence. If he did make a defence, he could have given his own
account of the transaction, or give an explanation of the charges made
against him. As to the insinuation that some of the witnesses examined
against him might have committed that crime themselves, counsel
scouted such an idea, and pointed to different portions of the evidence
in support of the theory of the Crown as to the guilt of the prisoner".

Because of Pistoria's greater commitment to the mutiny, he stood a
worse chance of winning his case than did Bombos. But at least in
Pistoria's case the real issues had been put to the Jury. Either the
English, who might well have mutinied themselves, provoked the
impressionable foreigners to do their dirty work for them, or the
Greeks and the Maltese were simply irrational monsters. If they were
monsters, why were they so lax with Carrick, Dunne and MacGregor?
Why had they not killed all the crew? It was said in this respect that
they spared the remainder because without their aid they could not
navigate the *Caswell*. Whatever the reason, surely this was a spurious
one; for If there was a real shortage of manpower, why were the Pistorias allowed to leave? No one even raised an objection to their
departure. And why, if they simply wanted to plunder the ship, did
they leave after they conquered it? Many of these considerations did
not make sense.

If, on the other hand, the English had skilfully taunted the unsuspect-
ing Greeks and Maltese, and had, at the same time, enlisted the natural
bellicosity of the captain to their aid - if, indeed, the unthinkable had
happened, and the English, in their fear and insecurity, had manipul-
ated the foreigners to mutiny against their captain and officers, how
could a tribunal so blunt as a criminal court of law distinguish the
guilty from the 'found guilty?'

Counsel for the Crown, Mr Murphy; put it plainly to the jury:

"What would be the feelings of the jury if they allowed this man, to
whom guilt had been brought home by the clearest and most irresistible
evidence that had ever been witnessed in a court of Justice - what would
be their feelings if they allowed him to go free? If they saw foul crime
committed and passed it by without saying anything, they became
participators in it themselves. If the jury disregarded the evidence of the
men who had been examined, if they put it aside and looked upon them
as foul murderers and perjurers, then they should acquit the prisoner;

174

but if they believed the evidence of such men as Carrick and MacGregor, they should find him guilty."

The brunt of the evidence against Pistoria revolved around the following concerns:

1. He ran from the wheel and shot the captain twice in the head (MacGregor). And if the others did not see this, they heard the shot and 'the cry of the captain.'

2. He shot the first mate who was crying out for mercy -- 'Not me, Joseph, Not me, Joseph,' to which Joseph replied 'Yes, you son of a sea cook'. (These words were heard even if the occasion was not seen by MacGregor and Carrick)

3. He shot the second mate in the arm (Ferguson). He called the Steward and fired twice at him, and then three times at him, chasing him into the arms of Big George who "cut the heart out of him." (MacGregor) "The Steward was shot in the head by Joseph" (Ferguson).

4. He forced MacGregor to his knees to swear loyalty to the mutineers (MacGregor, Ferguson, Carrick and Dunne)

5. He kicked the black cook in the head before throwing his body overboard.

6. He helped to throw the four bodies overboard.

The Judge's Summary

His Lordship told the jury that they were all "reasonable, rational men" and that they ought to " be satisfied beyond all reasonable doubt of the prisoner's guilt." He then pointed out that Pistoria was charged with having taken an active part in "one of the most terrible tragedies that was ever laid before a court of justice."

"He was charged with participating in the murder of four fellow beings, each within a few moments of the other, four transactions of which they had heard so much in detail could not have occupied many minutes to accomplish. Though the prisoner was accused with participating in the murder of four persons, he was now only formally charged with one, namely, the murder of William Wilson, the first mate. But it would be merely cavilling with the question and raising vague and perplexing

The Trial of Francesco Moschara

> crotchets to suggest that the tone of these transactions could be separated from the other. They were all one transaction, and the actors in one murder must have been engaged in them all."

His lordship then began to review the evidence minutely, and cleared away such difficulties as might have presented themselves to the minds of the jury.

The evidence in the case, he continued, was direct -- not circumstantial -- in its character, and four men came forward and stated that they saw with their own eyes the prisoner at the bar commit the crime laid to his charge, and it was for the jury to say whether they believed those men or not. If they did believe those witnesses they would be bound to convict the prisoner and, as he had already told them, if they had a reasonable doubt on their minds as to his guilt, they were bound to acquit him.

The jury retired at twenty-five minutes to seven to consider their verdict.

They soon returned and his lordship confessed that there was "one little matter" he had not mentioned. It appeared in the evidence, that Pistoria 'had saved the lives of the teenaged boys, MacDonald and Ferguson'. He also pointed out, however, that such evidence 'was not material to the issue now before the jury'.

The Verdict

After a further absence of twelve minutes the jury returned to court with a verdict of Guilty.

The prisoner, who during the earlier portion of the trial did not (according to the press) :-

> " appear much affected by the awful position in which he stood, was considerably moved during his lordships' charge to the jury, and seemed quite overcome when the verdict of the Crown put the usual question as to why sentence of death and execution should not be passed upon him, he appeared rather dazed and made no reply".

The Sentence

His Lordship then proceeded to pass the solemn sentence of death upon the prisoner. He said: -

The Trial of Francesco Moschara

"Joseph Pistoria, after a full and most patient trial, conducted according to the merciful laws of this country, in which you have had the benefit of the assistance of the most able advocate for your defence, you have been convicted by the jury of the wilful murder of this man Wilson.

No sane man who heard the evidence could hesitate for a moment to come to the conclusion of your guilt. You have been convicted of taking a prominent part in one of the most fearful tragedies of crime that has ever been disclosed in a court of justice. It is impossible to have listened to the narrative of the dreadful transaction, which converted that once peaceful ship on that day into a floating slaughterhouse, without feelings of horror and of awe.

It is not my purpose, it is not my duty to descant upon the enormity of your crime, or to add to the horror of the position in which you now stand - a convicted felon, awaiting the dreadful sentence of our law. That sentence it is now my fearful duty to pronounce upon you. Mercy in this world you cannot hope for, and I would recommend you to devote the short space of life that now remains to you in endeavouring to make your peace with that God whom you have so grievously offended.

His Lordship then assumed the black cap, and according to the usual form sentenced the prisoner to be hanged on Monday, August 25 within the precincts of the county Gaol.

With that the prisoner protested -

" It was to Nicholas I used the words - 'yes, you son of a sea cook' - and not to the chief mate. I would save the chief mate if I could, Sir, and I did stick up for all I could in the ship. It was Nicholas I wanted to kill when I saw him attacking the mate. I did what I could to save him, and I stood for the English and the ship. I did not raise a hand to the poor unfortunate man, but tried to save him"

His Lordship said - "Let him be removed now."

Joseph Pistoria was then removed.

======

Chapter 11

The Execution of
Francesco Moschara
(*Alias* Joseph Pistoria)

"On February 6, the four men on Pollard's boat , having
consumed the 'last morsel' of Samuel Reed, began to 'look
at each other with horrid thoughts in their minds,' according to one survivor, but we held our tongues. Then the
youngest of them, sixteen -year-old Charles Ramsdell,
uttered the unspeakable. They should cast lots, he said,
to see who would be killed so that the rest might live.

The drawing of lots in a survival situation had long been
an accepted custom of the sea..."

Nathaniel Philbrick: "In the Heart of the Sea,"
Publishers: Harper Collins, 2000

The Execution of Francesco Moschara
(*Alias* Joseph Pistoria)

Petitions

It was time for the petitions. One petition was signed by at least 34
persons including Members of Parliament, Justices of the Peace, Parish
Priests, and Patrick Kernan, a Huguenot.

Hitherto – and up to the time of his arrest in Monte Video -- he gave
the world to know that he was 'Giuseppe Pistoria' from Malta. Now he
'humbly prayed his Grace the Lord Lieutenant' that he was Francesco
Moschara, 'a native of Neu Castells in Sicily'. In the body of his petition
he blamed the Greeks for the mutiny, especially their ringleader 'a desp-
erate character named George Peno', under whose sole compulsion he
acted 'throughout that dreadful transaction'.

Amongst the reasons he felt he was deserving of mercy was the part he
played in saving the carpenter from certain death. When the Greeks tried
to force open the door and gain entry to the carpenter's house, he prevailed upon them to desist. The English, particularly John Dunne, acknowledged this virtuous deed. Moreover, practically everyone knew that he
also saved the lives of the two teenaged apprentices. So, if he had behav-
ed like a brute, he had also shown considerable restraint and mercy.

Pistoria claimed that he was the only foreigner on board who was able to
speak English and that he acted as an interpreter for the Greeks, and that
despite the threats of the Greeks, he managed the ship safely. Like Bombos, he reckoned that after the mutiny, George Peno was determined to
kill the remaining English, then sell or scuttle the ship when he arrived in
Greece. Pistoria claimed that he frustrated Peno in this and other enterprises : he restrained Peno from killing the English and by his diplomacy
had prevented him from scuttling the ship. He had also put the English
on their guard before he himself and his brother quit the *Caswell*.

Giuseppe Pistoria was a man who had done both vicious and virtuous things
in the same abnormal context, and the feeling in Cork city was such that most
people were a little nauseous at the thought of repeating a *Caswell* hanging.
In fairness to Mr Justice Barry, a most affable Judge , he, more than anyone ,
took the time to plead the merits of Pistoria's otherwise hopeless case. In
his longhand report to the Lord Lieutenant (dated August 11,1879), he started by setting out the facts of the case. Then he rounded adroitly on Pistoria's
virtues, which he listed systematically. "It will then be seen", he said, "that the
Prisoner took an active part in a most atrocious crime, but at the same time

The Execution of Francesco Moschara
(*Alias* Joseph Pistoria)

his case is not by any means devoid of mitigating circumstances."
With that he began to list the circumstances he had in mind:

"In the first place, there seemed to me strong reason to believe that Big George inspired everybody on board with terror and that he was the organizer of the piratical conspiracy and thus, although there was nothing to show that the part taken by the prisoner in the murders was the result of coercion, yet it is very possible the threats of Big George and the fear which he inspired had originally influenced the prisoners to form in the conspiracy.

The next point, which may be suggested in favour of the prisoner, is that at the first opportunity he left the vessel and abandoned the piratical enterprise. This also furnished some proof that the association with the Greeks was not altogether voluntary.

Further, in joining in the attack on the murdered men he was not guilty in any of those acts of barbarous ferocity exhibited by Big George - the prisoner used his revolver.

In the next place the prisoner saved the life of the carpenter – the Greeks would have killed him in a very few minutes but for the interference of the prisoner.

What the prisoner said to the Greeks to induce them to desist from this attack with compunction is unknown. What his motive was for interfering did not appear but he undoubtedly saved the man's life.The best point, however, in the prisoner's favour is that he saved the lives of the two splendid lads, the apprentices.

The Greeks were about to murder them when the prisoner resolutely and apparently from mere motives of humanity interfered and insisted that the 'boys' should not be harmed and they were spared.

In addition to these circumstances connected with the prisoner's conduct it will be remembered that the affair took place three years and a half ago and that seven human lives have been lost in the transaction in its results.

I feel the case is a difficult one for his Grace to deal with, for protection must be afforded to those engaged in our mercantile marine against the Cambasners of these desperadoes; at the same time I do not think I might avoid respectfully suggesting that his Grace be minded to adopt a course of mercy the circumstances to which I have adverted will furnish ample information for his doing so.

I may add that so far as my (of course somewhat limited) means of observation would enable me to form an opinion, the public sentiment in Cork is adverse to the sentence being carried out there."

The Execution of Francesco Moschara
(*Alias* Joseph Pistoria)

After such a strong recommendation one would have thought that a commutation might quite reasonably be expected; for generally speaking a Judge's words did not go astray -- nor were they made idly. In most nineteen cases, it is the Judge's opinion, short of the Lord Lieutenant, that determines the issue of mitigation. But not in this case!

All their petitions and appeals, including the appeal of the Italian Ambassador, had come to naught. They were now answered by the stock formula, which was even more final than the original death sentence. "After the most careful consideration," it seemed, his Grace the Lord Lieutenant could "see no reason for interfering with the execution of the sentence of the law." The only thing remaining, then, so far as the administration of criminal justice was concerned, was to carry out the sentence of the court.

In the interim Pistoria – or rather Moschara -- prepared a final declaration on the matter of the mutiny. He swore that neither his brother nor himself had anything whatever to do with the murders for which he was about to suffer. His account of the whole affair was recounted thus:

"On the morning of the mutiny, while lying in his berth, he thought something strange was about to happen. He said he observed the three Greeks 'speaking earnestly, and gesticulating violently.' He got up and asked Big George what was going on. Big George said -"Are you a friend of the captain?" He (Pistoria) replied that he was. Big George then said, "then you had better look out for yourself."

Alarmed at Big George's threats, Pistoria admitted that he went and fetched his revolver. He advised his brother to take a like precaution. When he was called on watch, he came on deck to take his turn at the wheel. The captain followed on deck shortly afterwards. Pistoria said that he then called out to the captain warning that 'something was wrong.' The captain replied that he was going as far as the main mast and would be back in a moment. With that the captain then went as far as the main mast, and he was then killed by Big George. He (Pistoria) ran forward to help the master but was too late. In the meantime one of the Greeks took hold of the mate, and he (Pistoria) called out to him: "Let him go, you son of a sea cook." But Big George was already at the mate's side, close enough to stab and kill him.

After the tragedy was over, Pistoria said he was called by Big George and asked whether he was with the mutineers or against them. Conscious of the position he was in, he, of course, replied he was with them, and to prove it, he helped to throw the bodies overboard. Because of his long-term fears, he asked Big George to leave the ship, and got leave to do so. Having received the letter from the Englishmen and having warned them of the danger they were in, he and his brother took their leave of the *Caswell*. The doomed man then concluded his declaration to Sir George Milero by saying,

181

The Execution of Francesco Moschara
(*Alias* Joseph Pistoria)

> " I solemnly declare and solemnly swear before the God I will see in forty eight hours, I never had anything to do to any Englishman on board - neither me nor my brother had anything to do with the murders, and what has been sworn against me is all false"

Because Pistoria had saved the lives of the apprentices, McDonald and Ferguson, some people were roused to "memorialize the Lord Lieutenant for a respite" of the sentence. And when no answer had been received for some three weeks, everyone's hopes were high. But then the news came and those hopes were inconsolably dashed. The *Examiner* went into denial of Cork's ensuing sense of despondency:

"Those who interested themselves on Pistoria's behalf perhaps were, no doubt, prompted by the best motives but one might have known that the request asked could not possibly be complied with by the Irish Executive.

"Humanitarianism in the abstract is all very well, and there are occasions when it is productive of great good; but it has limits, and the cold-blooded series of atrocities in which Joseph Pistoria took part, certainly removed his case outside its range. By some means the unfortunate man heard of the memorial having been got up in his favour (which was very injudicious to say the least of it), and although he was told to place no hope in its probable success, the poor condemned man naturally cherished the idea that it would be potent for good.

The gaol chaplain, the Rev. Father Cassidy, counseled Pistoria to abandon his hopes, and after a few days he became perfectly resigned to his fate. Indeed, according to the Examiner Pistoria became deeply penitent "from the moment he heard the words of doom rising from the lips of Mr Justice Barry in the County courthouse." Peculiarly enough Pistoria was described by those closest to him as one who was imbued with strong religious feelings. And during his time in prison he was known to have paid particular attention to the counsel of the chaplain. On occasions when he was alone with the two warders in his cell, he spent the greater portion of the day in prayer.

One of the warders informed the press that he knew him "to remain for five hours at a time on his knees praying for the forgiveness of his sins and for a happy death." Since he received his sentence, Pistoria's conduct was exemplary. He smoked a pipe for recreation. The Governor and the other prison officials spoke in the highest terms of the way in which Pistoria comported himself, and Dr. Beamish, the surgeon of the prison, was reported to have said "that a less exacting prisoner never passed from the condemned cell to the scaffold."

***

The Execution of Francesco Moschara
(*Alias* Joseph Pistoria)

At this juncture it behoves us to look at the business of hanging, and to try and understand the line of its legal authority. John Austin, the nineteenth century English jurist, believed that the law was no more than the command of the Sovereign. Having served in the army in Sicily and Malta, we can appreciate how such a "theory" of law impressed itself upon his mind. Nevertheless, the Austinian dictum has much to commend it; but it needs to be distinguished from an earlier notion called ' the social contract theory.'

Simply put, the social contract theorists understood that in return for citizenship all civilized societies of a European variety (except America) surrendered their arms to the Sovereign, in return for which the Sovereign would administer the laws on their behalf. The Sovereign, of course, had to behave himself (or herself). He had to govern fairly, impartially, and with 'due process' of law. To support this fiction, other attendant notions had to be given the respectability of a doctrine, rather than the rantings of propaganda. Citizens had to believe, for example, that 'everyone is equal before the law' and that 'no one is above the law.' These notions had more French than British in them, but they were mutually regarded as an excuse for running a capitalist economy. After two centuries of capitalism it is perfectly apparent that whatever else an underprivileged citizen has, it isn't a contract with his sovereign.

There is, then, much to be said for the Austinian view that all law, rather than being a contract, is simply the command of the sovereign. Under such a system, whether it is in the household, in the army, or under the constitution, one does what one is told to do by a superior force -- a superior force which implicitly carries more than the mere threat of personal physical violence – a bit like being on board the *Pilgrim* with John the Swede and Dana junior -- where it would hardly have served the crew members of the *Pilgrim* to remind the captain that they had a contract with him.

Austin's 'theory' is commendable on many grounds. It is not only simple, but it is also transparent and verifiable. Throughout the reign of Victoria most citizens – not just Thomas Crowe -- knew who had power and who hadn't, and indeed, why those who had power had it. Force of arms was a reality and was manifest and visible everywhere from the gathering at the Assize Court to the gathering at the occasional public hanging, from the Royal visits to the military strength in support of the police.

The Execution of Francesco Moschara
(*Alias* Joseph Pistoria)

That being the case, it was easy to comprehend one of the main constitutional principles, which intimated that one citizen, should not interfere -- even
minimally -- in the life and business of another, except in accordance with
positive law. What this meant was that anyone who purported to interfere
with another citizen or an institution (and thereby usurp the Sovereign's
power) had to point to some positive rule of law (or license) to justify it.

In the case of Pistoria, for example, it was apparent that written authority
backed up everything that occurred to him from the time of his arrest in
Monte Video to the time of his transfer in custody to Queenstown. On
arrest, he was charged and referred to the reason why he was arrested. On
May 12th, when he was transferred from Liverpool, the Crown Solicitor
for the County of Cork duly paid the Manager of the Pacific Steam
Navigation Company the sum of £30 for conveying Pistoria and Carrick
from Monte Video to England. In a similar fashion everything else had to
be legitimated. Pistoria's execution was obviously legitimated by the
sentence of the Judge of Trial. The Judge pronounced the sentence and
set the date and place and manner of execution quite carefully. We have
already seen that the sentence of Mr Justice Barry was passed with great
solemnity and deliberation, and if we did not recall the exact words of the
Judge, it wasn't just because they weren't printed in the local newspapers:
it was also because we know them practically by heart. Indeed, we know
them - or know of them so well - that, like all ritual, their repetition tends
to bore and irritate us. It is unnecessary to repeat these words, for we can
have no quarrel with them; the procedure is ritualized in every capital
case. The Judge of Trial wears the black cap and the famous words of the
death sentence are pronounced. Was this also by way of Sovereign license?

At local level it is the Sheriff who, as of old, represents the power of the
Crown and effects the sentence. It is he who, like the Judge, harnesses both
the Sovereign's power and her wrath. It is he who decides where and when
the iron fist behind the velvet glove of Her authority is released. In the instant case, the primary responsibility for carrying out the sentence of the
court fell to N.J O' Mahoney, the Under Sheriff, Co. Cork, and R Roberts,
the Governor of HM's Cork Male Prison.

If we look at the wording of the Warrant issued by Thomas Babington,
Clerk of the Crown for the County of Cork, we find much that is of interest.
Even in its archaic rhythms, which bear comparison with the most lugubri-
ous intimations of Gregorian chant, we sense a jurassic authority, a tone,
a tenor in which the most primordial and savage powers of the Sovereign
are couched! We can hear with what dogma the line of authority is drawn.

The Execution of Francesco Moschara
(*Alias* Joseph Pistoria)

Hidden in its free-flow punctuation, is the conferring of power coupled with the lethal injunction against failure to execute the warrant's intent.

County of Cork, to wit
Victoria by the Grace of God Queen defender of the faith and so forth.
To the sheriff of the County of Cork – Greetings

Whereas at the General Assizes and General Gaol Delivery holden at Cork in and for said County of Cork on Tuesday the twenty second day of July 1879, Joseph Pistoria otherwise Francesco Moschara was then and there Indicted tried and in due form of law found guilty of a certain felony and murder by him committed Whereupon judgment was given by the Court that he the said Joseph Pistoria otherwise Francesco Moschara should be taken from the bar of this Court where he now stands to the place from whence he came to the common Gaol of the County of Cork and that he be taken on Monday the Twenty fifth day of August in the year of our Lord one thousand eight hundred and seventy nine to the common place of execution within the walls of the prison in which he shall be then confined and that he be then and there hanged by the neck until he be dead and that his body shall be buried within the precincts of the prison in which he shall have been last confined after his conviction, the execution of which judgment yet remaineth to be done, these are therefore in her Majesty's name strictly to charge and command you the said Sheriff of the County of Cork that you cause execution of said Judgment to be done upon the said Joseph Pistoria otherwise Francesco Moschara in all points according to the tenor hereof and this you the said Sheriff is by no means at your peril to omit this being your Warrant.

Given at Crown Office Cork in said County this twenty fifth day of July in the year 1879 in this forty third year of Our Reign. Given under Seal of office

To the High Sheriff
Of the County Of Cork
And his assistants

But for all its encased certainty, its ponderous compulsion, the Warrrant could not embrace all phenomena. Judge Barry's Order did not say who should hang Pistoria, what kind of rope was to be used, how long the drop was to be, what kind of knot was to be used or, how or where the rope and knot were to be placed around the neck. The Judge only said that Giuseppe Moschara was to be hanged by the neck until he was dead. For centuries this general phrase gave enormous license to the Crown's executioners to do the most dreadful things in the name of justice. In this case, it was done by command of the Sovereign, Her Majesty the Queen.

The Execution of Francesco Moschara
(*Alias* Joseph Pistoria)

It was peculiar, to say the least of it, that this seemingly uncomplicated task could cause so much confusion. Governor O' Mahoney tried to secure the services of the most popular hangman in England, William Marwood. But it often happened in nineteenth century Ireland that one couldn't find a good executioner when one most needed one! A respectable Gaoler , as we shall see, would have to be fast off the mark to secure the services of a reliable hangman. That's why, when we find Marwood replying to O' Mahoney on August 8th in respect of an execution fixed for the 25th, we know that the alarm bells are sounding. With faltering and childish hand (See handwriting examples) Marwood tried to console the Governor.

To the Governor of H.M. Prison,
Cork, Ireland.

Sir,

Please this is to inform you that I received your kind letter concerning a Prisoner now under the sentence of Death at Hill Prison Cork, Ireland – I sent you a Telegraph Message stating that I would send you a letter this day to arrange for the time.

Sir. Please this is to inform you that Monday and Tuesday the 25th and 26th days of this month August is engaged in England. If you will be so kind as to arrange for time I will come over to Cork and Execute the Prisoner. Sir - I hope it will not make any difference to you in regard to the time please I should be very glad if you would be so kind as to arrange to appoint Friday the 22nd or 29th Day of August for the time for the execution to take place at Cork. Please, if you will arrange for the time you may depend on me to arrive at the time appointed and I will bring all things that is wanted for the Execution, rope and straps and cap. Please let me have your reply, as I shall return Home on Tuesday next from Exeter the 12th Day of August. I shall be very glad to hear from you in the matter in question

Sir I remain your Humble Servant

Wm Marwood
Church Lane
Horncastel
Lincolnshire
England

After a flurry of telegrams, it became evident that both Marwood and Gainsborough were unavailable. And, apparently, there was no one in Cork who could be induced to do the job. To make matters worse, by the

186

The Execution of Francesco Moschara
(*Alias* Joseph Pistoria)

time the letters and the telegrams had been answered, there were only three days left before the execution was due to take place. In desperation O'Mahoney turned to enlist the services of a Prison inmate. The County Sheriff confirmed his permission to do so. But this ran contrary to the terms of the Prisons (I.) Act, 1877. This was the act, which at last centralized prisons in Ireland. It dragged them out of the private and benevolent indifference of the eighteenth century. Unfortunately for the Governor of the Male Prison in Cork, the act also prohibited the employment of prisoners to hang other prisoners - at least not without the consent of the newly established Prisons Board. But time was running out, so the County Sheriff tried frantically to comply with the act and telegraphed the Prisons Board for the requisite permission. The County Sheriff's office received the following reply.

County Sheriff's Office,
Cork
22nd August 1879

Sir,

In the absence of the High Sheriff I have to acknowledge receipt of your telegraph of the 20th and letter of the 21st.

I have further to inform you for his Excellency's information, that every possible exertion has been made to obtain the services of an experienced Executioner and although the Governors of the Principal Prisons in the United Kingdom have been communicated with both by letter and telegraph the attempt has been entirely unsuccessful. One and all appear to recognize but the one Executioner, Marwood, whose services cannot be availed of on the present occasion for the reasons set out in the telegrams and letters herewith, which documents will more fully account for the Telegraph forwarded by Sheriff to you yesterday.

But one other Public Executioner appears to be known of in England and as you will observe by telegraph enclosed from Governor of York Castle Prison this man Gainsborough has been lost sight of.

No volunteers to perform this duty can be obtained in Cork.

On visiting the Male prison to day I ascertained that prisoners at present confined therein were willing to perform this duty but under the present Prison regulations all Prisoners are under the control of the Prisons Board who will not permit them to be made use of for this purpose. Formerly prisoners were under the control of the Sheriff who could and within my own knowledge often did make use of them for this purpose; I have therefore on the part of the sheriff to request that you may be pleased to direct that the Services of the Prisoners herein referred to may on the present

The Execution of Francesco Moschara
(*Alias* Joseph Pistoria)

occasion be placed at the disposal of the Sheriff with the view that the sentence may be carried out which otherwise will be utterly impossible.

With the view that this communication should not be made known to the Public through the means of the Telegraph I have arranged with the governor of the Male Prison that if he received a telegraph from you on tomorrow in the following words, he will understand that the request has been complied with and will allow the services of those men to be made use of.

A written communication from you would now be too late as they will be required to be instructed in their duty on to-morrow.

A telegram from the Chief Secretary to the Governor duly confirmed -- 'You are at liberty to act as Sheriff suggests'. On the 23rd August the Prisons Board wrote to the Under Secretary taking issue with matters as they stood. The Board pointed out that it had 'not been consulted in the matter', and that ' therefore the statement of this under Sheriff is not correct'.

While the County Sheriff was making a more formal application "for permission to employ two Prisoners, in the County Gaol, to act in the place of the Executioner Marwood," James J. Minton, the Under Sheriff, was making it known to all and sundry that as and from the 23rd of August all the arrangements were in readiness " for the execution of the convict on Monday next." Minton also realised that the time for protocol had run out. He needed to have the Lord Lieutenant's OK for the use of the convict/executioners and there was no time left to pussyfoot about. He contacted the Lord Lieutenant directly in search of authoritative cover to have Moschara executed. But was it too late?

County Sheriffs Office
Court House
Cork
August 25th 1879

Sir

I have to acknowledge the receipt of your letter of the 23rd inst. The governor of the male prison gave me distinctly to understand that certain duties having been assigned to prisoners under his charge, he would not permit the Sheriff to make use of any prisoner for the purposes of the execution without either the express authority of the Prisons Board or his Grace the Lord Lieutenant notwithstanding the 40th Section of the Prisons Act of 1877.

188

The Execution of Francesco Moschara
(*Alias* Joseph Pistoria)

It was two o'clock in the afternoon of Friday last before I had exhausted executioner. I deemed it inexpedient to communicate in the first instance with the Prisons Board, whose reply, if adverse, I could not have received before Sunday morning, when it would be too late to communicate with his Grace on the subject. I therefore think that I adopted a more prudent course in communicating direct with His Grace the Lord Lieutenant

I am, Sir,

Your obedient servant,

Jas J Minton Under sheriff,
Co. of Cork

The Under-Secretary

In the interests of thoroughness a Departmental Memorandum recorded that:

> "At seven minutes past eight o'clock in the morning Francesco Moschara alias Joseph Pistoria was hanged. Included in Governor Roberts notification to the General Prisons Board was the fact that, "A prisoner acted as Executioner on authority received by the Sheriff from the Chief Secretary."

***

On the Thursday before the hanging, Pistoria, "for the sake of good fellowship," tried to buy a drink for all present (the Doctor, two warders, and himself). When he was told that the prison regulations prohibited such a practice, he consented to take a bottle of porter himself — since when he received one daily. He took his meals regularly, and slept soundly every night.

Moschara had been made aware of his rights. Under Italian law a condemned man lost his civil rights. The Italian Consular Agent, Sir George Milero had made this quite clear to the court. In effect it meant that after his death Moschara could not legally dispose of his property as he might have wished.

With this in mind, he signed a Petition on Saturday addressed to the Italian government, praying that whatever property he had be given to his sister who was living at Acci Castello. After her death his property was to be divided and devolved upon his three children - Giuseppi, Fortunata, and

The Execution of Francesco Moschara
(*Alias* Joseph Pistoria)

Voluntina, who were at San Martino d'Albero under the care of Seirgi Marello, who was in the employ of the municipality of Genoa. Moschara wasn't sure how much property he owned, but he believed it consisted of some houses in Acci Castello, left to him by his father.

On Sunday, from early morning until late at night, he reserved his time almost exclusively for prayer. About three o'clock that evening he sent for the governor, captain Roberts; he wanted to dispose of the few shillings he had left in his possession. They were to be given to the Rev. Father Codd, to be distributed among the poor. And at half past eight, after Father Cassidy had left him, he retired to rest. He slept soundly until midnight, when he awoke again. He got up, dressed himself and told the warders of a strange dream he had had the night before. He thought he was at sea. Some distance away he observed a canoe containing Big George and the others. In his dream he thought that they would be swamped, so he made an effort to rescue them. Eventually he managed to do so. Then he adjourned and prayed from midnight until five o'clock in the morning, when he again retired to rest. He slept for an hour, got up again, and made his final preparations. The two clergymen, Father Cassidy and his confessor, Rev. Father Codd O.S.F., arrived at half past six to find him engaged in fervent prayer. Moschara made his last confession, and the two clergymen attended unsparingly to his spiritual needs.

At mass the rosary was recited and he received Holy Communion. He then joined in the responses to the prayers offered up. His confessor then addressed a few words of exhortation to him, and at ten minutes to eight the procession started, the condemned man bearing in his hands a little black indulgence crucifix.

On either side walked a clergyman and a warder and then came the governor, Captain Roberts, then Mr. Morrow, Deputy-Governor; Dr. Beamish surgeon, Mr. Johnson, Sub-Sheriff, and then the prison officials. The Litany of the dying was recited all the way, and Pistoria responded in a firm and clear voice. "In fact," reported the Examiner, "he seemed the least affected of all those present, neither his voice nor tread betraying any signs of faltering or indecision." Elsewhere the *Examiner,* (in terms already familiar to us) described the events that were to follow:

> "A procession to the scaffold is indeed a sorrowful sight to witness, and the stoutest heart might quit at the mere contemplation of it; but Pistoria seemed in every respect to be oblivious of everything but the making of his peace with God, and his countenance was lighted up with as cheerful an expression as if he had courted the dreadful death he was soon about to suffer. The melancholy procession wended its way a distance of about three hundred

The Execution of Francesco Moschara
(*Alias* Joseph Pistoria)

yards towards the place of execution, which is situate at the end of a very long avenue which leads to the portion of the prison formerly appropriated for the detention of those imprisoned for debt.

At the end of the wall, which leads to the southern extremity of the Gaol, there is a small gateway opening into an airing yard, forming a complete square, two sides being bounded by the prison buildings, and the other two by walls. In the furthest corner of the yard a scaffold was erected exactly in the same place as it stood when Tobin (*) was executed four years and a half ago, and Bombos and Crowe hardly three years ago yesterday. The yard has not been devoted to any purpose since, and it is now called the execution yard. The scaffold was so situated that the culprit could not see it until he entered the doorway leading into the yard.

It consisted of an iron frame, which, when not in use, can be lowered by means of a windlass to lie horizontally upon the ground, and it is the same iron frame, which was formerly used in front of the Gaol for public executions. When required for use, the iron frame is raised up and the top crossbar, having two hooks for the rope, then stands about 15 feet from the level of the yard, a rudely constructed platform with wooden supports was constructed around this, and a flight of wooden steps led up to the drop. The two hooks still remain at the top crossbar, and hanging from one of these was the rope, a white silk rope, about an inch in diameter (purchased in London) with a noose attached.

It was when the culprit arrived at the doorway of the yard that he caught the first sight of the dread instrument of death; but he did not betray any apparent emotion. There from a sidewalk in the yard through which emerged the executioner and his assistant, both having their faces veiled; and preparatory to the process of pinioning, the condemned man shook hands with the governor, the deputy governor, the doctor, the sub-sheriff, and the two clergymen.

The executioner then divested the culprit of his black hat and white neckerchief, but the coat was allowed to remain on the culprit wearing the same clothes as he did during the trial. The arms were then pinioned close to the sides with leather straps, and the procession again started for the scaffold, the executioner and his assistant leading the way. The condemned man ascended the steps leading to the drop without the slightest assistance, reciting in Italian with his confessor, a prayer for a person in agony.

On reaching the gallows he asked the executioner where he should stand, and after being placed in position under the rope, he said in a loud and firm voice, " May the Lord give me the grace of a happy death." The white cap was then drawn over his face, and when this was done the culprit was heard to say, "Goodbye, and God bless you." The clergymen were reciting the Litany all the time. The executioner then adjusted the rope, fixing the eyelet in the noose under the left ear (the same as Marwood). The next moment he stepped aside, touched a spring, a click was heard, accompanied by the rise

The Execution of Francesco Moschara
(*Alias* Joseph Pistoria)

of the running rope and the trap door flung open. Joseph Pistoria was launched into eternity.

Death was instantaneous, as the body made not the slightest quiver when the rope was fully distended. The length of the rope was seven feet, and the short drop was used by the executioner, three feet and a half being given, in contradistinction to the long drop of six, seven and eight feet used by Marwood. Who the executioner was is a little shrouded in mystery, and the proper name will, in all probability, never be known to the public. The officials of the prison say his name is Standhouse, or Gainsborough; but the prevalent opinion among outsiders, some of them asserting it on good authority too, is that the executioner and his assistant have been for a short period under surveillance in a place not a hundred miles from here. The bolt was drawn at eight minutes past eight o'clock, and a black flag hoisted on the tower. At ten minutes past eight I informed a lot of curious people (about a hundred) standing on the road leading up to the gaol that justice had asserted itself, and that the majesty of the law had been vindicated. The prison bell pealed from a quarter to eight until the black flag had been hoisted.

A posse of police was stationed outside the Gaol door, but their services were not required. No person was allowed into the Gaol until the flag was hoisted except those we have mentioned, and at a quarter-past eight the representatives of the Press were admitted. After Pistoria's body had remained suspended for an hour, the body was cut down and at the same minute the black flag was lowered. The body was then conveyed to a shed in the yard where it was viewed by the jury, and in the course of the day it was enclosed in a rude coffin and buried in the portion of ground set apart for the bodies of those who die on the scaffold."

(*) William Reevins, alias Tobin, was a convict on ticket of licence. At midday on the 1st August 1874, he entered the house or Johanna Cotter, farmer's wife, and struck her on the head repeatedly with a two-pronged fork. Robbery appeared to have been the motive. Reevins was arrested immediately after the murder, and convicted at the Spring Assizes, 1875. He was sentenced to death and executed on 19th April 1875.

***

Chapter 12

AFTERMATH
AND
EPILOGUE

" He - man or people -who, putting his trust in the friendship of the
sea, neglects the strength and cunning of his right hand, is a fool! As
if it were too great, too mighty for common virtues, the ocean has no
compassion, no faith, no law, and no memory. Its fickleness is to be
held true to men's purposes only by an undaunted resolution and by
a sleepless, armed, jealous vigilance, in which, perhaps, there has
always been more hate than love."

> *Joseph Conrad: The Mirror of the Sea*

The Aftermath

At ten o'clock in the guardroom of the gaol the Coroner, Mr Horgan,
and a jury, held an Inquest on the body. Mr Thomas Morrow, Deputy
governor, in reply to the Coroner, recited the details antecedent to the
hanging. He said that the deceased, Joseph Pistoria, alias Francesco
Moschara, was committed to the gaol on the 1st day of April 1879. He
was then lodged in custody and charged with the murder on the 4th of
January '76 on the British ship *Caswell* of George Edward Best, William Wilson, Allan McLean, and Edward Griffiths. He was tried on
the 22nd July at a Special Commission before Judge Barry at the last
assizes, and he was found guilty on the same day of the murder of
one Wm. Wilson, on the high seas. The sentence of the judge was that
he be hanged in the County Gaol on the 25th August, and that his body
be buried within its precincts. That sentence was carried out at 8 o'clock

that morning; he (Mr. Morrow) saw Pistoria executed and killed in accordance with the sentence.

Dr. Wm. Beamish, surgeon to the gaol, said he was also present at the execution of Pistoria that morning. He said he saw the sentence carried out as Judge Barry pronounced it. The drop was between three and four feet. Pistoria was instantaneously killed. He also made an examination of the body after death and ascertained that one of the superior cervical vertebrae was fractured, which caused instant death. The deceased was a healthy man between twelve and thirteen stone weight, and in his (Dr. Beamish's) opinion he could have suffered no pain.

Accordingly, the jury found --

"That the said deceased came by his death by hanging on Monday, the 25th day of August, 1879, in the County Cork Gaol, in obedience to the sentence of the law passed on him on the 22nd day or July, 1879, for the murder of William Wilson, first mate of the British barque *Caswell*, on the high seas"

The Inquest over, the body was taken away and buried according to the Judge's sentence. Even if some questions remained unanswered, the process was over. Everything that could be done to mortal life was done. All else was consigned to another world, and all that remained was the curiosity of those marginally effected.

First of all there was the Italian Consul. Did he know that Moschara had been executed by two of his fellow prisoners? Notwithstanding the very comforting description of the execution by the reporter from the Examiner and Dr. Beamish's reassurance that Moschara did not suffer, there must still remain some doubt as to whether the hanging itself was as perfect as described or -- on the contrary -- if it was a botched job. Did he make any enquiries about the matter? After all it was he who made the other arrangements; he hired Counsel for Moschara, and he generally directed affairs in his interest. Did he not know who was hanging Moschara? Was he informed? Indeed, did the authorities feel that they had any obligation to inform him of how, and by whom, his fellow citizen and, to some extent, his charge was to be executed? Or did he choose not to take issue with the hanging arrangements? Did the Consul in fact witness the hanging, and, if so, what were his opinions on the matter?

On these considerations we can only speculate…

Contemporary science knew that there are at least three vital elements involved in the calculus of an efficient execution. The first is the prisoner's weight; the second is the nature and tautness of the rope chosen; and the third is the amount or length of the fall of the body weight. We cannot speak for the second item, and we can only assume that it was a reliable rope of the kind recommended by hangmen like Marwood or scientists like Samuel Haughton. Apart from this assumption, we know that "The deceased was a healthy man between twelve and thirteen stone weight." We also know that although the rope was some seven feet in length, the drop was as short as three and a half feet. We also know that this drop was done "in contradistinction to the long drop of six, seven and eight feet used by Marwood."

Given these observations, how is it possible to have faith in the conclusion that -- "Death was instantaneous, as the body made not the slightest quiver when the rope was fully distended"?

By 1879, Marwood, who was not presently available, had taken over from Calcraft as chief hangman in the British Isles. In some ways it marked a revolution in the technology of capital punishment. What this meant was that Marwood, using the sub-aural knot, hanged people, as the *Cork Examiner* had rightly pointed out, from a drop of 6 or 7 feet. Both of these innovations - that is, the placement of the knot under the ear (as opposed to behind the neck, the 'occipital knot'), coupled with a drop of between 6 to 7 feet (as opposed to the 2-foot drop of Calcraft), were revolutionary in that the more efficient knot and the more efficient drop tended to bring about a more efficient or less painful State-killing. The principle in question approximated what happened to a rabbit when it was struck on the back of the neck. It came into popular parlance as the "rabbit-punch," but in effect it was as deadly a *coup de gras* as the guillotine. In contrast the short drop, as has already been described in Bombos' case, tended to kill by strangulation or suffocation and prolonged the pangs of death. The victim is left to dangle on the end of the rope until his life is expired; the vertebra is not broken at all or broken inefficiently.

The Drop, worked out by the scientist, Dr Samuel Haughton, and approved by successive governments, recommended a length of rope to suit the poundage-weight of the prisoner. Nowhere on the recommended scale does a body- drop of 3 feet occur, simply because people in excess of 284 lbs are not envisaged. The greatest weight

appearing on the recommended scale is 284 pounds, when a drop of
4 feet 6 inches is recommended. Similarly a drop of 4 feet is recommended for a body weighing 210 pounds, but this would be quite
in excess of Francesco Moschara's stated weight of 182 pounds. At
182 pounds weight the recommended drop was – and is - 6 feet 11
inches, not between 3 and 4 feet, which is half that of the efficient
or appropriate drop. Yet from the description in the *Examiner* the
execution was perfectly executed.

At the Inquest Dr. Beamish testified that Pistoria was killed "instantaneously" and — after examination of the body — "that one of the
superior cervical vertebrae was fractured, which caused instant death."
He does not say which vertebra was fractured. That being the case, the
only area of doubt remaining as to the efficiency of the hanging revol-
ves around the length of time it took before Pistoria's vertebrae became
fractured.

Given these considerations, how are we to conclude with Dr Beamish
-- or the reporter -- that "Death was instantaneous, as the body made not
not the slightest quiver when the rope was fully distended?" This description purports to come from someone who actually saw the hanging and
would ideally reflect the hanging of Pistoria from a drop measuring 6 feet
11 inches.

The question is: could two prisoners with no experience whatsoever,
and using half the recommended drop, and God–knows-what- kind-
of- knot, have got it precisely right? It should be remembered that the
very purpose of introducing the recommended drop-tables by the
government was to avoid the indignity -- not to mention the cruelty --
attending upon hangings that promoted the short-drop. It was also one
of the reasons why before 1868 hangings were carried out in public –
that is, to deter criminals (by their gruesomeness) and to satisfy the
perceived demands of 'justice.' In this connection it should be remembered that in an earlier age the sentence of "hanging, drawing and
quartering" was intended as a gruesome spectacle to deter felons and
their accomplices. It was left to a later age to find this procedure inhu-
mane and unacceptable.

Things had even changed since 1876.The Irish General Prisons Board,
for example, had been set up in 1877 and had radicalized the Prison
Service. Over the three years preceding 1879 the attitudes to the Press
had also changed. In the Bombos case, the authorities were welcoming;
journalists were invited to the execution - a demonstration of the Prison

Board's professionalism, openness and transparency. From the Press' description of the 'double execution,' the public realised that the criminal justice system operated on a kind of hit-and-miss basis. A capitally sentenced prisoner could be either 'launched' peaceably into eternity or, alternatively, he might be launched kicking and screaming into either Hell or Heaven. It wasn't so much where a person went as how he was dispatched that mattered.

Everyone knew that the good went to Heaven and the bad went to Hell's torments. It was only the very few remaining atheists who – like all the aboriginal Gaelic and pagan Irish – went into oblivion. No: the question in Francesco Moschara's case was "how" one was dispatched rather than to "where".

It was outrageous! All civilisation depended upon it, yet the State simply could not hang a person properly. No wonder that three years after the Bombos fiasco, the erstwhile transparency of the Prison's Board had evaporated. The new idea was to conceal the execution (and the identity of the executioner) from the public's gaze. And what if -- towards this end -- steps had to be taken to confound the Press and deceive the public? After the hanging of Moschara, for example, the *Examiner* followed up its account of the hanging with the following note:

The Executioner's Exit

"About half-past nine o'clock a good number of persons were still lingering about the prison gate, in order to catch a glimpse of the executioner, as it was thought he (being a Yorkshire man) would naturally try to get out of the city at the earliest moment - namely, by the 12.30 mail train for Dublin. However, they waited in vain for the appearance of anyone likely to be a hangman; and when three persons emerged from the prison - a man and two boys handcuffed together - in the custody of two policemen, the commiseration of the quidnuncs for the unfortunate trio diverted their thought for a time from the consideration of anything appertaining to the craft of which Marwood is such a deft master. It is unnecessary to say that the centre figure of the three quondam prisoners was the executioner of Pistoria, and thus did he make his exit from the gaol. We believe he found a resting place in Tuckey-street police station; but whence or when he departed thence is unknown to us."

***

Epilogue

At the end of the *Caswell* story, we are almost as confused as we were at the beginning. The riddle remains with us. Why did five foreigners who had never been obviously or grossly slighted by either the captain or his officers mutiny against them and kill them? This has always been the Riddle of the *Caswell*. Her secret was further compounded by the fact that the British sailors who signed up in Buenos Aires were the ones who had been treated most cruelly by their captain, and, on that account alone, were most likely to mutiny. Why did they not mutiny? It was easy to see why they insisted upon going over the captain's head to see the Consul. But having been beaten into sub-mission and put in irons, why did they not attempt to mutiny or to stop the Greek mutiny? And why, having taken flight during the mutiny, did they emerge from their hiding places unscathed? Why, indeed, were they spared after the mutiny? Much was made of MacGregor being made to swear allegiance to the Greeks and then being spared. But were the others so humiliated? Was Carrick or Dunne ever really forced to swear allegiance in the same or a similarly convincing manner?

It is obvious that some aspects of the *Caswell's* story remains unres-olved -- particularly in those areas where the facts simply do not gel, or where contradictions abound, or where oddities in evidence, or disparate accounts of the facts, prevail. In a word, the amalgamated facts lack something at their centre, something that would make them more amenable to reason and more enlightening in their detail. And yet if we adjust some items we arrive at a more compelling picture of what probably happened.

But first let us enumerate the more obvious inconsistencies. The following nine points are either ambiguous or unconvincing :

> 1. The reason why a group of foreigners mutinied against their captain and his officers, when they were never seriously threat-ened by them;
> 2. The notion put about at the trial that these foreigners wanted to seize the *Caswell* and sell or scuttle her;
> 3. The rationale behind the conflicting evidence respecting the initial time of entry on board the *Caswell*;
> 4. The missing logbook;

5. The contents of Bombos's unique statement concerning -
   a. The fear of Big George Peno;
   b. The intentions of captain George Best;
   c. The good terms at times between Greek and British – and as especially evidenced between Bombos and Carrick;
   d. The various plans that were periodically put forward for the relief of the *Caswell* after the mutiny;
6. The need for Bombos' second trial;
7. The letters written by Carrick for the Pistorias and Bombos ;
8. Pistoria's cordiality with the British before leaving;
9. The wearing of the captain's clothes, not by the mutineers, but by the counter-mutineers.

We could repeat the riddle ad nauseam, but we cannot close this book until we try and reconcile these nine points with the facts. What needs to be adjusted, perhaps, is both our view of the temperament of those on board and the initial refusal of the British to sail with the Greeks ; for neither are consistent with the facts surrounding the mutiny. This is not to say that the objection to sailing with Greeks was not true, but rather that if it was true, it was not the sole truth. And where it is advanced as a sole or predominant truth, it appears to be neither complete nor unvarnished.

On 'Greek' -- or rather Turkish -- temperament all one can say is that one feels that they were a pretty gullible, irascible and superstitious lot. Perhaps their religious fervour in the face of death gives us a clue to their superstition, although it is apparent that had they shown as much faith in their fellow man, maybe the mutiny might not have happened. There is no reason at all for us to support the view that they conspired to bring about the mutiny as a long-term project, although it was, by any account, more than a spontaneous occurrence. We must conclude that either the mutiny was pre-arranged, or, what was more likely, that pathological violence was quite close to the surface of all the mutineers, especially Big George. The so-called fear of Big George was without doubt very real, but could not of itself have driven the mutiny. Nevertheless our view of Big George probably requires substantial adjustment. The one thing that no one could predict was his volatile and inflammable nature. And before the mutiny occurred, who could have suspected it?

The second adjustment is much more difficult to see, and has to do with the objectors themselves. To support our skepticism in this respect we must begin with the known facts and after that the reliable ones. That captain George Best wanted a mixed crew is coercive.

There is no evidence to show that he cared where they came from, so long as they were mixed. As Edward Warner stated, maybe he felt that it augmented his power over the crew, or simply that it minimized their capacity to organize against him. In either of these cases it would seem that the captain anticipated trouble or, alternatively, that he became aware of his own limitations in handling men, and accordingly, thought to minimize the worst aspects of those limitations by mixing the crew, thereby diminishing their communicative skills, their linguistic fluency and, derivatively, their capacity to plot and conspire against him.

Further, whereas the British probably discovered something of the captain's personal history, there is no reason to believe that the Greeks did. They had to take him as they found him. They also had to content themselves with whatever the British crew told them of his intentions.

Secondly, and not unconnected with the foregoing, the *Caswell* spent a full six weeks in Buenos Aires. On reflection it appears highly probable that at some stage during this period the British sailors found out about captain Best's very belligerent disposition. MacGregor or any of the mates or apprentices could have told them, but that was hardly likely when we consider that MacGregor in fact wanted to enlist people as much as the captain did, and, in any event, he still had a good opinion of his captain. It is also significant that MacGregor was never put in irons – nor did he at any stage object to sailing with Greeks or anyone else. And if the crew heard nothing critical from MacGregor it is also unlikely that they heard anything from the mates or indeed the apprentices. Why? Because, in the first place, the British were unlikely to befriend either the mates or the apprentices socially before they had enlisted, the one being above and the other being below the dignity of an ABS (Able Bodied Seaman). Secondly, if indeed they did mix socially, there is no evidence to suggest that either the mates or the apprentices found anything critical to complain of in the captain's style of management. On the contrary, they remained loyal to him. Even if there were now two irascible monsters on board (Best and Peno), only one of them was known to the crew to be so.

So where else could the new crew have heard about captain Best and the desertion of his old crew?

The most likely answer is that Carrick, Dunne, and Rourke -- and possibly others -- were out drinking, either socially or as part of the sailor's habitual manner of enquiring into the state of the labour market. Or, perhaps, after they were recruited, they drank in anticipation of the long journey home. Carrick, for example, stated that when he came off the *Seabird* he spent "a few days" in Buenos Aires before enlisting. And this is not to rule out the possibility that Carrick or the others found out after they had signed on. It is also quite likely that some of the crew of the first voyage, having quit the *Caswell*, also hung about Buenos Aires for some time, perhaps for days, weeks or months; and it does not strain the imagination to conceive that Carrick, or Dunne or Rourke, or all three, met up with those sailors, who – as one might expect -- told them all about their skipper and the trip out from Glasgow. A ship does not lie in dry dock without sailors swapping all kinds of information about it. So, there can be little doubt but that the British were informed of the *Caswell's* first trip and why it was that 13 out of 19 men quit after the Glasgow/ Buenos Aires voyage. More to the point, what was said about the *Caswell* and captain George Best?

Whatever was said, it more than likely did not suit the expectations of Carrick, Dunne and Rourke. That being the case, it is every bit as probable that their objection was as much to sailing with captain George 'Bully' Best as it was to sailing with Greeks.

In this respect, it is pertinent to ask: when did the objectors learn, first, about captain Best and, secondly, that Greeks would form part of the crew? Obviously if the British knew both these things, or that they were required to sail with Greeks, before they enlisted, then they simply would never have enlisted. Whichever fear was greatest, it is logical to infer that they had enlisted before they found either out.

So, after enlisting, which fear predominated? Their fear of Greeks or their fear of captain Best? If, after enlisting Carrick, Dunne and Rourke, now heard about captain Best's character, would they not have tried to leave ship? And if they were prevented from leaving by the captain, what then?

Logically, they needed to figure out how to get off the ship, even at the expense of their contracts. At this stage, and in the absence of any other excuse, the British would be very likely to fix their objections on the 'Greeks', not just because it was a good excuse to get out of their indentures or to see the Consul, but also because it was a compelling issue and an opportune gripe.

The objection to sailing with Greeks also had the advantage of being irremediable – for what captain, having hired some men, would now discharge them at the request of other seamen: and Johnny-come-latelies at that? If the captain had said; "O.K. We will sail without any Greeks; we'll only take a Maltese or two", would the objectors have been satisfied?

Or would they have invented another objection in order to get to see the Consul? Or was it a ruse to get off the ship? Indeed, if they had not been put in irons, would they have sailed at all on the *Caswell*? It should also be recalled that none of the objectors ever made any reference, good, bad or indifferent, to any past experience(s) involving Greeks. And even if the question cannot be answered, it is pertinent to ask whether the objection to Greeks really meant an objection to all foreigners, including Greeks, Turks, Maltese and Italians?

What prompts this line of reasoning is the ease with which it explains several if not all the outstanding matters in our nine-point list above.

When they failed to get to see the Consul a confrontation must have ensued. The captain felt compelled to beat them into submission and then put them in irons. Whatever advantage the captain thought he had gained by demanding a mixed crew, it was now lost to him when the British were put in irons. Why he would have proceeded with them can only be put down to his sense of desperation; for now the objectors' relation with him -- and his with them -- was not only soured but was likely to remain so throughout the long voyage home. Did they then recklessly slip into such disrespect for their captain that they actually wanted a mutiny to occur? Did they promote the mutiny, or did they just become recklessly careless whether one occurred or not? At least this would explain the doubts they created in the Greeks, who unknowingly sympathised with their plight.

What is of some significance to us is the fact that the accusers could not remember when, precisely, they boarded the *Caswell*, or in what order they had been recruited. So vague were they on this information that their purported reason for not wanting to sail with Greeks becomes highly suspect. On the basis that people are most apt to forget or ignore details only when those details are of little importance to them, it is pertinent to ask whether the real chronology of recruitment supports one proposition over the other. In other words, while the official complaint was that they did not want to ship with Greeks, was it used to disguise the more real complaint of not wanting to ship with captain Best?

We know that the six remaining crewmembers after the Glasgow trip comprised the captain, the first and second mates, the carpenter, and the two apprentices. Leaving out Emmanuel Griffiths, the black Welsh steward (19) who was probably recruited by the captain personally, nine others have to be accounted for. The recruitment drive had to take place between the 10th of September (the date of docking in Buenos Aires) and the 24th of October 1875 (the date of departure). On the assumption that the British, including the German Cook, Rook Agineau, were recruited on or about the same date, we can tabulate and suggest the following recruitment dates, the underscored entries representing the more accurate order of events.

In the absence of the logbook these things cannot be proved. The only remaining alternative then is to piece together the oral evidence—as we have done -- and sift the most reliable evidence from the least reliable. Even still we find a remarkable degree of variation between those who testified to their arrival on board.

What we can rely upon is the evidence of Daniel Johnson, the 36-year-old Shipping Master at Buenos Aires, who gave us the date when Pistoria was recruited. This date is firm

Carrick's date of recruitment is also reliable in so far as it applies to himself, but *contra* Carrick defence counsel's dates with respect to the recruitment of Bombos and Big George are firm.

If we just refresh our memory on the respective evidence given, it will be apparent that there was no common understanding of when precisely everybody came on board. According to the Cambrian -- which gave no dates for recruitment -- " the Captain shipped two Maltese seamen… three Britishers and a Greek named Christos Baumbos." It then continued:

> "As they were two short, Baumbos asked to go ashore to fetch two men. He was granted permission and returned with George Peno and Nicholas Morellos, two men of ill repute. (Greeks)."

This very plausible view we have accepted throughout our story, and we still have no reason to deviate from it. Accordingly, from the date of arriving in Buenos Aires the captain waited nine days before recruiting the Pistorias on the 19th of September. These were first. Four days later he recruited Bombos, and a further five days later he recruited Carrick, and -- arguably (since they were put in irons together around the same time) -- Dunne, and Rourke, and probably the German Cook, Agineau as well. It is then quite plausible that he sent Bombos to recruit Big George and Nicholas Morellos. Since Bombos is on board a week before Big George and Nicholas Morellos are recruited, he could – in theory -- have had a whole week to recruit them. But "As they were two short…" (the Cambrian) suggests that all the crew had been recruited before Bombos was detailed to recruit the remaining two. This meant that it had to be on the 28th of September

Recruitment Dates

	Cambrian	MacGregor Nic. Mor.	Carrick (Seabird)	Defence Counsel +D.Johnson
19.09.75 19.09.75	Ga. Pist. Giu. Pist.	.Ga. Pist. Giu. Pist.		19.09.75 19.09.75
23.09.75	Bombos			23.09.75
28.09.75	Carrick (Dunne?) (Agineau?) (Rourke?)	(Bombos) (Big Geo.)	(Bombos) (Big Geo.)	
30.09.75 30.09.75	Big Geo. Nic. Mor.			30.09.75

Obviously, on the 28th or the 29th the captain could have sent the British to recruit the two remaining crewmembers he sought to make up the complement. Why didn't he send the British? Probably because it was easier for a Greek to recruit other "Greeks". And if Bombos had little English, he could easily get by with Italians and Turks. But it could also have been because the objectors had already made their feelings known and, consequently, he did not trust them to carry out his wishes.

The captain could also have sent the 'Maltese', but as the *Cambrian* says, it was Baumbos who "asked to go ashore to fetch two men." In his own statement Bombos is silent on this whole matter, save to say: "When I went on board I saw Dunne and Carrick in Irons."

Unfortunately, this statement is neither time- nor date- specific -- and we simply do not know from the context when it occurred.

Against this order of recruitment (underlined), Peter MacGregor has Nicholas Morellos coming on board as the first of the foreigners. In his testimony he said:

> "Of the foreigners shipped at Buenos Aires Nicholas was the first who came on board, and then the Maltese; the prisoner and Big George came on board together."

Nothing could have been further from the truth. Yet MacGregor – since he was part of the first crew -- was arguably in the best position to know when the crew was successively recruited. But until Daniel Johnson's account was recalled, he was of the opinion that the Maltese followed Nicholas Morellos, and that they accompanied Big George on board. In so far as he thought that Bombos and Big George came on board together, he was again quite wrong, but he was in agreement with Carrick and, possibly, the others as well. On this view there could be no suggestion of a conspiracy between Nicholas and Big George or any suggestion of any previous relation between them. It was more likely that MacGregor collaborated with Carrick in order to cement a unified version of their evidence for the court. Unfortunately they were unified in their inaccuracies.

Carrick was the only witness to venture the dates for the recruitment of others, and for a man who was applauded for his devotion to detail, his inaccuracies on this point are remarkable. He testified as follows:

> "I shipped at Buenos Aires. I was there a few days, having arrived there from Liverpool in the *Seabird*. Big George and the prisoner joined the same day (as I did)."

When counsel challenged Carrick's evidence, he (counsel) produced the relevant crewmembers' articles in court. He pointed out in no uncertain terms that Bombos enlisted on the 23rd, whereas Big George signed on a week later, on the 30th of September. So, quite clearly Bombos and Big George did not join together. They joined in a rotation, which again gives credence to the view that perhaps Bombos did recruit Big George and Nicholas Morellos on the instructions of captain Best. Carrick in fact joined with neither Bombos nor Big George, but as the Table of Recruitment Dates shows, five days after Bombos and two days before Big George.

Whatever objections were made to the captain, they had to be made on or after the 28th of September and more particularly they had to be made between, possibly the 28th of September and the 11th of October, a period of around two weeks in which to meet with members of the old crew. Because the *Caswell* did not sail until the 24th of October, and if the British spent up to 13 days (at most) in irons, on the basis that they were released with the hoisting of the anchor, then it had to happen between these dates.

It should be remembered that MacGregor was on board all the time and was in agreement with his captain. He could not — and did not – claim any anti-foreign bias. If anything, he must have been in support of the foreigners and must have been by the same token, somewhat distant from those the captain put in irons. Carrick's interests and MacGregor's could only have gelled after the mutiny, throughout the counter mutiny, and during the trip home and in preparation for the trials.

Moreover, after the departure of Rourke, only two of the original objectors remained, Carrick and Dunne. Because he received the greatest punishment, we might infer that Rourke was the strongest objector. He was also the very first to desert the *Caswell*. Was this because of Greeks or because of captain Best? Carrick and Dunne could also have deserted, but they chose not to. Desertion would have afforded them an escape from Greeks, but not from the long shadow of British law.

By realizing that the real complaint was against the captain and that the Greeks were only used for the purpose of getting out of a foolish contract, the anomalies already enumerated can be explained.

First of all it explains the false and foolish notion the British had of the recruiting dates. How could the British have such strong objections to the Greeks when they could not remember them coming on board? First impressions are important! And if the objection to sailing with a mixed crew is mere cover-up for their fear of captain Best, then this kind of slipshod regard for first impressions are be expected.

Secondly, if the logbook had survived, perhaps it would have recorded the fact of the real complaint, and, therefore, explains why Carrick would want it thrown overboard. Of course the logbook would not have recorded the fact of their objection to sailing under captain George Best, simply because they never made that complaint. At least we do not know whether they made that complaint or not. Maybe they did, or maybe captain Best saw through their motives and made entries that could have shed light on that issue, and on why he put them in irons. It should be borne in mind that if the British objection was to captain Best, it has ramifications that go to the heart of the mutiny itself, and the plausibility of the British engineering it. And this is perhaps why one of the jurymen at the first trial simply did not believe the witnesses. And their testimony with respect to the time and the order of recruitment could not have inspired confidence in their honesty.

It is clear from his statement that Bombos knew no more than what he was told. There is a reciprocal fear engendered in the crew by both captain Best as well as George Peno, but the fear of Big George can only be realised after the mutiny, whereas before the mutiny the only fear is engendered by the captain -- and the Greeks, as we have repeatedly said, had no reason to hate the captain, whereas the British did. Did the German, Agineau, and the Irishman, Michael Rourke, go AWOL because of George Peno or because of George Best? Did they flee from something that might happen or from something that had already happened?

Thirdly, such an explanation tallies with Bombos' account. For sailors who would not ship with Greeks, the British seemed to get on quite well with each of them before the mutiny. And as for Big George? He was last to enlist, and people had little or no truck with him. So the objectors cannot read the future complaints back into an original fear of specific Greeks. The main complaint against Big George was that he threw his knife in a dangerous fashion. The other complaints against the Greeks occurred coincidentally with the counter-mutiny, when pea soup was thrown by the Greeks as a pretext to assassinating the British.

Fourthly, it goes some way to explain the need for the Pistorias' request for a letter from Carrick -- a letter of support, indemnifying them as to their role in the mutiny. In this respect Carrick could not indemnify them howsoever; but he could give his evidence now in a letter. He could say that George Peno was a brute. But Pistoria hardly sought that kind of evidence from him. He could say that the captain was a brute, that he had planned to kill the Greeks, all of them, when he got them out to sea. Carrick could have written that the British also wanted the captain dead, and that they inspired, encouraged, and welcomed the mutiny; and that they connived with the very foreigners they first objected to, to have it done. The letter could contain some explanation as to why the foreigners, who were never beaten or put in irons by the captain, mutinied. The Pistorias must have believed that the British did at one time support them in the mutiny and ought now, before their departure, to be prepared to indemnify their actions by way of a letter, a permanent reminder, as it were.

For much the same reasons, only this time in collusion with Bombos, would a similar letter explain Bombos' claim. Bombos' letter was meant to be collected and sent to the authorities. Was it ever written?

This alleged cordiality between the crew and the Greeks at this time could, of course, be explained by means of terror while in captivity. But then, why did the Pistorias quit the ship? And what avail would a letter from Carrick be under circumstances in which he wrote it out of terror? Surely the Pistorias wanted the letter as an instrument of evidential value -- just in case the British changed their minds about what had really happened? What happened to the letter eventually no one knows. After three years Giuseppe Pistoria probably thought he would have no use for it again and discarded it.

Of course, no one could have guessed how gullible, superstitious, inflammable and self-igniting the foreigners were, especially Big George.

If this was how it happened, if the initial objection was really against captain George Best, and the Greeks were used as a ploy to vent the crew's spleen, it would also explain the jubilation when, at the counter mutiny, the British – according to Bombos – took to wearing the captain's clothes. Arguably, it could have been done as a gesture to the memory of the captain – a gesture which suggested that justice on his behalf, and on behalf of the three other murdered crew members, had been done. But such feelings of retribution suggest a quieter, more refined, dignified, elevated and, perhaps, solemn celebration – not a garish display of triumphal transvestitism. The wearing of the captain's clothes, suggested a degree of triumphalism, not just over the mutineers, but also over their captain and his officers.

It explained the mutiny itself. It was a British mutiny carried out by 'Greeks.'

208

AFTERMATH AND EPILOGUE

***

Finally, it is time to ask what ever happened to the *Caswell*?

Apart from the mutinous events above recited - events which
were documented contemporaneously with the mutiny itself and the
ensuing trials -- there was very little written by way of extended treatment of either the mutiny or the *Caswell*. Periodically, of course, the
story has been repeated in miniature, invariably with little inaccuracies or unsupported opinions. At other times additional information
was added. Some curiosity lingered regarding those who got away.
What ever happened to Gaspari Pistoria, for example? Rook Aginau?
And the Irishman Michael Rourke?

Gaspari Pistoria was never discovered or brought to justice and
nothing was ever heard from either Rook Aginau or Michael Rourke.

What about the relatives of the surviving crew?

With one exception no reference could be found to any relatives of
either the 'Greeks' or the British. The exception appeared on the
following website: <:http://www.airmuseum.ca/mcgregor.html> and
reads:

> "For the last 8 years I have taught basic English as a volunteer tutor in
> Kwantlen College in Richmond and managed to have a historical novel
> published about my grandfather's involvement in a bloody 1876 mutiny-
> at-sea. The book is titled the Caswell Mutiny. "

Unfortunately, the website furnished no email address, and without
the publisher's name or place or time of publication, all hope of getting a copy of the Novel before going to print had to be abandoned.

What then about the *Caswell* herself? What ever happened to her?

> "The later history of the *Caswell*," wrote J.G. Lockhart, "marks her as a ship
> of ill-luck. After changing hands two or three times, in February 1899 she
> sailed from New South Wales to Guayaquil with a mixed crew. Her fate is
> unknown, but she never reached port." (The "Mary Celeste", London, 1952)

According to Lloyds the *Caswell* sailed from Newcastle, New South
Wales, for Guayaquil on 18th February 1899. She was loaded with a
cargo of coal, and she sailed with a crew of ten men and two appren-

209

tices. En route she disappeared and nothing more was ever heard of her. She was posted missing on 30 August 1899. Unfortunately, this account differs markedly with the only other report available, namely that of the Board of Trade. The difference lies in the estimated number of crewmembers lost on the final voyage.

When the Board of Trade enquired into the disappearance of the *Caswell* , it prepared a report that did not exceed three paragraphs in length. The report (No. 5958) is entitled:

> "Report and decision of the Local Marine Board of Newcastle, New South Wales, in the matter of the missing barque "*Caswell*", of Swansea, Official No. 70492."

This report, issued in London on the 1st day of December 1899, recited briefly:

> "An inquiry was held by the Local Marine Board into the condition of the barque *Caswell* when she left this port, and they ascertained that she was an iron vessel of 499 tons register, built on the Clyde, and owned by Messrs. Simpson Brothers, of Swansea, and commanded by Henry Lewis, a capable and experienced ship master. She had a crew of 15 men all told. The vessel sailed from this port on the 18th February last with a cargo of 756 tons of coal - she was not over laden - bound to Guayaquil, South America, and has not since been heard of.
>
> The Board reports that when the *Caswell* left Newcastle she was well found in every respect; a first class vessel; fully manned, and perfectly seaworthy, and provided with good shifting boards.
>
> There is no evidence to account for the loss of this vessel; the weather was fine at the time of sailing, and continued so for some considerable time afterwards.
>
> J H Veitch
> Secretary
>
> Office of the Local Marine Board, Newcastle, 20th September, 1899"

***

Appendix A

Narrative of C.E. Bombos

I, Christos Emanuel Bombos, shipped from Buenos Ayres with the barque *Caswell*. When I went on board I saw Dunne and Carrick in Irons. The Captain had put them in, and after 13 days gave them their liberty. Previous to this the Captain had broken their heads. The Cook (Rook Agineau) also heard him swearing and using bad language and would not work. We were ordered to scrape the rust. The captain then ordered Rook to go to the wheel and kept to the wind. Said he to the captain: "I cannot go nearer to the wind as the sails 'won't draw'". The captain used bad language about his (Rook's) sister. He (Rook) then asked him how did he know that he had a sister. The captain in reply rushed at him, caught him by the head and threw him on the deck and he remained there insensible for three hours. It was Carrick's turn to go to the wheel, and he said to Nicolas Morellos of Samos, 'I will give 6 (six pounds) to whichever of you will kill the Captain - to which he replied: "Why don't you kill him yourself?"

We arrived at Valparaiso and stopped there three days and sent Rook on shore without giving him a penny of his wages. Rook then went to the Consul and told him how the captain had treated him and the Consul sent him away without listening to him. We arrived at Antofogasta and loaded with Saltpeter, and we were half loaded, (when) two boys went with a boat to fetch the captain on board and he ordered them to go back with only him, as he intended coming with another boat. And they brought it back. We took it on board.

The mate McClean spoke to the Maltese Giuseppe Pastori (who could speak English) and told him that the captain intended killing them and throwing them overboard as soon as we sailed from the place. Pastori came to the forecastle and told it to us in Italian, We then saw the captain bring in three other English captains to dinner. And when they came on board the mate came to the Forecastle while we were in our bunks and said:

"Get up, till I tell you something -- (Giuseppe Pastori who spoke English, Dunne and Carrick were there) -- I heard your captain tell to the other captains that he would kill you and throw you overboard, as soon as the ship leaves Antofogasta. Then Giuseppe Pastori turned round to us and said: 'This strange mate says the same things as the mate McClean says.'"

At midnight when the captains were going away, Gaspari Pastori stole up to the cabin to find if they were saying anything. He heard the captain repeating accusations and he then came back and told us. Then we said to the English crew, "We cannot work tomorrow but go and tell the Consul."

They refused. Then G.Pastori said, "I will not go ashore either, since there is no English consul, but only an interpreter who used to attend English ships." Consequently we commenced to work.

I Christos E. Bambos heard that myself, and when I heard more (of) those words, I asked a boatman to take my clothes, and take the boat onshore - offering him a pound at the same time. I then asked permission of the captain to go on shore on the pretence of buying cigars, intending not to return on board again; but he would not allow me, or anyone to go on shore and got a watchman to watch us all the night through.

We sailed on Friday evening, and on the whole of next day (Saturday) we were kept at work, without getting any food. On Sunday evening I felt unwell and the first mate came and told Big George to come and release me. George said he would not come, as he could not speak English, George said he could not go, as he did not know English and it would not do for the whole watch to go on as he could not speak the English language, and said: 'Let others go.'

Then the first mate said:" You must go, because if you wont I shall go and tell the captain." Big George repeated again: "I wont go." The first mate then went to the captain, and the captain came to the fore below with the mate and a revolver in his hand and ordered Big George to his watch. He still refused, saying: "Let other men go because I cannot speak English." The captain insisted on his going. Then Big George said to him: "Why have you come to the forecastle with a revolver? To kill me? It is usual for captains when they want the sailors, to send for them on the cabin, and if they do not obey orders to write their conduct in the logbook or put them in irons until we arrive in England." The captain then went off.

On Monday when we were at work Carrick said to Giuseppe:"The captain wants to kill you -- as he killed a French man in the same way on the main yard, and, at another time, a boy at Autofagosta. He will do the same thing to you."

That evening he sent me weekly provision and some bread and sugar (but) G. Pastori spoke to the first mate and asked him (because) they did not get the usual provision. The mate said you will get us butter or oil for the lamp.

On Tuesday morning the watch of the captain (and Carrick) came, and when Carrick came to give his work to Big George and I gave mine to Dunne and G. Pastori went to the wheel, the captain went where Big George was working and spoke to him. But I did not hear what he said. But I heard the captain cry out and going up I saw the captain standing on deck with his stomach ripped open. G. Pastori left the wheel and fired his revolver at the captain's head. And as the first mate was coming on Nicholas Morellos ran out of the galley and stabbed him twice. Big George did the same and G. Pastori fired at him and finished him.

Then George caught the Steward by the neck and dragged him in the Cabin to show him where the arms were kept. I then said to George "Don' kill any more." He then turned round and told me, "If you say more I will kill you too." And he then dispatched him with his knife.

Then Giuseppe Pastori called out for the second mate who was hiding in the cabin and where he came up he fired at him and finished him. At the same time Big George was holding him and hacking him with his knife. Giuseppe fired at him twice and when the second mate fell he lay near the captain.

Then George took a rope, and gave it to G. Pastori, and they tied all the feet of the slain together. Then Giuseppe ordered us to take the anchor and tied the rope with the bodies on it and pitched it overboard -- in which we all helped except the boy McDonald who was at the wheel.

Appendix A

The carpenter who was locked up in the Galley saw nothing of this except the commencement. When he saw the captain pulled down by Big George.

Then Giuseppe Pastori ordered Nicholas Morellos and Carrick to go down to the cabin and find out the whereabouts of the ship. In the meantime we washed the decks. They then went down in the cabin. George and Pastori locked themselves in the captain's cabin. What they did I cannot say. Then George came out and brought Nicholas Morellos in (and) locked the door again. I heard the clinking of coin. They then came out and Carrick followed them up. Pastori ordered breakfast and said we will go to Valparaiso. Then the two Maltese with George and Nicholas went down into the Cabin, and in about half an hour they called me up, and I went down and asked them what did they want. George said to me "We will tell you -- do you value your life?"

"Ho", says I "of course I do. Who does not?"

Says he: "We will go to Valparaiso, scuttle the ship and kill the Englishmen and yourself -- but if you wish to save your life you can if you like".

Says I: "I will neither kill anyone nor let you scuttle the ship -- for these men have done nothing to me and I have no spite against the owners".

Then George said: "Since you do not wish to do as you are told, you will share the fate of the others".

"Be it so", says I. I then came on deck and went foreword and told Carrick what Nicholas and George and the Maltese wanted to do, i.e. to kill us and sink the ship, So we had better be on the look out. Gaspard Pastori came up then and asked me what was I grieving about. And I replied: "Why should not I grieve considering you are going to slay me?"

"Oh", says he, "You need not be afraid"

I then asked him why did they wish to commit this frightful act. Says he: "Which other way can we escape?"

Says I: "You do not know the coast -- as none of you have been here before. And if you scuttle the ship, you will be caught by the agents of the owners of the ship and cargo wherever you happen to go to. But listen to what I suggest". Then I spoke thus:

> "We will take the ship back to Buenos Ayres and you can go on shore with Nicholas and Big George. Then the five English men and myself can take the ship back to England".

"Well" said he, "I will speak to my brother about it".

He did so -- but his brother made no reply. Then I went up to them and repeated what I said before. And he said: "I will think about it "-- but that George, he was sure, would not listen to such a proposal.

"We are in the majority", says I, "and we could carry it out since there are only two of the other side. If you mind what I say you need not care as I understand their language and will listen to what they say and can report it to you, and then both yourselves and the ship will be saved".

They assembled and came below with me, and we told Nicholas and George we would take the ship to Buenos Ayres; and the four of them could go ashore and I with the other Englishmen would take the ship back to England. Then George took out his revolver and tried to fire at me, but the Maltese prevented him. Then he told them not to mind what I said as he (Christos) wants to have you arrested. We argued the point for over an hour, and came on deck.

In the evening I stole into the cabin, where Nicholas and George were. And I tried to make out what they were talking about. And I heard George say:

> "We must kill the Maltese and Christos and afterwards the Englishmen, scuttle the ship and go to Valparaiso, and in case we are arrested to say that the ship caught fire and that all perished. And we will be believed since a Greek and Maltese were asleep".

I then came up on deck and spoke to the Englishmen and the Maltese on the forecastle: "I will tell you something both for your good and for mine; if you do not wish to sink the ship I will tell you".

Appendix A

"Tell us", says they, " and we will not sink the ship". I then repeated what I had heard.

The Maltese then hailed me as a brother and Gaspari said: "You take a revolver", and he gave me one. Says I: "Let half of you sleep, but be wide awake". Then I told Carrick and Dunne the whole thing. And Carrick said to me, "I have no arms".

"Take a halibut", says I, "and in addition, you have your own knife. I have a revolver since Gaspari gave me one. But you had better be on the lookout".

The whole night we kept watch. In the morning George came and spoke to the two Maltese and me, and asked us what did we intend to do? "Have you", says he, "agreed with Christos and the Englishmen?"

"Christos will play the deuce: he will eat your head with you".

Gaspari said: "It is you that wants to play the deuce with us, and not Christos."

Then George said to the Maltese: "We must do what I told you or else we shall have a general fight."

Then Gaspari said: "We four will go on shore at Buenos Ayres and then Christos with the Englishmen can bring the ship back to England."

Then George said: " If we go back we will scuttle the vessel".

The Maltese said: "We will see about that".

When we came to St Antonio I said to the Maltese: "George will propose to you to land at Monte Video. You can persuade him to go out with you. We can then set sail for England".

They said: "Very well".

And when we approached, George said: "When you go to Monte Video take care you do not take Christos Bombos with you for as sure as you do, he will go and inform on you." And they agreed. Gaspari came and told me that "George would land at Monte Video and you could go back to England".

Then I said: "If George does not come on shore, will you take me with you?" And they said: "Yes".

I went then to Carrick and said: "You must write a letter to the Consul and I will take (it) to him (as I am going on shore with the Maltese) -- that he might send a man of war to arrest Nicholas and George. But do not let them see you write it".

He did so and gave me the letter. Then Giuseppe Pastori said: "We will not take you ashore and George will land at Monte Video with Nicholas."

Then said I: "This is all the thanks I get. But for me George would have killed you".

Said he: "My brother told me that George told him that you would inform on us, and that is the reason".

Says I: "If you do not wish to take me on shore, at least do me a favour."

"What is that?" says he

Says I: "I wish you would take a letter for me to a certain coffee house, and my brother's cousin will get it."

Says he: "I will think about it."

I then told Carrick that I could not go on shore since they would take me, but I could have the letter conveyed, if you hold your tongue. When they launched the boat to go on shore I asked Gaspari in tears to take the letter and he took it and left it on shore. This letter came to Queenstown and I saw it. They then landed. For the past three months I had slept in the forecastle along with the English crew, Nicholas and George had slept with the Maltese in the cabin, and when the Maltese left, George ordered me to bring my chest into the other cabin and not to speak or mix with the English. If I did he would kill me. Then I went in the forecastle and sat on my chest and said to Carrick:"This is no good, bad for all men".

Appendix A

He then helped me to bring my chest in. Then George spoke and said: "If you ever come down in this cabin whilst I am asleep, I will kill you."

One day Carrick came into the cabin and he saw the logbook on the table and said, "Throw the book overboard, it will tell against us".

But I did not do so. He then took the book and pitched it into the sea out of the cabin window. After that I said to Carrick and Dunne that when George and Nicholas were asleep, we would (go) down below, tie them and bring them to England in that condition. But they would not agree to this.

That evening I felt unwell and I asked the carpenter for two potatoes and some coffee, which he gave me. I then went and slept with Nicholas. George slept on deck, but I did not see him as I slept below.

Then, as Dunne afterwards informed me, he made the appointed sign by pulling a cap on his head -- and they went at George with hatchets and finished him. The carpenter then came below and cut Nicholas Morellos' head off with an axe, as he was asleep in the captain's berth. (The pillow still bears the mark of the axe) I was asleep when I was awakened by a blow on the head from an axe, which was succeeded by a shower of blows from the same quarter. I staggered and fell in the middle of the cabin. I had besides the four (cuts?) on my head, one on the neck, two on the hands and two on the back. Then I asked Carrick: "Why are you trying to kill me? I have not harmed you, but on the contrary I saved your life and the ship."

They then caught hold of me and dragged me on deck where George was lying down; then he was heard to groan, and Dunne 'taking the axe from Carrick broke George's skull in three places. Then MacDonald brought his (George's) revolver from the cabin and Carrick discharged it at the body, and pitched him overboard.

They seized me and locked me in the carpenter-house, where I remained half insensible for the next ten hours, I weltering in blood. They came then and asked me (if?) I was dead. I replied "Is this the return I get for saving you! I proposed that George Nicholas should be seized, and brought to England in Irons. I repeated to you faithfully what I had heard, and you promised me, that if I saved your life you would give me anything I wanted when we returned to England, and hailed me as a brother -- and now you want to kill me."

They then said; "We will cure you, and not kill you". Then they brought a needle and stitched up my wounds and anointed them with oil, and in a fortnight I began to mend. At the end of that time they put me in irons and gave me very little bread and water, and very often I (went) without getting anything to eat the whole day, and they used to beat me on the face with their clenched fists, which made the blood run from my nose and mouth I used to ask them (why?). They would then reply: "Because you are a Greek". And I said: "Is that the reason? Because I am a Greek? There are good and bad amongst all nationalities." I then asked for bread, and they struck me, and repeated the treatment when I demanded some water. Says I:"If you do not give me something I will die".

Said they: "That is precisely what we wish".

Said I: "You had better take another and finish me, rather than torture me in this manner".

One day we met an English ship, and the captain came on board, and Carrick told him everything about the mutiny. And the captain came up where I was tied up and said: "Did you do anything?"

"No", says I -- and Carrick confirmed my statement. Then the captain went away.

In about ten days we came across a French ship and Carrick went on board and stayed the whole day to set the ships chronometer, and came back in the evening. On the French there was an English boy who was dissatisfied and he jumped overboard and swam to our ship, when he came on board MacDonald told him everything. One day when the boy was passing me with the plates I begged a piece of meat from him, and (he) refused, saying that he had orders to that effect, and went and told Carrick. Then Carrick came up to me with a piece of raw pork about 9 lbs weight and hit me across the face with it -- and struck me in the nose with his clenched fist and said: "If you ask for anything more I will kill you".

"I want to return to England because I have not done anything, if I say anything it will be but the plain truth and nothing to your disadvantage".

Appendix A

And they said: "You will not be rewarded by the owners. So you had better, when we are nearing home, to take a small boat and land on the French coast." But I refused, and he took a stick and began to strike me.

Then he took a marling-spike and poked it in my eyes. McDonald came up and said: " If you do not land on the French coast, Carrick will kill you."

I still refused. And day and night I used to be beaten, and when I tried to sleep they used to pour cold water on me, and I was kept constantly drenched. The French ship's boy could testify to the truth of the statement regarding my ill treatment.

Dunne, Carrick and the carpenter wore the captain's clothes.

This is the truth and I Christos Bombos, imprisoned here have written this statement.

Translated at this Hellenic Majesty and Consulate, Queenstown

A True translation

G Yourdi etc
Consul for Greece.

The *Caswell* Calendar

Built at Dumbarton in 1875 and Registered in Swansea: -

Official Number: 70492
Signal Code: N.W.T.H.
Gross Tonnage: 517
Net Tonnage: 499
Length in feet: 156.5
Breadth in feet: 28.0
Depth in feet: 16.8
Builders: McKellar, McMillan & Co of Dumbarton in 1875.
Owner: W.H. Tucker & Co., Swansea

Date of Arrival in Glasgow: 1st July 1875.
Date of Departure from Glasgow (at 8am) to Buenos Aires: 1st July 1875
Date of Arrival in Buenos Aires: 10th September 1875, after 73 days:
Date of Enlistment of New Crew: 19th -30th September, 1875
Date of Departure from Buenos Aires to Valparaiso: 24th October 1875
(MacGregor says the 23rd.)
Date of Arrival: 1st December 1875 (Michael Rourke, an Irishman,
jumped ship; the ship stayed 3 days)
Date of Departure from Valparaiso to Antofogasta: Circa 4th December
(Rook Agineau, a German, jumped ship) (MacGregor says the Irishman
left here)
Date of arrival at Antofogasta -- circa Boxing Day, 1875
Date of Departure from Antofogasta to Queenstown: 1st January 1876
Date of Last Log Entry: 3rd January 1876
Date of Mutiny: 4th January 1876
Date Pistorias left *Caswell* and up River Plate: 18th/19 February 1876
Date of Counter Mutiny: 11th March 1876
Date of Arrival in Queenstown:(8.20 am) May 13, 1876
Date of Bombos' First Trial: Thursday July 27 1876
Date of Bombos' Second Trial: Monday the 31st of July
Date of Execution: 25th August 1876
Date of murder of John Hyland: 30th of March 1876
Date of Trial of Thomas Crowe: Tuesday morning July 25th, 1876

221

Date of Execution: 25th August 1876

Dates Appicable to Giuseppe Pistoria:
Date Giuseppe Pistoria First Spotted in Monte Video: 21st January 1879
Date arrested: 27th January 1879
Date of Departure for Liverpool: 18th April 1879
Date of arrival: 20th March 1879
Date Pistoria given in custody, Queenstown: 1st April 1879
Date of Pistoria's Trial: 22/4th July 1879
Date of Execution: 25 August 1879
Last Voyage of *Caswell*: On February 18, 1899, the Caswell sailed from Newcastle, New South Wales with a cargo of coal, a crew of ten and two apprentices. Nothing more was ever heard of her.
On August 30, 1899, The *Caswell* was posted missing.
Board of Trade Report: September 20, 1899

REFERENCES

Newspapers

The (London) Times:

May 16, 1876
July 28, 1876
July 29, 1876
August 1, 1876
March 21, 1879
March 27, 1879
April 2, 1879
April 21, 1879
August 21, 1879

The Cork Constitution:

May 16, 1876
May 23,1876
August 1, 1876
July 26, 1876:
July 27, 1876:
August 21, 1879
August 26, 1879

The Cork Examiner:

July 26, 1876
July 27, 1876
July 28, 1876
July 29, 1879
August 1, 1876
August 21, 1879
August 25, 1876
August 26, 1879

The Cambrian, Swansea,

12th May 1876
19th May 1876
28th July 1876
4th August 1876

The Illustrated News
The *Illustrated News*, 27 May 1876

REFERENCES

The *Illustrated News*, May 1875- October 1876

The Archives, Bishop's St., Dublin

CRF 1879 B - 26 –1876
CRF 1879   M – 26 -1879
CSORP 8080/78
CRF C-36-76

Home Office Files:

HO45/9545/SS307/90777

Journals:

Sea Breezes v 15 Nov 1931
Sea Breezes number 236, August 1965
The Mariner's Mirror, Vol 74,Feb. 1988

Reference Books:

Ball, F. Ellington, The Judges In Ireland, 1221-1921, (The Round Hall Press, Dublin
    1993, Vols 1 & 11)
Bateson, Charles, and Loney, Jack, Australian Shipwrecks 1622-1990, 5 vols.
    (Various Publishers, 1972-91). 656.61.085.3(94)
Berman, Bruce D, Encyclopedia of American Shipwrecks (Boston: Mariners Press,
    1972). 656.61.085.3(73)
Bevan, Bryan, The Great Seamen of Elizabeth 1, London, 1971
Burney, James, History of the Buccaneers of America, London, 1949
Chapelle, H.I.: The Search for Speed under Sail. New York, 1967.
Cooper-Pritchard, A.H., The Buccaneers, London, 1929
Cooper, James Fenimore: The Red Rover and:
    The Pilot, A Tale of the Sea (Two Vols. New York, published by Charles
    Wiley, 1823)
Cordingly, David, Women at Sea in the Great Age of Sail, NY, 2001
Cruikshank, E.A., Life of Sir Henry Morgan, London, 1935
Course, Captain A.G., Pirates of the Eastern Seas, London, 1966
Course, Captain A.G., Pirates of the Western Seas, London, 1969

Dana, Richard Henry, Jr., Two Years before the Mast, 1840
    The Seaman's Friend, 1841
Earle, Peer, Corsairs of Malta and Barbary, London, 1970
Forester, C.S., The Barbary Pirates, London, 1956
Goldsmith, John, Voyage in the Beagle, London, 1978'
Gosse, Philip, The History of Piracy, London and New York, 1932
Hocking, Charles, Dictionary of Disasters at Sea during the Age of Steam
    (London: Lloyd's Register of Shipping, 1 016.656.61.085.3)
Hooke, Norman, Modern Shipping Disasters 1963-Z987 (London: Lloyd's of
    London Press, 1989). 016.656.61.085.3'1963/1987
Lane, F.C.: "The Mysterious Sea," Doubleday, New York, 1947
Lockhart, J.G., The "Mary Celeste" (and other strange tales of the sea),
    London, 1952
Lubbock, Basil, The Last of the Windjammers, vol. 1, vol. 11 and
    Vol.111, Glasgow, 1975
Lubbock, Basil, The Opium Clippers
Lubbock, Basil, Round the Horn Before the Mast, Glasgow, 1986
Luring, Thomas, The Fighting Sailor Turn'd Peaceable Christian
    (HTML at voicenet.com)
MacGregor, D.R.: Fast Sailing Ships. Nautical Publishing, 1973.
Mason, A.E., Life of Francis Drake, London 1941
Philbrick, Nathaniel, In the Heart of the Sea, Harper Collins, 2000
Pringle, Patrick, Jolly Roger, London and New York, 1953
Raban, Jonathan, *The Oxford Book of the Sea*, OUP, 1992
Ran away to Sea, Reid, Capt Mayne,Private (Ticknor and Fields),1859
Rhadamanthus : Our Judges, Dublin, 1890
Sailing Alone, Slocum, Joshua, Penguin ,1999
Sailor's Life, Hartog, A Jan de, Harper and Brothers, 1955
Saunders, Margaret Marshall, Her Sailor: A Love Story
    (Boston: L.C.Page, 1900)
Sauer, C.O., The Early Spanish Main, Los Angeles, 1966
Stammers, Michael K.: The Passage Makers, Teredo Books,
    Brighton, 1978.
Under Sail (Swansea Cutters, Tallships and Seascapes 1830 - 1880)
    Published by the Glynn Vivian Art Gallery, Swansea City Council
    on the occasion of the exhibition 'Under Sail'), 20 June - 1 August, 1987
Wallace, Frederick William: Wooden Ships and Iron Men. London, 1924.
Williams, Neville, The Sea Dogs, London, 1975
Woodworth, Francis C., Stories by Jack Mason, the Old Sailor, (NY: Clark, Austin
    & Co., 1851; see also: HTML at merrycoz.org).

Websites:

Most Websites lead elsewhere. The following handful of sites is both self-explanatory
and provides a wealth of other links to further maritime sites:

    http://www.cus.cam.ac.uk/mhe1000/intro
    It also leads on to the Naval and Maritime Museums pages at
    http://pc-78120.udac.se: 8001/WWW/Nautica/Museums/mm.html
    And to Naval and Maritime Museums in Europe at
    http://pc-78-120.udac.se: 8001/www/Nautica/Museums/MMEU.html
    And to the Maritime History Virtual Archives at
    http://pc-78-120.udac.se: 8001/WWW/Nautica/Nautica.html

Other sites, such as
<http://www.bbc.co.uk/wales/southwest/swansea/categories/pages/museums.sht
m>
And the Project Gutenberg at <ftp//ftp.biblio.org >ed. By Logan Marshall
<http//ihr.sas.ac.uk/gh>)
carry their own rewards.

See also:

<http//www.cityoflondon.gov.uk/history/archiheritage>
and the National Maritime Museum (Greenwich, London SE10 9NF), which
provides all kinds of historical information relating to Lloyd's registers, muster
rolls, crews, captains, ships, agreements, etc all variously referred to at several
of the following sites:

http://www.nmm.ac.uk
<http://www.port.nmm.ac.uk/research/c8.htm>
<manuscripts@nmm.ac.uk.>
<(http://www.nmm.ac.uk)>
< (http://www.nmm.ac.u k) >
< http://www.mun.ca/mha/>
See also *<http://www.pro.gov.uk>*
and <http://www.AandCorg> and
<http://www.aandc.org/member_pages/ims/sb_236_571.jpg>
P.O. Box 125, Picton, Ontario, K0K 2T0, Canada!
Phone 1 613 476 1177 — Fax 1 613 476 7598
Visitors — 2, Gladstone Avenue, Picton, Ontario

Book Index

A

A Double Execution 140, Ch 8
A Man Named Clayton 167
A New Crew 16, 17 159
Abdül Hamid II 20
Agaera 23
Alexander Selkirk 7
Algeria and Tunisia 21
Alias JOSEPH PISTORIA 168 et. seq.
Allan McLean,
  the second mate 14, 36, 40, 42, 181,
    208
An Irish mate 24
Archimandrite 29, 141, 145, 146, 147,
    148, 149, 151
Argentina 16, 32, 56, 158
Armistice 22
Attica 1, 23, 141

B

Bahia 10, 159
Baumbos 11, 12, 13, 44, 48, 54, 63,
    66, 82, 83, 84, 85, 86, 90, 102,
    103,106, 107, 111, 152, 220
    See Bombos
Belfast 10
Big George 13, 26, 32, 36, 37, 38, 39,
    40, 41, 42, 43, 44, 45, 46, 47,
    49, 50,51, 52, 54, 56, 57, 58,
    60, 62, 64, 65,66, 67, 68, 84,
    86, 87, 88, 89, 90, 93,94, 99,
    102, 109, 183, 184, 187,
    192,193, 194, 203, 215, 219,
    220, 221, 222,224, 227, 228,
    229, 230
Big George Peno, 31, 37, 43, 44, 45,
    46, 47, 48, 49, 50, 51, 52, 54,
    55, 56,59, 60, 61, 63, 65, 66,
    68, 69, 70, 73,

75, 77, 78, 79, 80, 81, 100, 101, 103,
    104, 105, 106, 107, 108, 111, 112, 118,
    121, 129, 209, 210, 214, 219, 220, 221,
    231, 244, 249, 250, 251, 252, 253, 255,
    259, 260, 261, 262
Big Harry 29
boatswain's locker
boatswain 8
Board of Trade, 15, 181, 187, 192,
    198, 241, 270
Bombos 2, 12, 13, 15, 19, 26, 27, 28,
    32, 34, 36, 37, 38, 39, 40, 41, 42, 4346,
    47, 49, 50, 51, 52, 54, 55, 56, 57, 58,
    59, 60, 62, 63, 64, 65, 66, 67, 68, 69,
    70, 71, 72, 74, 75, 76, 78, 80, 81, 83,
    86, 87, 88, 90, 93, 94, 96, 98, 99, 100,
    101, 102, 105, 108, 109, 110, 125, 140,
    142, 145, 146, 147, 148, 149, 150, 151,
    156, 157, 160, 162, 164, 168, 171, 173,
    176, 181, 183, 184, 185, 186, 191, 204
    Christos Emmanuel, 1, 2, 14,
    15, 16,17, 18, 23, 30, 32, 37,
    40, 42, 43, 45,46, 48, 49, 50,
    51, 54, 55, 56, 58, 59, 60, 61,
    62, 63, 66, 67, 68, 69, 70, 71,
    72, 73, 75, 76, 77, 78, 79, 80,
    81, 82, 83, 84, 85, 86, 87, 89,
    90, 92, 94, 96, 97, 99, 100, 103,
    104, 105, 106, 108, 111, 112,
    113, 115, 116, 117, 118, 119,
    120, 121, 124, 125, 127, 128,
    129, 130, 135, 145, 146, 162,
    163, 164, 167, 168, 169, 170,
    171, 172, 173, 174, 179, 180,
    183, 186, 187, 191, 195, 198,
    201, 206,208, 209, 210, 211,
    212, 218, 232, 238, 239, 244,
    248
Brazil 16, 161
Brigandage 23
British crew 19, 216

British soldiers 22
Brothers Pistoria 37, 163; Chs. 10,11
Buenos Aires 1, 4, 5, 9, 10, 11, 14, 15,
16, 18, 19, 31, 48, 49, 50, 51, 52, 54,
57, 58, 59, 79, 85, 86, 102, 151, 156,
157, 158, 160, 161, 162, 163, 169, 170,
172, 174, 177, 214, 216, 218, 219, 220,
221, 223, 236
  Buenos Ayres, 1, 5, 6, 11, 12,
  16, 17,18, 19, 21, 22, 36, 57,
  58, 61, 63, 65, 70, 72, 95, 101,
  102, 103, 104, 121, 174, 179,
  180, 181, 184, 186, 193, 194,
  197, 199, 202, 243, 245, 246,
  248, 249, 250, 251, 253, 269

C

Cape Horn 1, 2, 3, 54
capital punishment 96, 101, 130,
152, 210; Ch.8,11
Captain,
  Sea-captain, 1, 2, 3, 8, 9, 10, 12,
  13, 14, 15, 16, 18, 19, 20, 21, 22,
  23, 28, 29, 30, 31, 32, 33, 35, 36,
  37, 38, 39,40, 41, 42, 44, 45, 47,
  48, 49, 50, 51,52, 53, 54, 55, 56,
  57, 58, 59, 60, 61,67, 72, 73, 83,
  84, 85, 86, 98, 99, 100, 101, 102,
  103, 104, 105, 106, 107, 108,
  117, 118, 119, 121, 122, 123,
  124, 125, 126, 172, 174, 176,
  185, 190, 192, 201, 210, 211,
  213, 220, 221, 231, 242, 243,
  244, 245, 246, 247, 248, 249,
  250, 252,254, 255, 256, 257,
  258, 259, 260, 261,267

  Captain Best
  11, 12, 17, 18, 26, 28, 31, 32, 34,
  46,82, 86, 90, 98, 99, 153, 216,
  217, 221,223

  Captain George Best 16, 99, 103,
  105, 215, 216, 217, 218, 223,225

Captain Hatfield 24
Captain R. D. Peattie 30
Captain Tullock
  of the Glynliffon, 162, 166
Carrick and Dunne 38, 45, 48, 49, 52,
57, 64, 65, 169, 184, 185, 187, 222,
231, 232
Caswell mutiny Ch.3 2, 68,175, 176,
213
Hue And Cry The Caswell Ch.9 178
Charles Darwin 15
Charles McDonald
  an apprentice 14, 60, 87, 99,
183
Constable Nugent, 149, 150, 161
Crown Solicitor, 90, 97, 203, 224
Christos Bombos 2, 13, 58, 63, 75,
145, 232, 234
  Christos Emmanuel Bombos 1,
  12, 14, 35, 74, 81, 95, 108, 115,
  141, 150, 151, 152
Constantinople 21, 77
Copper Ore 3
Cork 72, 74, 75, 76, 78, 81, 83, 93,
94, 100, 101, 111, 112, 119, 120, 122,
123, 124, 125, 131, 133, 136, 137, 138,
140, 141, 145, 150, 151, 152, 157, 160,
170, 173, 180, 181, 182, 193, 196, 197,
198, 199, 200, 201, 202, 209, 210, 238
COUNTER MUTINY Ch. 4, p 90 et
al.
Chapter 4 62
Cyprus 21

D

Dana 6, 7, 105, 240
Dr Denis Donovan 150
Dr. Beamish
  medical officer, 150, 204, 209,
211
Dr. F. H. Smith 150
Dr O Neill. See Chapter 7
Dr. Stratuli
  Greek Archpriest. See Bombos,
  and Execution, Chapter 8

Dublin Castle, 131, 180, 182, 193, 194
Dunne, John.
Dumbarton 3, 14, 183, 236
Dylan Thomas 155

E

E. Pinatel
    a Frenchman, 160, 165, 167
Emmanuel Griffiths.
    the black steward 11, 14, 41, 74
English crew 15, 19, 62, 95, 102,
227, 232
Edward Warner, 12, 118, 124, 244
Execution 2, 25, 29, 48, 95, 97, 98,
107, 111, 119, 123, 140, 141, 142, 145,
146, 150, 152, 156, 168, 173, 188, 193,
196, 197, 198, 199, 201, 202, 204, 208,
209, 210, 211
    Executions Ch. 8/1165, 98,
    141, 142, 147

F

Foreigners 19, 33, 34, 46
FRANCESCO MOSCHARA
    the trial of Ch. 10/11 180, 190,
    200 et al.

G

Galtee
Galtees, Galtee Castle. See Chapter 7.
Galtee evictions. See Galtees, Chapter
7, p. 144 et al.
Gaspari 13, 14, 19, 26, 33, 34, 36, 37,
38, 39, 40, 41, 42, 45, 46, 47, 49, 51,
59, 60, 83, 109, 161, 163, 172, 184,
225, 227, 228, 229, 232, 237 and
George Peno 12, 13, 14, 26, 36, 39,
40, 47, 50, 51, 58, 66, 71, 93, 99, 183,
191, 215, 220, 224 See Big George and
    Greeks
Gilbert and Sullivan
    Chapter 2.
Giuseppi 13, 203

Giuseppe Pistoria 13, 14, 47, 50, 157,
212 See
George Edward Best 14, 74, 104, 105,
181, 208
Greeks 12, 13, 17, 18, 19, 20, 24, 25,
26, 28, 30, 34, 35, 36, 38, 43, 44, 45,
47, 48, 49, 50, 52, 53, 54, 59, 60, 62,
63, 64, 65, 66, 67, 71, 77, 85, 86, 87,
88, 89, 94, 102, 106, 151, 159, 173,
176, 182, 184, 186, 191, 192, 193, 214,
215, 216, 217, 218, 220, 221, 222, 223,
224, 225
    Greco-, 1, 13, 15, 17, 21, 26,
    27, 28, 29, 31, 34, 35, 43, 51,
    65, 66, 72, 76, 77, 79, 83, 90,
    91, 92, 93, 94, 105, 106, 113,
    118, 120, 122, 125, 126, 127,
    130, 131, 132, 162, 163, 164,
    168, 170, 172, 173, 175, 176,
    192, 206, 249, 254, 263, 265,
    266, 267
Glasgow 4, 5, 9, 10, 11, 14, 15, 49,
82, 83, 99, 162, 183, 217, 218, 236,
240
Goshawk. See Caswell, Queenstown.
    See Caswell, Queenstown. See
    Harbour, Queenstown
Guano phosphate 175, 176

H

H. PinckneyWalker
    , of the Charleston Consulate 160
Hafod Copper Works 3
Hanging in the 1870s. See Letters And
    Petitions, Chapter 6
Heron Q.C. See trials of Bombos
Herzegovina 21
High Court 7
High Seas,
    Murder on, crime on, 12, 35,
    41, 181,236, 237
HMS Pinafore 17
Horn, The 2, 18, 31, 52, 54, 96, 240
HUE AND CRY THE CASWELL
Chapter 9 146 et. al.

South America
    America 3, 9, 104, 152, 153,
    159, 161,170, 214
        South America. 3, 104, 159
        South Carolina 160, 162
Straits of Magellan 31
Sub-constable Jones, 141, 161
Swansea
    Swansea 1, 3, 4, 12, 75, 76, 158,
160, 213, 236, 239, 241
        Old Swansea town, 1, 2, 3, 4, 5,
        14, 90, 92, 181, 183, 242, 269,
        272, 273, 274
Swansea pioneers 3
Swansea's North Dock 2, 3

T

T. M. Healy 141
The 1870s 3, 5, 13, 15, 31, 97, 98,
158, 176
The *Beagle* 15, 39, 240
The *Cambrian* 4, 12, 15, 36, 63, 68,
101, 239
The Cape 31
The *Caswell* 1, 2, 3, 4, 5, 7, 8, 10, 11,
14, 15, 18, 24, 25, 26, 27, 28, 31, 32,
33, 34, 47, 49, 51, 54, 55, 57, 58, 59,
60, 62, 65, 67, 68, 69, 70, 72, 73, 74,
76, 77, 78, 82, 83, 85, 99, 100, 105,
106, 108, 110, 112, 114, 125, 141, 145,
151, 156, 158, 159, 160, 162, 167, 168,
171, 172, 173, 175, 176, 177, 178, 182,
183, 184, 185, 186, 191, 194, 212, 213,
214, 215, 216, 217, 218, 222, 237
The Charleston Suspect 160
The Chief Mate 7
The Commissioners of Customs 159
The Cook
    Rook Agineau, *10*
The Cork Constitution 160
The Cork Examiner 111, 152, 182,
238
The Cork Herald 141
The Drop,
    scaffold 149, 209

The English Government 23
The Executioner 149, 205
The Foreign Office 158, 163, 168,
174, 175, 178
The Gallows 146
The High Seas 74, 80, 152
The Home Office á 157, 158, 159, 160,
161, 163, 168, 173, 174, 178
The Illustrated News 63, 72, 73, 75,
239
The Leicester Castle, 35
The Old Bailey, 33
The Lennie 18, 24, 25, 26, 28, 29, 78,
79, 82, 100
The Lennie Mutiny 24
The Marquis of Salisbury 175, 178
The Pistorias 12, 51, 52, 55, 56, 57,
59, 62, 64, 156, 157, 158, 160, 162,
163, 164, 167, 172, 173, 181, 184, 186,
220, 224, 225
The Port of Swansea 2
The River Plate á 54
The *Sea Gull*,
    Baltimore, 164
The Second Mate 24, 25
Thomas Crowe 79, 110, 111, 119,
120, 121, 122, 123, 124, 125, 127, 131,
133, 134, 140, 141, 142, 143, 144, 145,
149, 151, 152, 153, 154, 196, 237
The Times 22, 29, 100, 106, 153, 160,
177, 181, 238
Turkey and Servia 22
Turks 22, 24, 25, 77, 217
The Washington Consulate, *187, 190*

V

Valparaiso 27, 30, 31, 32, 33, 47, 49,
51, 79, 151, 227, 229, 231, 236
Victorians 180

W

Wales 2, 4, 98, 101, 160, 213, 237
Walter Chisholm Ferguson,
    an apprentice 14, 86

I

Illustrated News, 4, 76, 87, 88, 89, 90, 272

Irish court 26 I Chs.5,7,10

J

J. M. Synge 62

James Carrick,
able seaman 2, 11, 12, 14, 26, 27, 28, 34, 39, 41, 57, 73, 76, 109, 114, 158, 172, 174, 175, 176, 179, 183

James H. Wood
detective, 165

Jasper Kelsoe and William Kelsoe. See Chapter 9. See Chapter 9. See Chapter 9

John Dunne,
able seaman 11, 12, 14, 26, 27, 86, 166, 183, 191, 213

John Henry Vivian and Sons 3

John Hyland
A servant. See Chapter 7

John Ryan
Tenant. See Chapter 7

John Masefield's 6

Joseph Moschara chs. 10/11 pp. 200,210
an able seaman.
See also Joseph Pistoria 14

Joseph Pistoria 32, 43, 44, 58, 85, 162, 163, 167, 168, 169, 171, 173, 174, 181, 188, 189, 194, 197, 202, 205, 208

Joyce's Ulysses 5

Juan Fernandez islands 32

Judge 7, 47, 90, 94, 99, 111, 136, 154, 181, 187, 193, 196, 198, 208, 209

K

Kourkoubas 23

L

La Plata 161, 163, 166

Leicester Castle, 28, 30

Lord Jim 16

M

Maltese 11, 12, 13, 33, 34, 43, 44, 47, 48, 49, 50, 51, 52, 54, 55, 56, 57, 58, 60, 62, 85, 106, 107, 109, 110, 159, 163, 170, 171, 182, 186, 217, 219, 220, 222, 223, 227, 229, 230, 231, 232

Marwood
the executioner, 112, 118, 148, 149, 150, 198, 199, 200, 201, 205, 210, 212

Masons 163, 164, 166

Mate
The first mate, the second mate, chief mate, 8, 9, 10, 16, 28, 35, 39, 40, 43, 44, 47, 48, 49, 50, 51, 52,54, 55, 58, 99, 100, 102, 103, 108,123, 124, 213, 214, 216, 221, 237,259, 260, 261

Matteo Cargalia 29

Merchant Navy 158

Merchant Service 153

Michael Rourke
an able seaman 14, 15, 26, 27, 212, 236

Midhat Pasha 20

Mitchelstown Murder 121

Mitchelstown. See Chapter 7,

Mr Patten Smight Bridge. See Chapter 7, also pages 125, 145

Mixed crews 30

Monte Video 16, 56, 58, 59, 109, 172, 174, 175, 178, 191, 196, 231, 232, 237

Montenegro 22

Morachlis 62

Morellos 13, 46, 66, 88, 226, 229

Mr Cartwright. See Interpreter, trials of Bombos, trial no. 2

Mr Joseph Cartwright
Interpreter Chapter 7

Mr Justice Lawson.
See trials of Bombos ch. 5,p. 108 et al.

See also chapter 7 p. 144 et al.
Mr M. J. Horgan Coroner.
See Chapter 8
Mr Murphy
     Crown Counsel.
     See Trials of Bombos and of
Moschara.
Murderers 23, 25, 77, 147, 159, 186
Muslim 20
Mutinies 13, 26, 28, 100

N

N. L. Thomas 9
Nicholas 12, 13, 14, 28, 40, 44, 46,
47, 49, 50, 51, 54, 57, 58, 59, 60, 62,
63, 64, 65, 66, 67, 68, 72, 84, 86, 87,
88, 94, 145, 189, 220, 221, 228, 229,
230, 232, 233
Nicholas Morellos 12, 13, 14, 28, 40,
44, 46, 47, 54, 57, 58, 60, 62, 64, 65,
66, 67, 87, 88, 94, 220, 221, 228, 229,
233
Nineteenth century 2, 5, 7, 8, 20, 30,
143, 195, 198
Norse blood, 4
Notice to Quit. See Thomas Crowe,
     John Ryan, Chapter 7.

O

Objections,
     to Greeks 20
Oropos 23
Osama Bin Laden 143, 144
Ocean River, 5
Ottoman 20, 21, 24
Ottoman Empire, 24, 25, 27

P

Paratjime 22
Peloponesia 23
Peno 41, 42, 43, 47, 49, 55, 60, 62, 63,
85, 93, 99, 100, 191
Peter MacGregor

the carpenter 14, 40, 41, 43, 55,
     79,83, 183, 213, 220
Pinatel , E, 160, 161, 162, 163, 164,
166, 167; Pitatel's signature 162
Piratical object 47
Pistoria's Counsel 57

Q

Queenstown 4, 10, 28, 30, 36, 47, 57,
59, 67, 69, 70, 72, 73, 74, 75, 76, 77,
81, 102, 106, 108, 125, 157, 159, 173,
181, 182, 196, 232, 234, 236, 23
     Queenstown harbour, Cork, 4, 11,
     33, 35, 42, 57, 68, 69, 72, 81, 83,
     85, 86, 87, 88, 89, 90, 91, 92, 97,
     98, 121, 126, 128, 146, 180, 181,
     182, 183, 198, 206,208, 224, 265,
     268, 270
     Queenstown Magistrates 157/8

R

Resident Magistrate 157, 170
Rio de Plata, 16
Plate 16
Robert Frost 156
Rook Agineau,
German cook 12, 14, 15, 27, 32, 33,
226, 236
Roman, 4, 50, 93, 151, 165, 167, 171
Rustchuk 22

S

Salonica 24, 77, 78
Scotsmen 9
Secretary of State 29, 158, 177, 178
Sentence of death 29, 95, 101, 108,
110, 111, 140, 145, 188
Shakespeare 79, 180
Sicily 13, 181, 182, 191, 195
Sir Edward Thornton
     From the Washington Office,
164
Skyros 23

Welsh waters 3
William O'Brien,
        a young reporter, 140
William Tobin 152
William Wilson,
        The first mate 14, 36, 39, 40,
        181, 187, 208, 209

Printed in the United Kingdom
by Lightning Source UK Ltd.
9615300001B